Pre-Raphaelite Treasures
at National Museums Liverpool

Laura MacCulloch

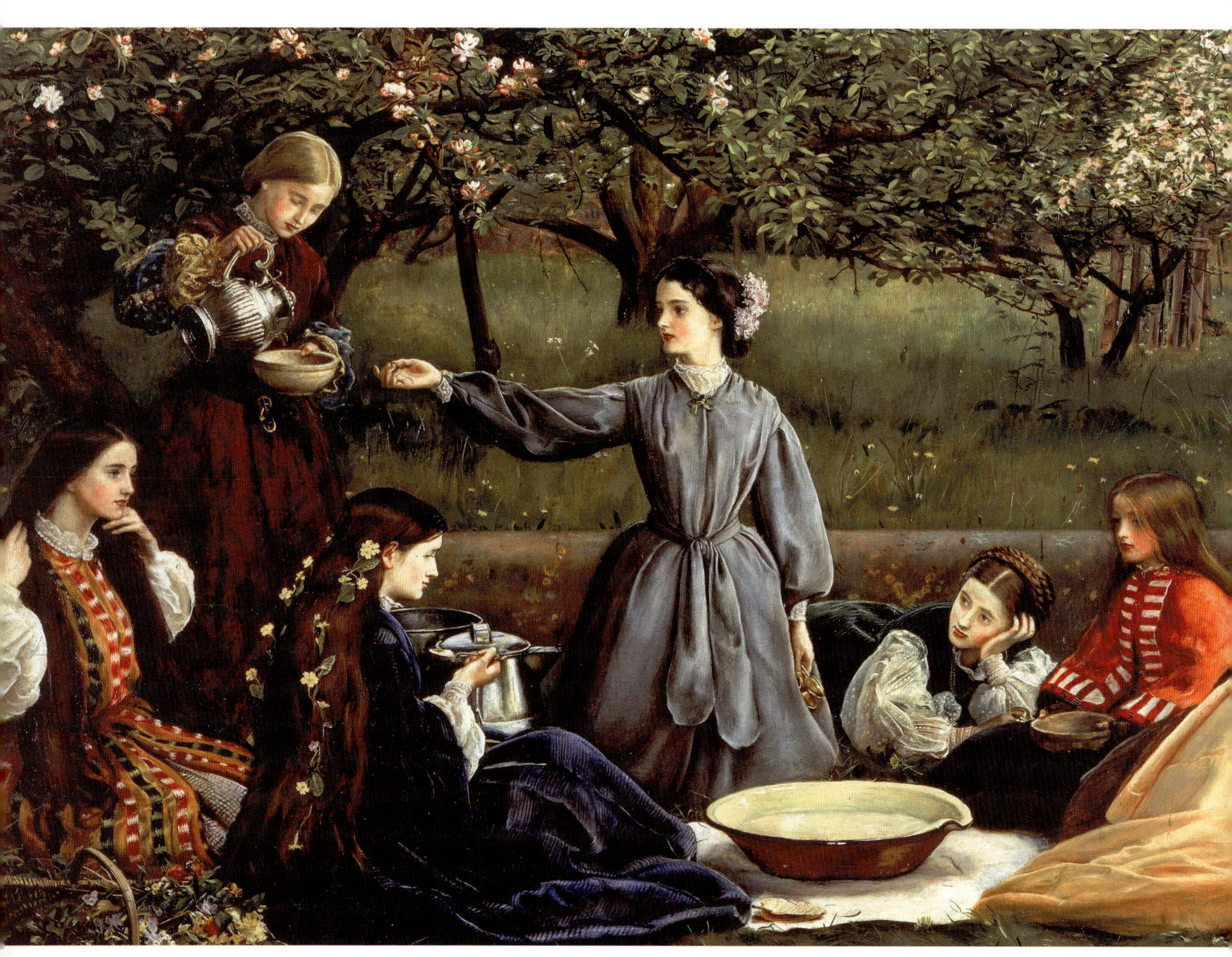

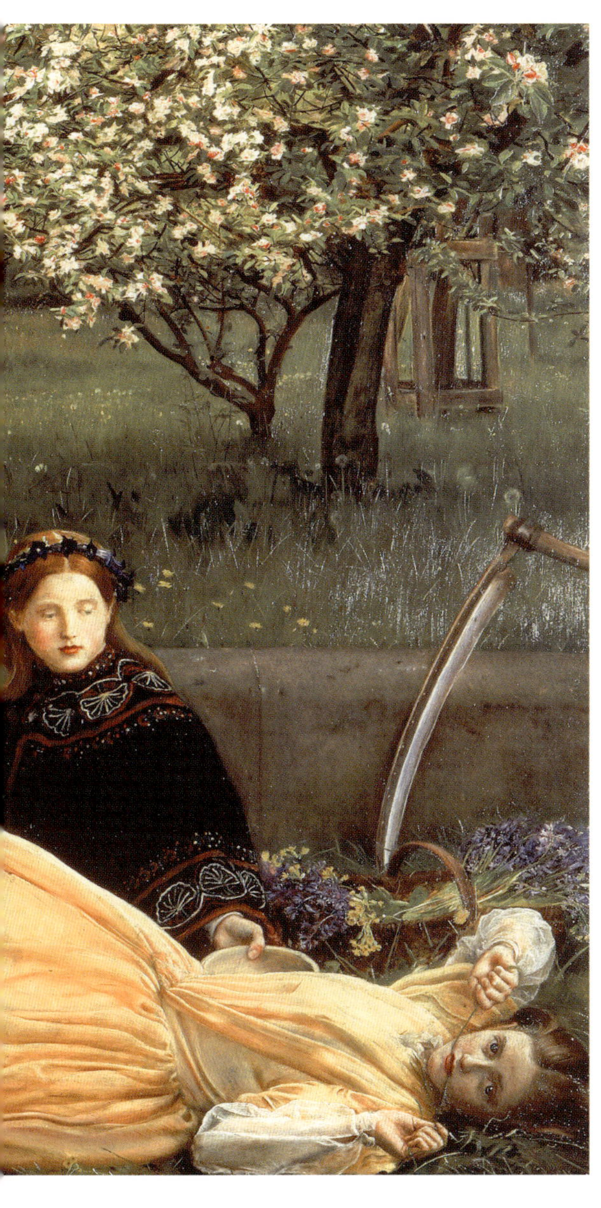

Pre-Raphaelite Treasures

at National Museums Liverpool

Laura MacCulloch

For Darren

Published by
Liverpool University Press
4 Cambridge Street
Liverpool
L69 7ZU

and

National Museums Liverpool
127 Dale Street
Liverpool
L2 2JH

ISBN 978-1-84631-897-9

Designed by Carnegie Book Production

Printed and bound in the UK by
Henry Ling Ltd

Owing to limited display space, outward
loans and the effects of light on
watercolours and drawings, the works
featured in this publication are not always
on display. Please contact the Gallery
before travelling to see a particular piece.

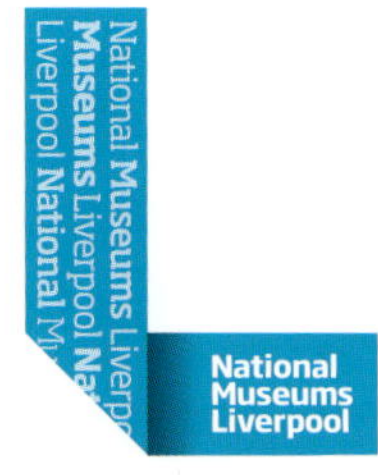

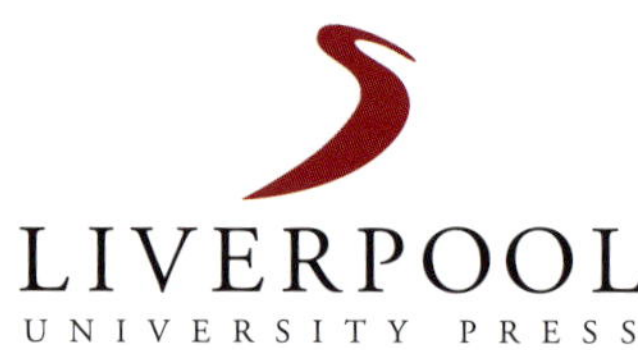

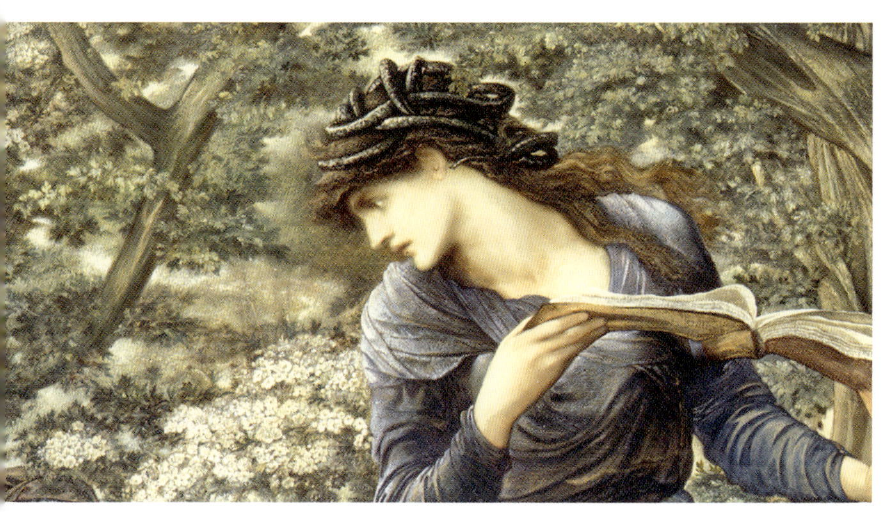

Contents

Introduction 7

The Pre-Raphaelite Brotherhood 11

The Later Pre-Raphaelites 37

Liverpool Pre-Raphaelites 77

Further reading 95

Index 96

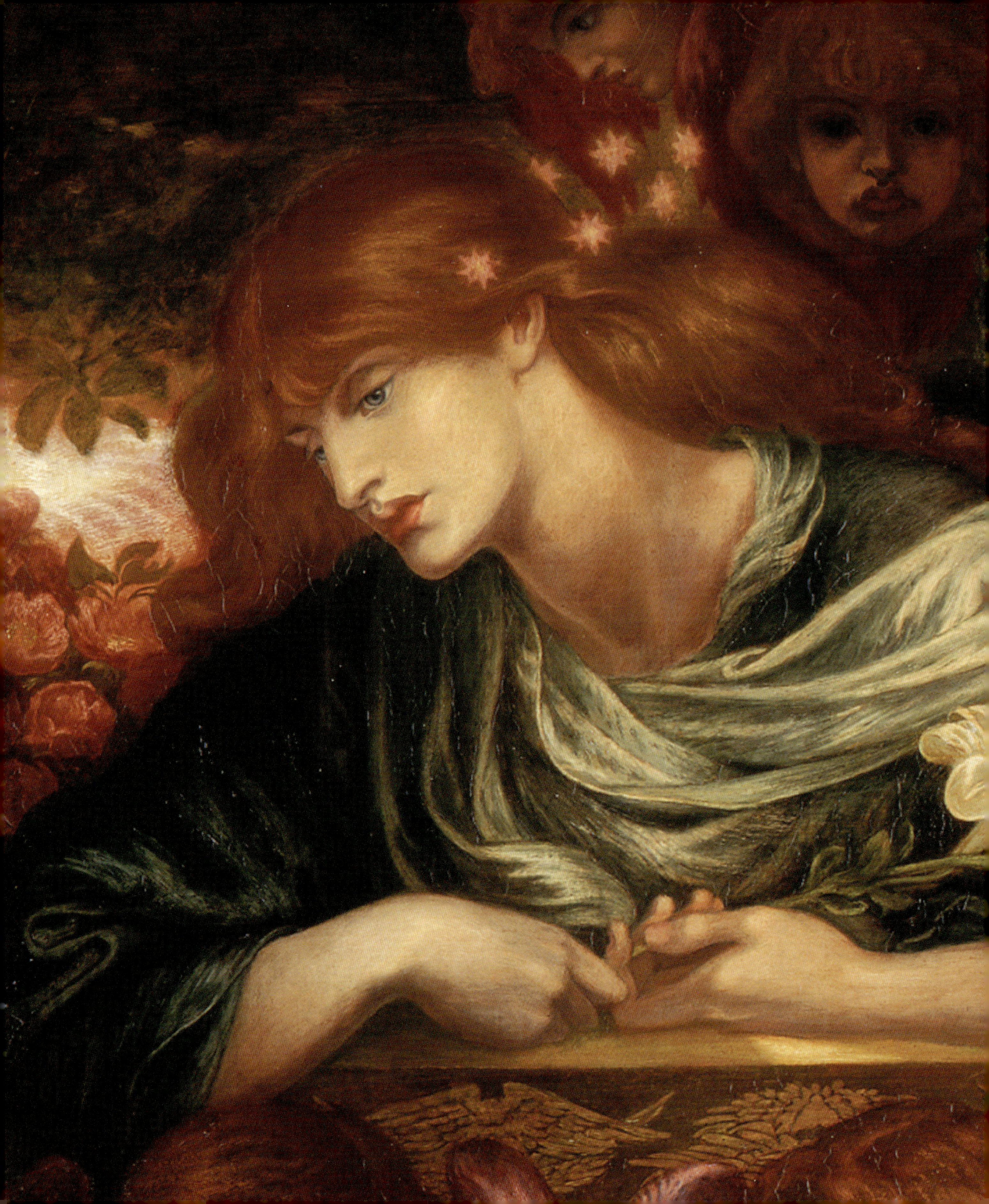

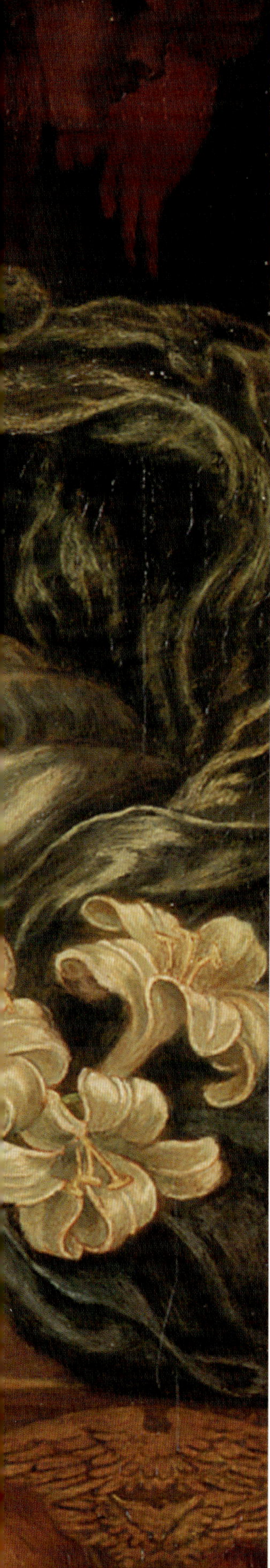

Introduction

National Museums Liverpool holds one of the most significant collections of Pre-Raphaelite art in the country. Founded in 1848, the Pre-Raphaelite Brotherhood sought to change the face of painting in this country. Dissatisfied with the traditional teaching methods of the Royal Academy, the group challenged artistic conventions. The artists advocated a fresh, highly coloured palette, meticulous detail, and the keen observation of nature. They extolled a more imaginative focus on narrative, depicting often- represented themes with a new sense of vigour, and sought new subjects, many of them literary. Their work, which was charged with symbolism and hitherto neglected references to modern life, appealed to the Victorian merchant class keen to invest its new found wealth on art. The group came to influence a large number of contemporary artists and indeed inspired a whole new generation. The style was still popular with buyers and practised by some artists well into the 20th century. The history of Pre-Raphaelite art is both fascinating and complex.

The paintings, watercolours, drawings and sculptures held in the Walker Art Gallery, Lady Lever Art Gallery and at Sudley House provide insights into all the key moments of this Pre-Raphaelite history. They also reveal the incredibly important role Liverpool had to play in supporting what was, in its early days, regarded as a radical and challenging artistic faction. From the late 1840s onwards, the town and its collectors exhibited, commissioned, bought, encouraged and advocated the work of John Everett Millais, William Holman Hunt, Dante Gabriel Rossetti and their followers. Here at National Museums Liverpool, the legacy of this time is a superb collection that traces the story of Pre-Raphaelite art from the early experiments in detailed colouring and narrative exemplified in Millais' early works, to the grand religious symbolism of Holman Hunt, and the romantic and decorative later works of Rossetti.

The history of the Walker's Pre-Raphaelite collection is entwined with the history of the annual Liverpool Autumn Exhibitions, set up to emulate the Royal Academy Summer Exhibitions in London. Held from 1871, the shows, which were initially at Liverpool Museum, provided a new opportunity for living artists to showcase work. In 1877, the Walker Art Gallery was built to house the exhibition. Liverpool's Library, Museum and Arts Committee soon began to purchase works of art for its permanent collection. Examples of work by the leading figures of Pre-Raphaelite painting were inevitably among their collecting aspirations. So, in 1881, just over 30 years after the formation of the Brotherhood, the Walker Art Gallery acquired its first major Pre-Raphaelite painting, *Dante's Dream* by Rossetti. It was closely followed in 1884 by the purchase of Millais' *Isabella* and then in 1891 by *The Triumph of the Innocents* by Holman Hunt. The Walker's collection now includes examples of paintings and drawings by all the major Pre-Raphaelite artists: John Everett Millais, William Holman Hunt, Dante Gabriel Rossetti, Ford Madox Brown, Arthur Hughes, John Brett and Frederick Sandys. Complementing these pictures is a wonderful group of landscapes and figurative paintings by the 'Liverpool School' artists William Windus, Daniel Alexander Williamson, William Davis, John Ingle Lee and James Campbell.

The Lady Lever Art Gallery was founded in 1922 by William Hesketh Lever (1851–1925), later first Viscount Leverhulme, to house the best of his huge and diverse personal art collection. Lever, who made his fortune from soap, had a special interest in Pre-Raphaelite painting. He acquired more than 20 works by Millais, his favourite, including *The Black Brunswickers* with its beautiful detail and colour and the more contemplative picture *Spring (Apple Blossoms)* with its commentary on life and death. Lever was willing to pay high prices for Pre-Raphaelite work, even in the second and third decades of the 20th century when arguably Pre-Raphaelite art was out of favour. He bought Millais' *Sir Isumbras at the Ford* for over £8,000 in 1913 from the George McCulloch collection. Then, as late as 1923, he was willing to pay almost £5,000 for Holman Hunt's *tour de force* of Victorian religious symbolism, *The Scapegoat*. For Lever, collecting was always about having the best examples of work he could possibly acquire. His pursuit of Pre-Raphaelite art was no exception.

Lever was also interested in the histories of collecting, seeking out works acquired by

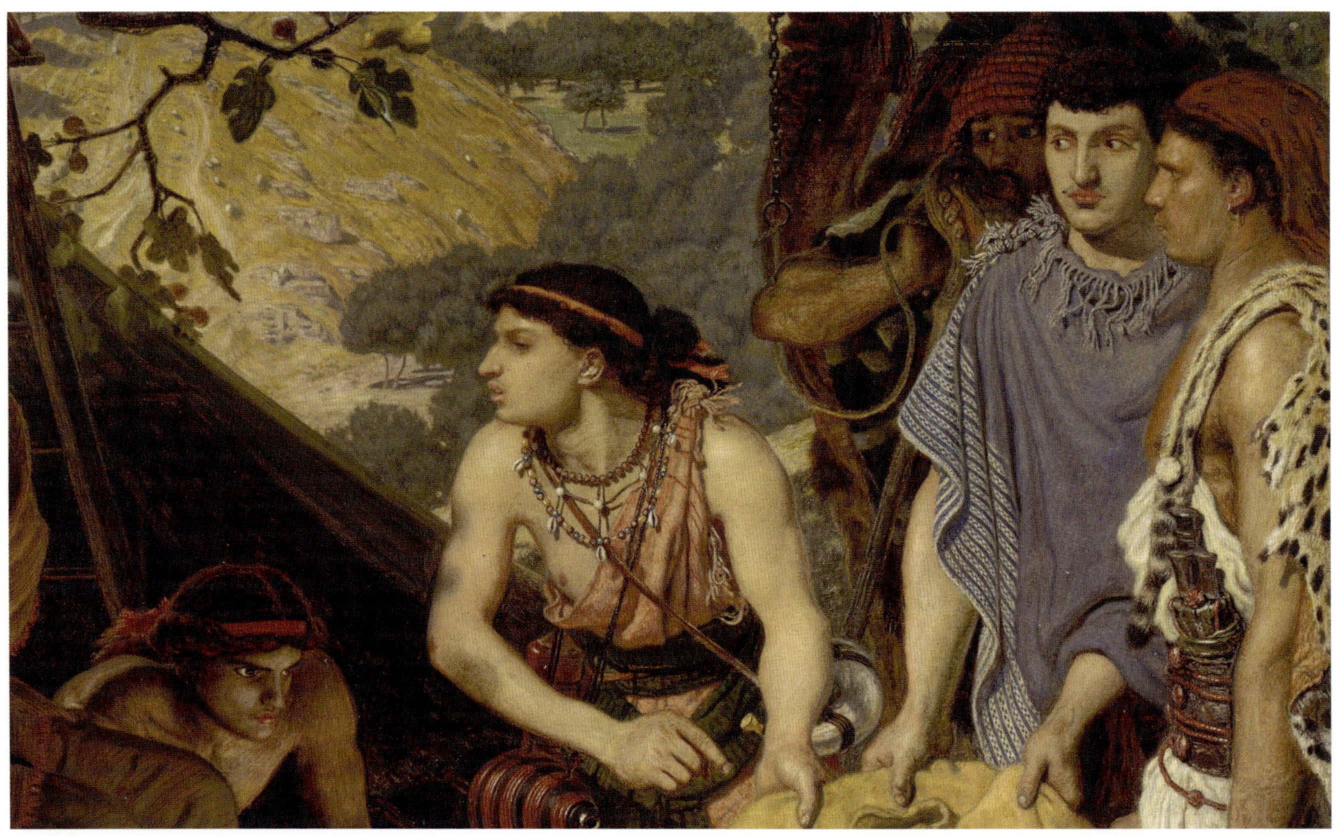

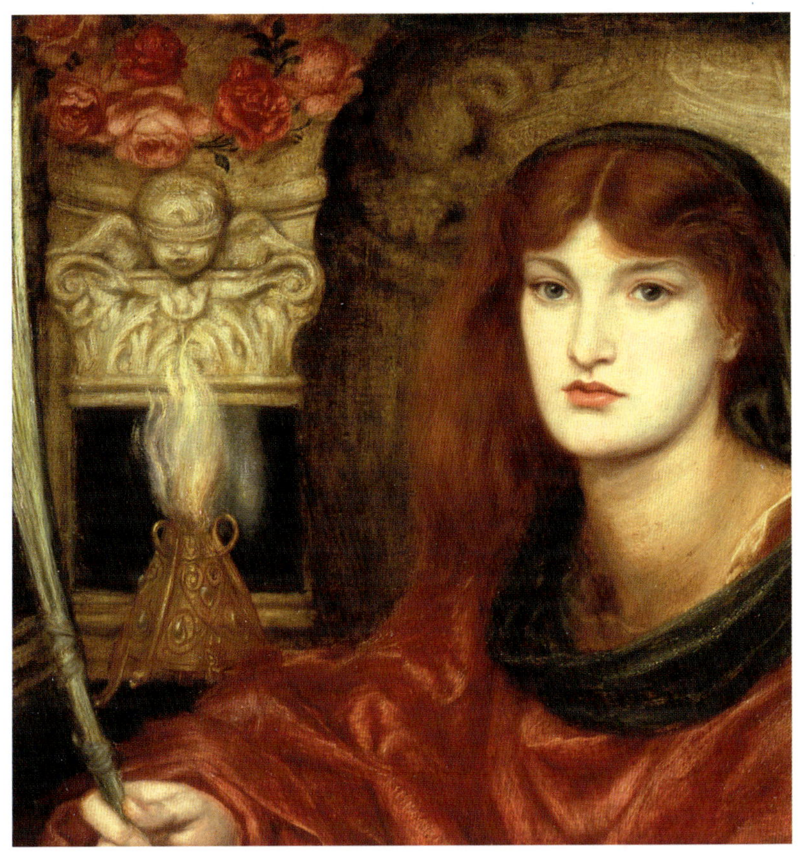

other significant collectors. In this vein, his purchase of *The Beguiling of Merlin* by Edward Burne-Jones and *Sybilla Palmifera* by Rossetti was completely understandable. *The Beguiling of Merlin* was one of the works Burne-Jones selected to display at the first ever Grosvenor Gallery exhibition in London in 1877, but it was also a work commissioned by Frederick Leyland, the great collector of aesthetic works who had strong links with the Liverpool area. Rossetti's female beauty *Sybilla Palmifera* was commissioned by George Rae to create a trio of beauties by the artist for his Birkenhead home. Lever no doubt greatly appreciated the local associations of these two paintings.

Sudley House was owned by George Holt (1825-96), a ship owner, who like many Liverpool merchants of the later 19th century collected art to decorate his home. As was typical of the mercantile collectors, he focused primarily on contemporary or near contemporary art, only later expanding his collecting to embrace earlier British painting. Among his purchases was a small but significant collection of Pre-Raphaelite works. This included the exquisite *Angel Playing a Flageolet* by Edward Burne-Jones and *The Finding of the Saviour in the Temple* by William Holman Hunt. Holt went on to be patron of John Melhuish Strudwick, a later Pre-Raphaelite whose highly stylised and tonal paintings were inspired by Burne-Jones.

This guide to the Pre-Raphaelite collections of National Museums Liverpool has been written by Dr Laura MacCulloch. The book gives a succinct but highly informative overview of Pre-Raphaelite history and the Liverpool Pre-Raphaelites as well as detailing individual pictures. Laura has brought a fresh insight into these much-loved works and provided us with an excellent starting point for appreciating this highly significant collection. Ann Bukantas, Head of Fine Art, edited the guide and helped uncover new facts, in particular on the Liverpool painter John Ingle Lee. Karen Miller, Publications Manager, has also edited and as usual has expertly guided the production of this book. We would like to thank Heather Birchall and Colin Simpson who kindly agreed to read through aspects of the text at an early stage. No publication on the Pre-Raphaelites and Liverpool would be complete without acknowledgement of the ground-breaking work carried out by Mary Bennett from the 1960s onwards. Mary's extensive research on all aspects of Liverpool and the Pre-Raphaelites forms the basis of our study today. Thanks must also go to Edward Morris and Julian Treuherz who have done much to extend our knowledge of the Liverpool Academy, Liverpool collectors, Rossetti and Ford Madox Brown. This guide is sure to be a much-loved resource for all those studying Pre-Raphaelite art and those with a passion for what is today a much admired group of Victorian artists.

Sandra Penketh
Director of Art Galleries
National Museums Liverpool

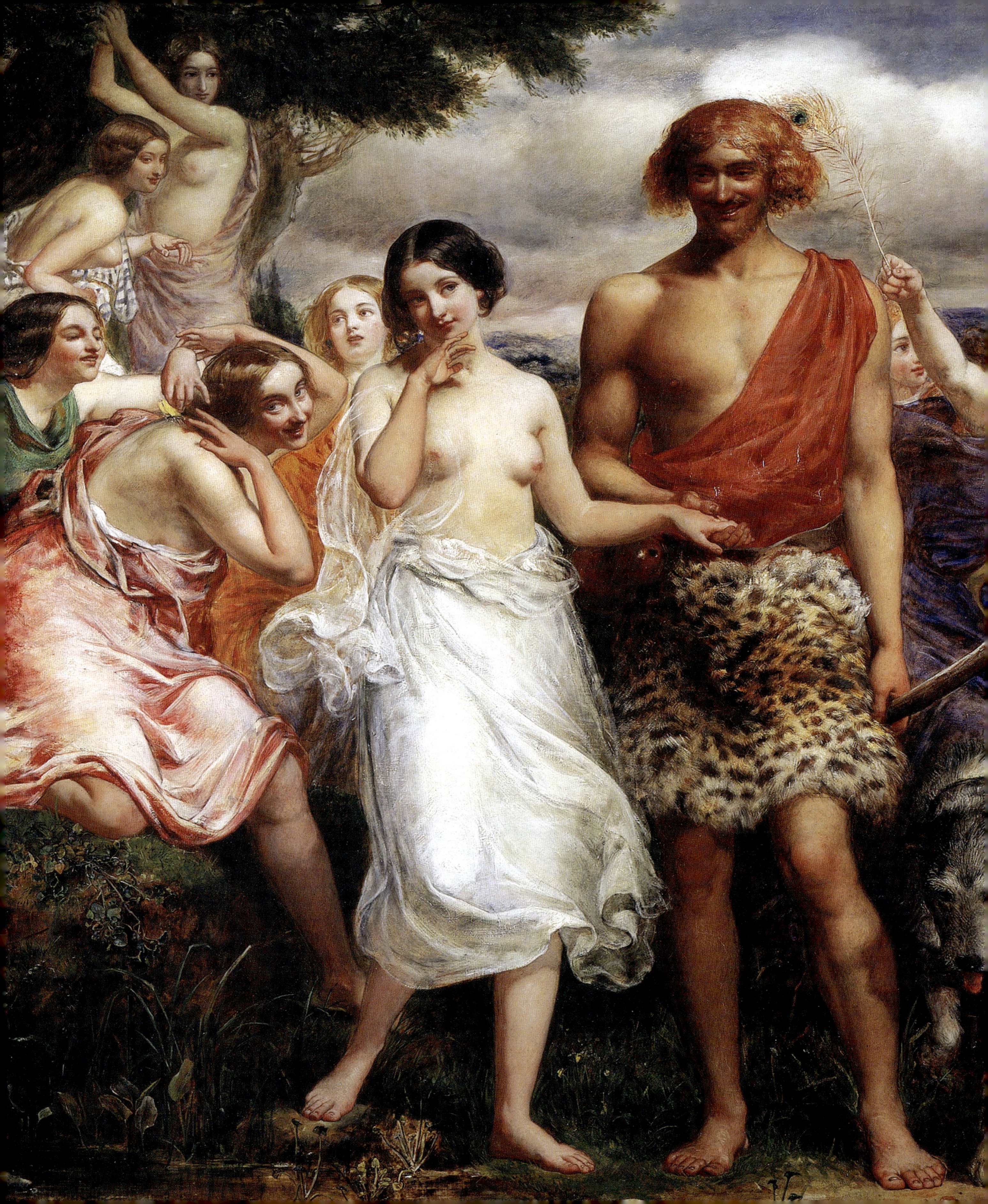

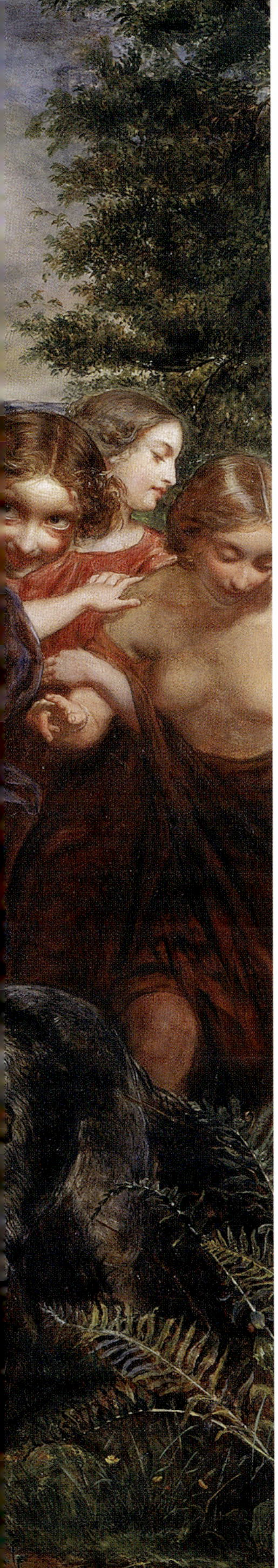

The Pre-Raphaelite Brotherhood

The Pre-Raphaelite movement grew out of the Pre-Raphaelite Brotherhood. This initially secret group was formed in September 1848 by seven young male artists who were drawn together by their mutual dissatisfaction with the state of contemporary British art in the mid-19th century. The three founder members of the group were 20-year-old Dante Gabriel Rossetti (1828–82), 21-year-old William Holman Hunt (1827–1910) and 19-year-old John Everett Millais (1829–96). They met while studying at the Royal Academy Schools in London, at that time the country's leading art school.[*] At the age of eleven Millais became the youngest ever student to be accepted to the school and a star pupil. In common with Rossetti and Hunt, he became increasingly dissatisfied with the teaching he received. The curriculum was based on a traditional art training which had evolved from Renaissance art practice. On first entering the academy schools students focused on learning to draw simple objects before progressing to the copying of plaster casts of famous ancient and Renaissance sculptures. Once a student had mastered a

plaster cast they were admitted to the life-drawing class, and having learnt to draw the human figure they progressed to the painting course. There, students were urged to follow the traditional formula of using one-third light to two-thirds dark in their paintings, creating a spotlight on the most dramatic element of the picture. Rossetti, Hunt and Millais found this training stifling and were keen to set up a group in which they could experiment and learn from each other, away from the prescriptive traditions of the Academy.

The founder members enlisted three fellow students to join their group: the painters James Collinson (1825–81) and Frederic George Stephens (1828–1907) and the sculptor Thomas Woolner (1825–92). Rossetti's brother, William Michael (1829–1919), who worked for the Excise Office (later the Inland Revenue Board), was enlisted as Secretary to record the proceedings of the group. Later in life he recalled that their aims were:

1   To have genuine ideas to express;
2   To study Nature attentively, so as to know how to express them;
3   To sympathise with what is direct and serious and heartfelt in previous art to the exclusion of what is conventional, self-parading and learned by rote; and

---

[*]   The Royal Academy Schools encompassed schools of Architecture, Sculpture and Painting.

4   and most indispensable of all, to
    produce thoroughly good pictures and
    statues.[*]

The group named themselves the Pre-Raphaelite Brotherhood in reference to the early Italian artists they admired who were working before the Renaissance artist Raphael (1483–1520). At the Royal Academy Schools Raphael had been held up as the model artist to whom all artists should aspire, but the Brotherhood felt that art made after Raphael, although technically sophisticated, was vapid, lacking in sincerity and repetitive. They wanted to radically change the direction of contemporary art by looking to earlier artists whose paintings they felt had truthfulness, creativity and spiritual integrity. They drew up a list of their artistic heroes including Fra Angelico (born about 1395, died 1455) and looked at prints of 14th- and early 15th-century Italian fresco paintings. They were also heavily influenced by the writings of the influential art critic John Ruskin (1819–1900) and in particular his book *Modern Painters: Their Superiority in the Art of Landscape Painting to the Ancient Masters*. The second volume particularly inspired the Brotherhood. Among his descriptions of nature's elements Ruskin wrote that artists should look directly at nature, 'rejecting nothing, selecting nothing, scorning nothing'. This led the Brotherhood to copy nature in minute detail. They used their skills to reproduce individual blades of grass, the small creases in fabric and the tiny wrinkles on a face. Since each element was copied so diligently, those in the background appeared as detailed as those in the foreground. It also led them to seek out real backgrounds and interiors for their pictures; Millais used a real carpenter's shop for his painting *Christ in the House of his Parents* (1849–50, Tate).

Ruskin's ideas also influenced the group's use of symbols in their works to add greater meaning. He highlighted that this had been common in medieval and Renaissance pictures in which each object was not just an accessory in the scene but added deeper meaning to the painting. The Brotherhood used colour and religious symbolism as well as the popular language of flowers. In Millais' painting *Isabella* (1848–9, Walker Art Gallery) he illustrates an early scene from Keats' poem *Isabella and the Pot of Basil* in which the doomed lovers Lorenzo and Isabella eat alongside members of her rich merchant family, including her two brothers who later murder Lorenzo. To allude to the disastrous consequences of their love Millais uses symbols such as spilt salt and a falcon with a dove's white feather in its mouth.

Two of the most striking aspects of the Brotherhood's new style were their insistence on natural lighting and their use of bright colours. In their desire to be truthful to nature they rejected the rules that they had learnt about employing a dramatic contrast between light and dark. They preferred to give their pictures an even lighting much closer to real daylight. They also rejected the conservative, muted tones and yellowy varnish favoured by more established mid-19th century artists. Instead their admiration for 14th-century painters led to their preference for bright, pure colours and the adoption of the new chemical dyes, which created a range of jewel-like paint colours. The members of the Brotherhood were also eager to experiment with fresco painting in which paint is applied directly to wet lime plaster. This method was used to decorate walls by many of the early Italian painters that they admired such as Fra Angelico. Fresco inspired the Brotherhood to apply a wet layer of white gesso, or plaster, to their canvases. They then painted onto the gesso which made their colourful palettes even brighter.

It was not just the style and technique of their paintings that broke from tradition. The subjects they chose to paint, and how they approached them, was also radical. The Brotherhood painted scenes from the Bible and literature. These were both traditional subjects, but they painted biblical scenes without idealisation of the characters and

---

[*]   WM Rossetti, *Dante Gabriel Rossetti: His Family Letters, with a Memoir*, 1895, I, p. 135 (Rossetti's numbering and his use of a double 'and' have been retained in this quotation).

chose modern poets, notably Keats and Tennyson, as inspiration for their pictures. Rather than creating sentimental or saccharine images of the Holy Family they preferred to use real people as models and match these as closely as possible to the characters being represented. When painting *The Girlhood of the Virgin Mary* (1848–9, Tate), Rossetti used his pious teenage sister Christina as a model; when depicting Joseph for his painting *Christ in the House of his Parents*, Millais used a carpenter to model for Joseph's body and his own father to model for the head. They also believed everyday life could be a serious subject for contemporary art and painted scenes from modern life with the same dedication, and on the same scale, as their religious works. They also applied their new principles to landscape painting, reproducing nature in minute detail, and often worked on their canvases outdoors instead of the conventional method of painting in the studio from sketches.

Between 1848 and 1849, Hunt, Millais and Rossetti worked on pieces to exhibit in London at the Royal Academy Summer exhibition and the Free Exhibition at Hyde Park Corner. Both were high profile venues for the young artists. They signed these early works with the initials 'PRB' and early reviews of work by the Brotherhood were generally positive. This changed in 1850 when art critics finally noticed the mysterious initials. They were furious that a secret group of young artists would have the audacity to criticise contemporary art. Their reviews were savage and it was not until John Ruskin wrote two letters of support to *The Times* in 1851 that the art world and the public began to accept the Brotherhood and their ideas.

The Brotherhood were not the only young artists who wanted to break away from the constraints of their art training. Ford Madox Brown (1821–93) studied in three art academies in Belgium before settling in England in 1846. He began experimenting with new ways of painting that year and had works on show in several London exhibitions in the late 1840s. Rossetti noticed Brown's work in these exhibitions and wrote to him asking if he could become his painting student; Brown was seven years older with considerably more experience. He agreed but the lessons were short-lived as Rossetti did not take to his teaching methods. Despite this, a life-long friendship began. Although Brown was never a member of the Brotherhood he was closely involved with the group. They were inspired by the work he had already produced in which he had begun to use natural lighting, to work with meticulous attention to detail and to include highly accurate backgrounds. Likewise, their new technique of painting on a wet, white ground to achieve more luminous colours influenced Brown's working methods. Other artists, notably Arthur Hughes (1832–1915) and John Brett (1831–1902), admired the aims of the group and began to paint in their style.

By the mid-1850s the Pre-Raphaelite Brotherhood had broken up owing to the members' desire to pursue individual goals. Hunt travelled to the Middle East to find authentic settings for his religious paintings, Millais began to favour a looser painting style, perhaps due to his love of the medium of oil painting, and Rossetti wanted to pursue his medieval-inspired painting and poetry.

Frederic Stephens gave up painting and became a highly respected art critic and art historian. William Michael Rossetti continued to work for the Inland Revenue Board while remaining involved in the arts. He became an art critic, literary editor and art collector. In 1874 he married Ford Madox Brown's eldest daughter Lucy (1843–94), who was an artist in her own right. James Collinson was the first to leave the Brotherhood in 1850 to train as a Catholic priest but within four years he had abandoned this vocation and returned to painting. Thomas Woolner left England to join the Australian gold rush in 1852 before returning two years later to continue working as a sculptor. Despite the Brotherhood coming to an end by the late 1850s their style and artistic principles had created a major contemporary art movement.

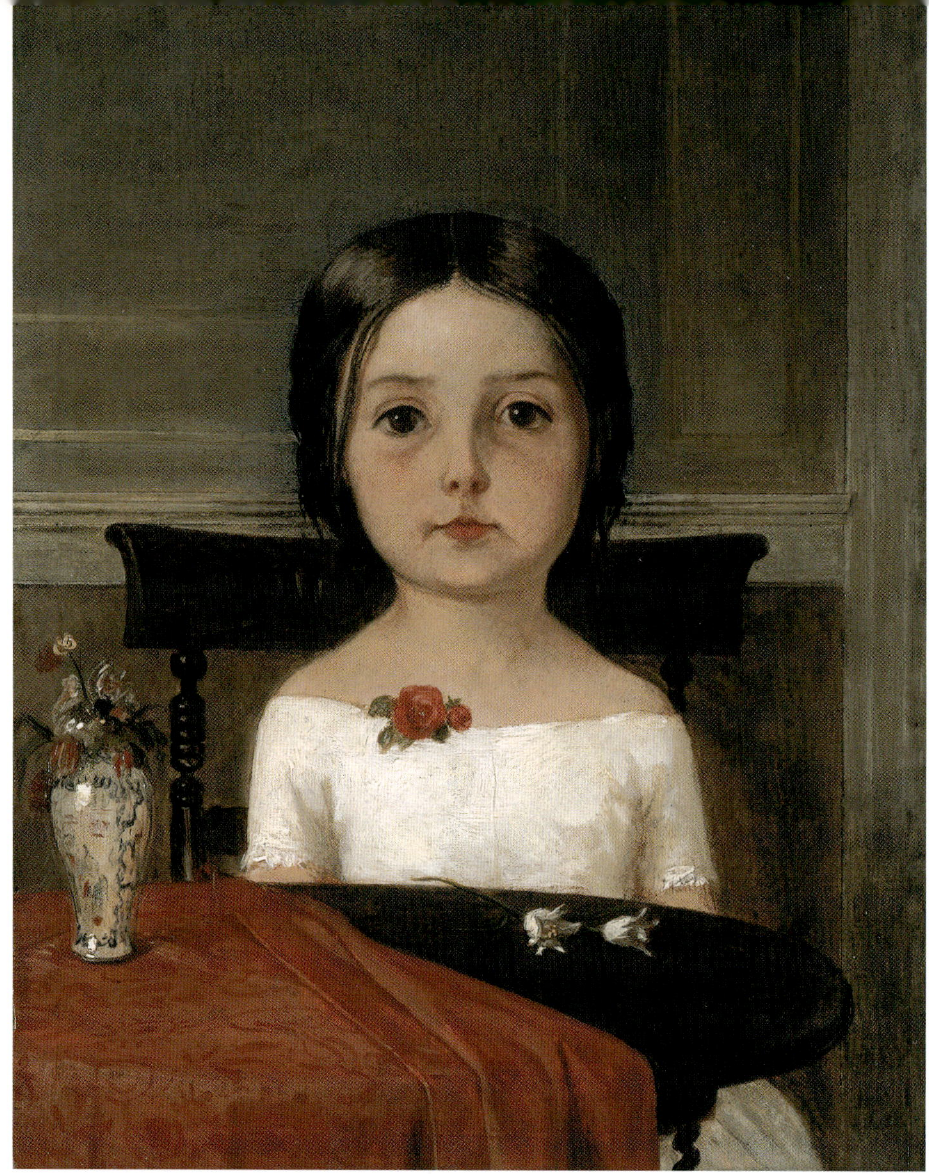

Ford Madox Brown (1821–93)

Millie Smith, 1846

Oil on paper on panel, 22.9 × 17.5 cm

Purchased in 1972; inv. no. WAG 7804

Brown's small portrait of his daughter's playmate is an early experiment in breaking away from mid-19th century art conventions. It shows Brown moving towards the style which would be championed by him and the artists in the Pre-Raphaelite Brotherhood. He has deliberately abandoned the sophisticated shading and modelling that he mastered as part of his art training. He uses a more naïve style to highlight the simple innocence of the little girl. Brown painted this portrait when he was on holiday in Southend with his daughter, Lucy, following the recent death of his first wife. Amelia (Millie) Smith was the daughter of the landlord in whose lodgings they stayed. She was about five years old when she modelled for Brown. The portrait suggests that the painter found solace in seeing Lucy happily playing with another child despite the shadow of grief under which they were living.

John Everett Millais (1829–96)

Self-Portrait, 1847

Oil on mill-board, 27.3 × 22.2 cm

Presented by Miss Eleanor Prior in 1977; inv. no. WAG 9240

This is Millais' first self-portrait. It was painted a year before he joined the Pre-Raphaelite Brotherhood and shows the confident 18-year-old artist with the tools of his trade, looking straight at the viewer. The style is painterly and in keeping with the training he had undertaken at the Royal Academy Schools. He uses the deep tones, thick paint and broad brushstrokes which were favoured by fashionable painters of the 1840s. The light focuses on his head, the source of his creativity. His dark clothing, made blacker by his use of bitumen in the paint, heightens this effect.

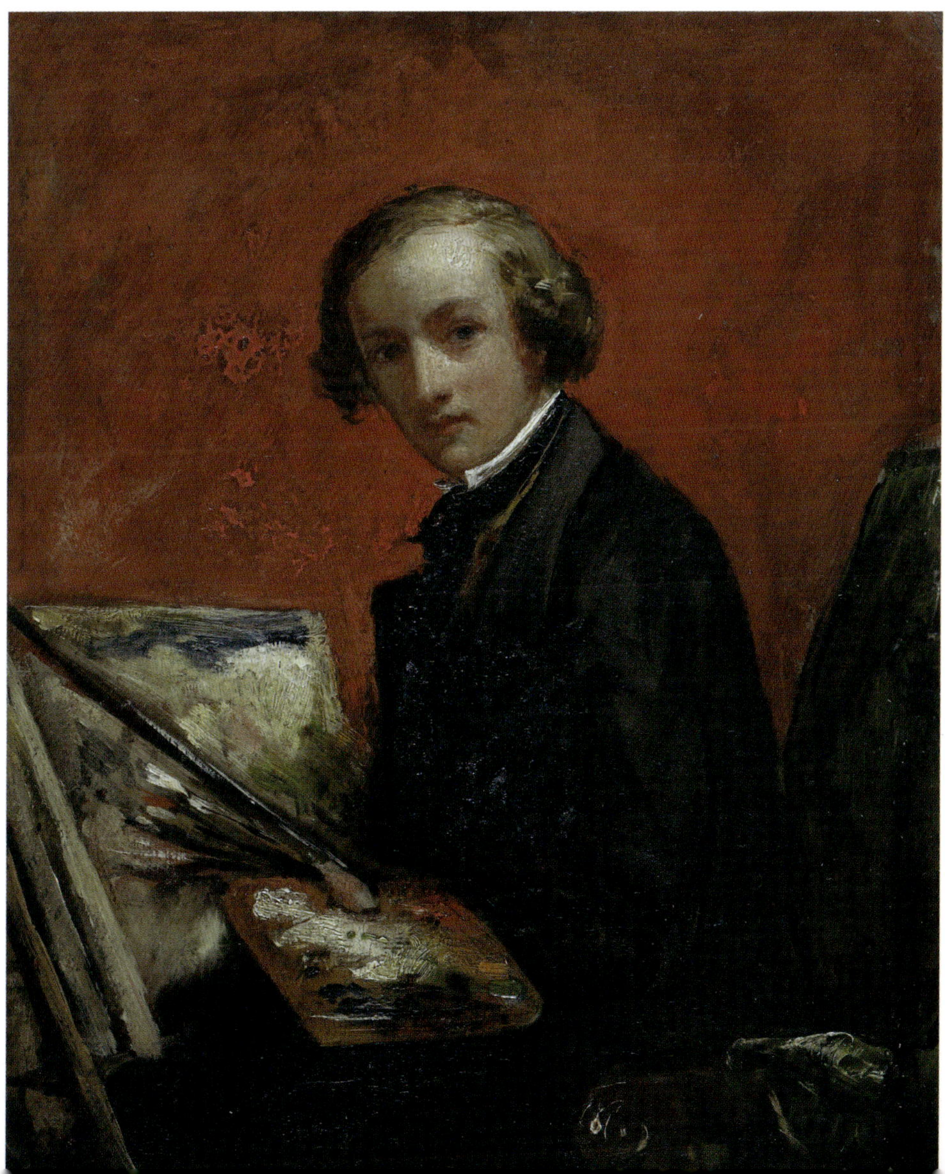

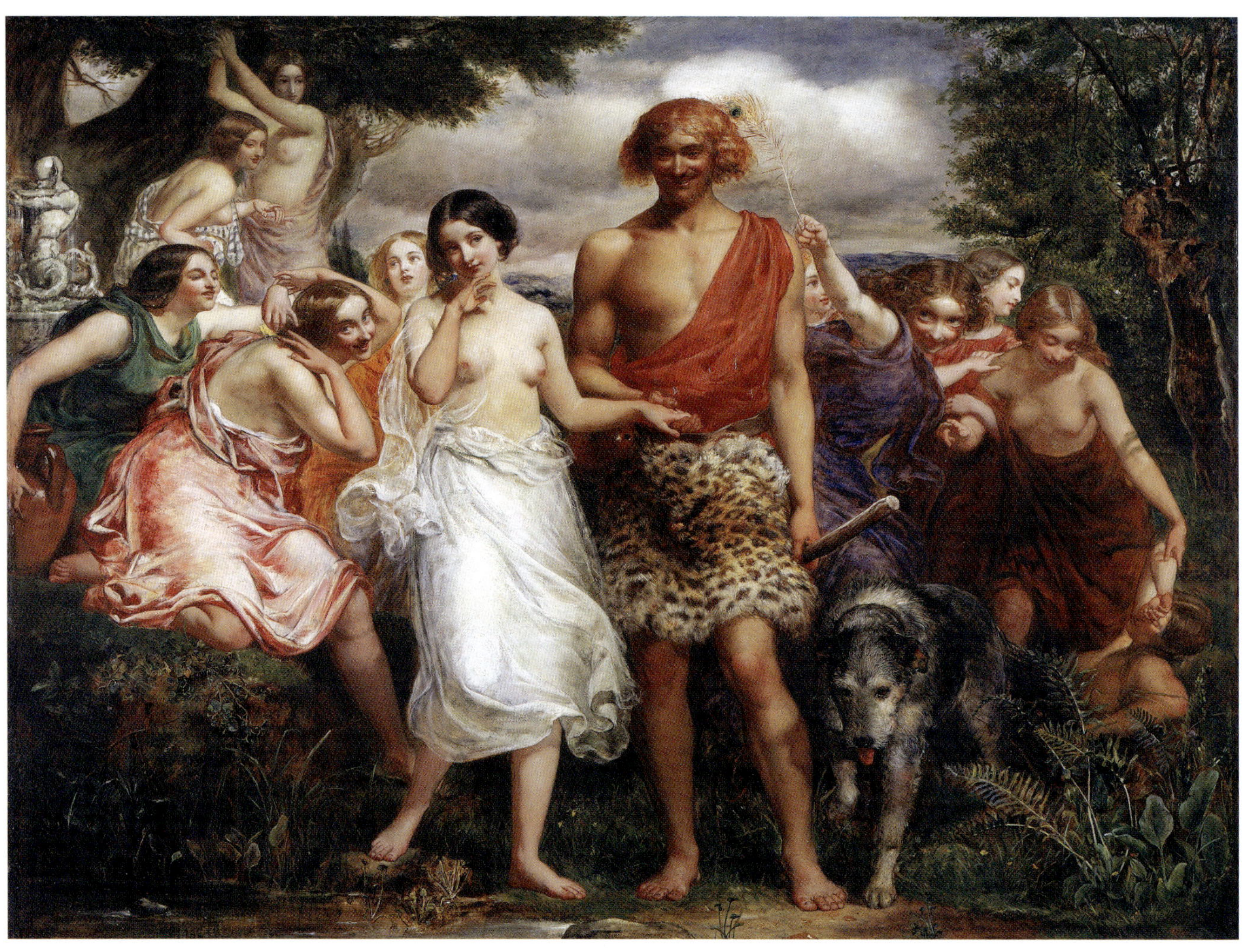

John Everett Millais (1829–96)

Cymon and Iphigenia, 1847–8

Oil on canvas, 114.3 × 147.3 cm

Accepted by HM Government in lieu of Inheritance Tax and allocated to National Museums Liverpool in 2004; inv. no. LL 10336

This was the last picture Millais painted before joining the Pre-Raphaelite Brotherhood. Millais depicts Cymon, a boorish country youth, who falls for the beautiful Iphigenia and is transformed by her love into a sophisticated young man. The story was first written by the medieval Italian poet, Boccaccio, but Millais drew his inspiration from John Dryden's 18th-century version. The generically pretty faces of the women with their fashionable hairstyles show the influence of the older artist William Etty (1787–1849) who was well-known for painting fleshy beauties. These women contrast with the awkward, minutely realistic figure of Isabella who appeared in Millais' next picture of the same name [see p.21], painted when he had joined the Pre-Raphaelite Brotherhood.

John Everett Millais (1829–96)

Ferdinand Lured by Ariel, 1848

Ink on paper, 28.4 × 20 cm

Presented by Miss Sylvia Crawshay in 1983; inv. no. WAG 10364

Before the Pre-Raphaelite Brotherhood was founded Millais was a member of the Cyclographic Club in which young artists circulated drawings for peer criticism. This drawing may well have been made to be exhibited to members of this club as it is highly finished and signed with Millais' monogram in the bottom left corner. The scene is from Shakespeare's play *The Tempest*. It shows shipwrecked Ferdinand, son of the King of Naples, being misled by Ariel, a sprite disguised as an invisible sea nymph, who sings into his ear the false news that his father has died. As well as a painter, Millais was the most prolific of the Pre-Raphaelite illustrators. He designed hundreds of illustrations for novels and poems. His delight and skill in the graphic arts can be seen in this line drawing.

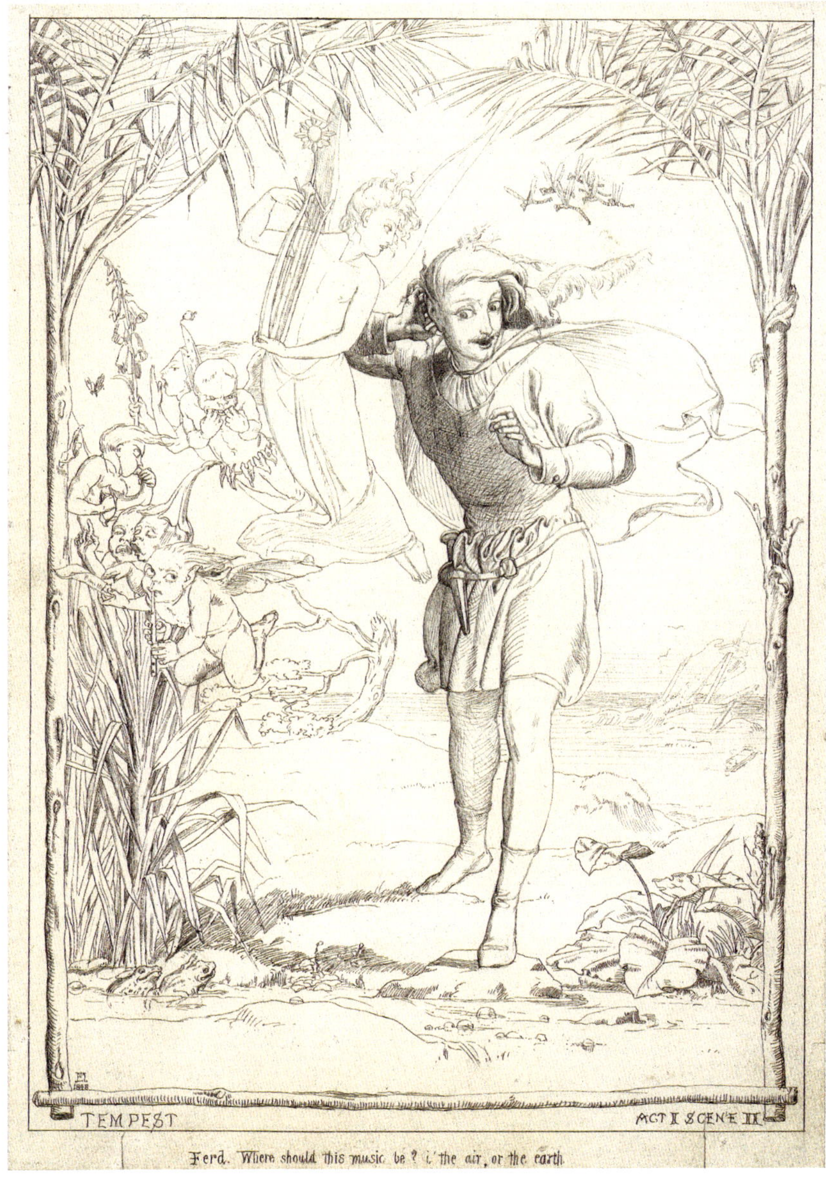

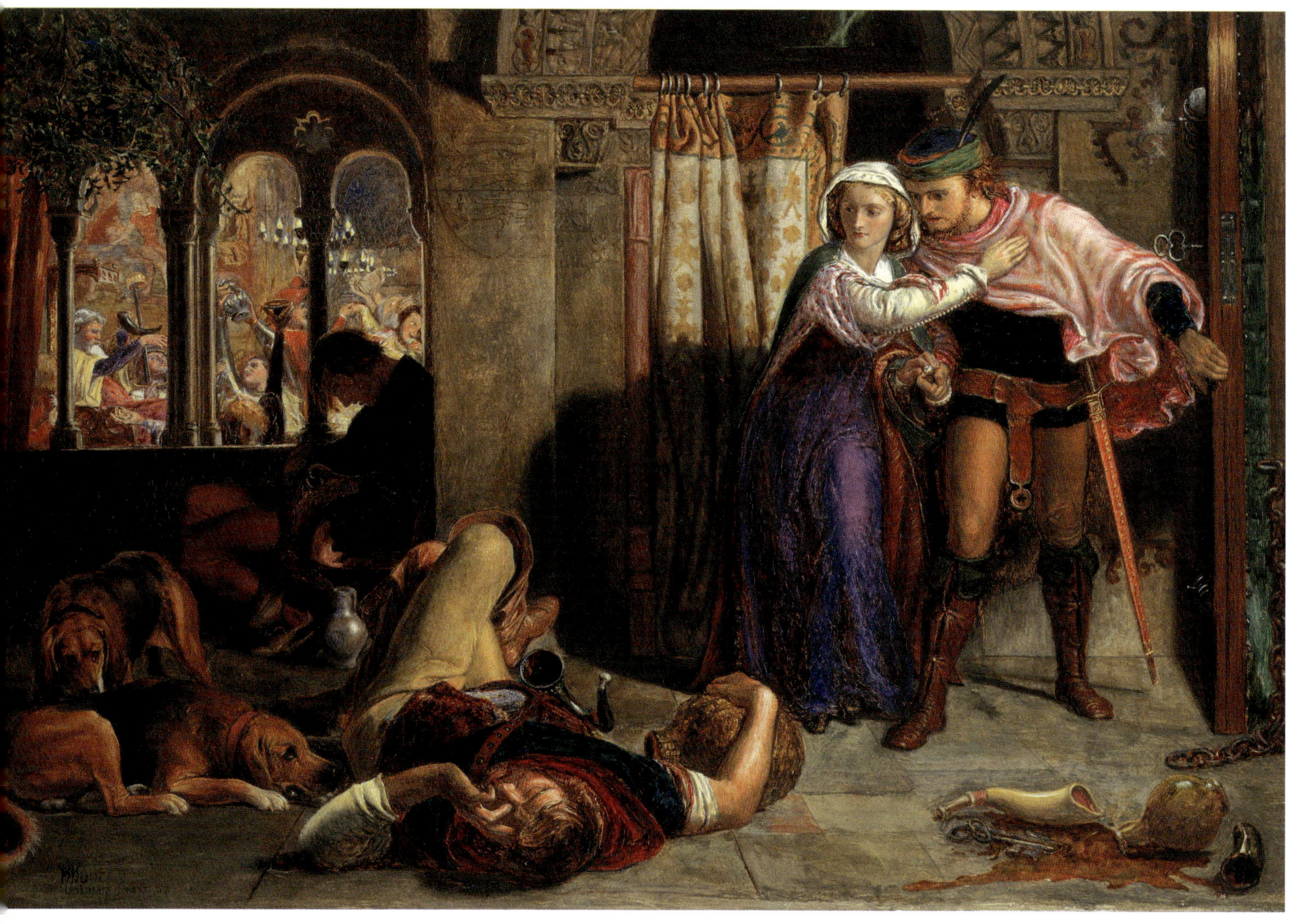

William Holman Hunt (1827–1910)

The Flight of Madeline and Porphryo during the Drunkenness attending the Revelry (The Eve of St Agnes), 1847–57

Oil on mahogany panel, 25.2 × 35.5 cm

Bequeathed by Miss ME Munn in 1948; inv. no. WAG 1635

The jewel-like colours favoured by the Brotherhood shine out of this picture of two lovers making a night-time escape. Madeline and Porphryo tentatively pick their way through drunken revellers while the party continues in the top left corner. The scene is taken from Keats' poem *The Eve of St Agnes*. Hunt was drawn to the subject as it allowed him to show innocent, pure love in contrast to frivolity and drunkenness.

This is a smaller version of the painting which Hunt exhibited at the Royal Academy in 1848. It began as an outline drawing for the bigger picture but in the 1850s Hunt finished it for his patron John Miller of Liverpool.

William Holman Hunt (1827–1910)

Sheet of figures and compositional studies connected with Dr Rochecliffe performing Divine Service in the Cottage of Joceline Joliffe at Woodstock, Christ and the two Marys, *The Flight of Madeline and Porphryo during the Drunkenness attending the Revelry (The Eve of St Agnes)* and other subjects, 1847–8

Pencil on paper with one figure outlined in red chalk, 34 × 48.3 cm

Purchased with the assistance of the Art Fund, the V&A Purchase Grant Fund and the Friends of Merseyside Museums and Art Galleries in 1985; inv. no. WAG 10534

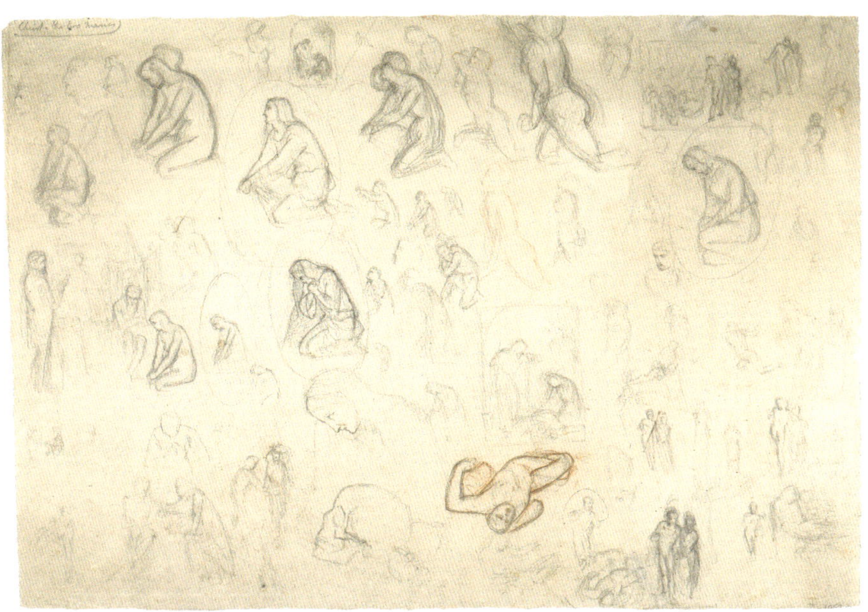

This double-sided sheet of studies gives an insight into Hunt's working process. There are several sketches which he has boxed in with borders that represent the edge of the canvas. The loose sketching style suggests that he used the sheet to work out initial ideas for compositions. Several of these compositional studies are for his painting *The Flight of Madeline and Porphryo during the Drunkenness attending the Revelry* [see p.18]. These drawings show that even at this early stage Hunt had a clear idea of the main points of the composition, with the lovers on the right and the drunken revellers on the left. The sheet is also littered with figures which reveal Hunt trying out various poses for individual characters. In the top left section of one side Hunt has worked out the pose of a kneeling figure. He has first drawn them nude and then redrawn them wearing clothes. This was the method of working that he was taught as an art student as it was believed to be the best way to make figures proportionally and anatomically correct.

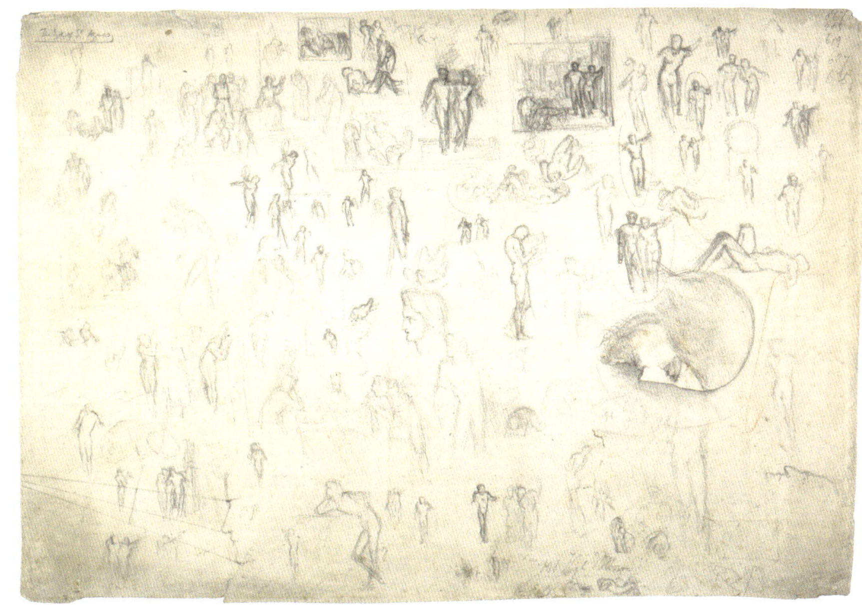

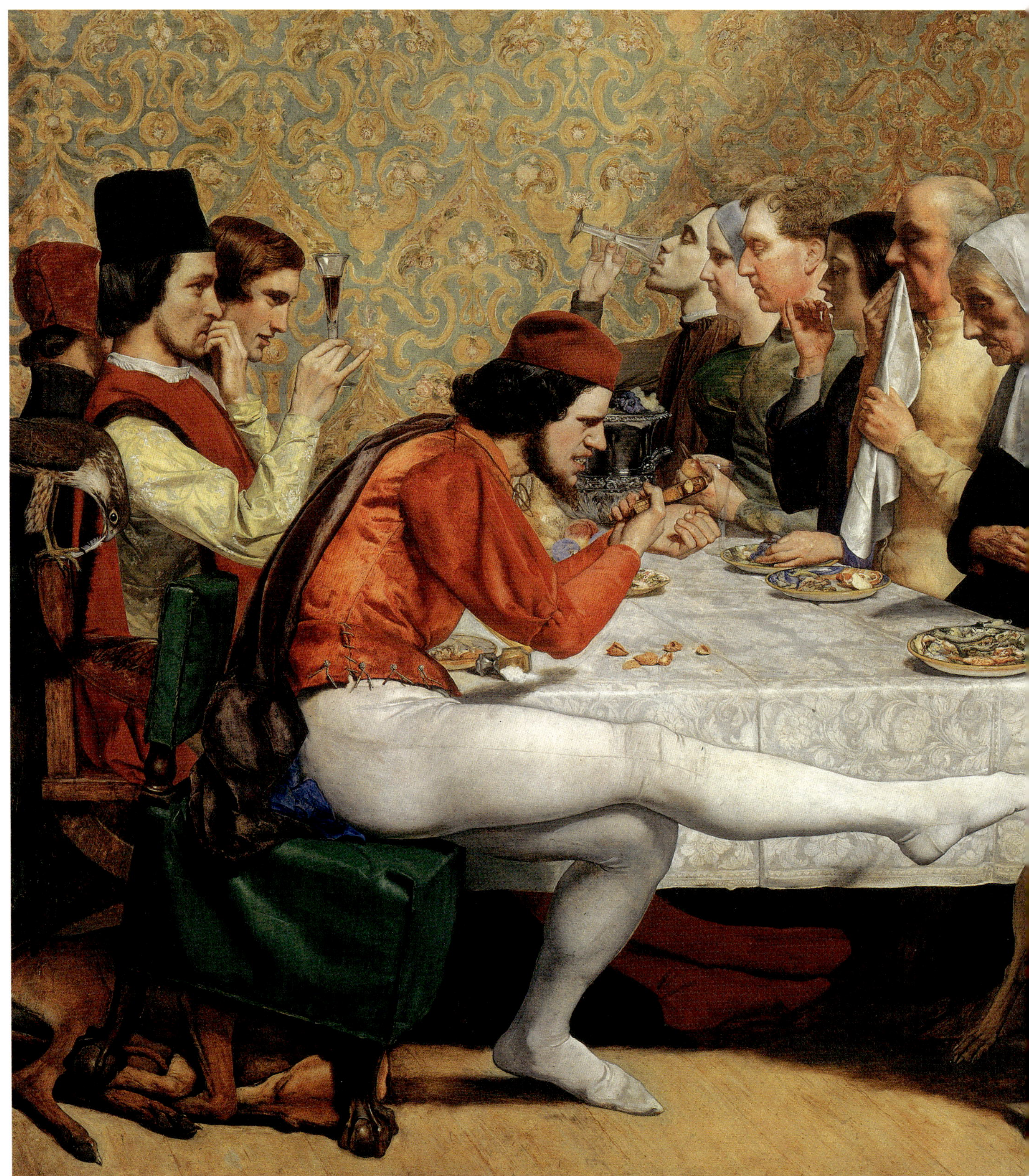

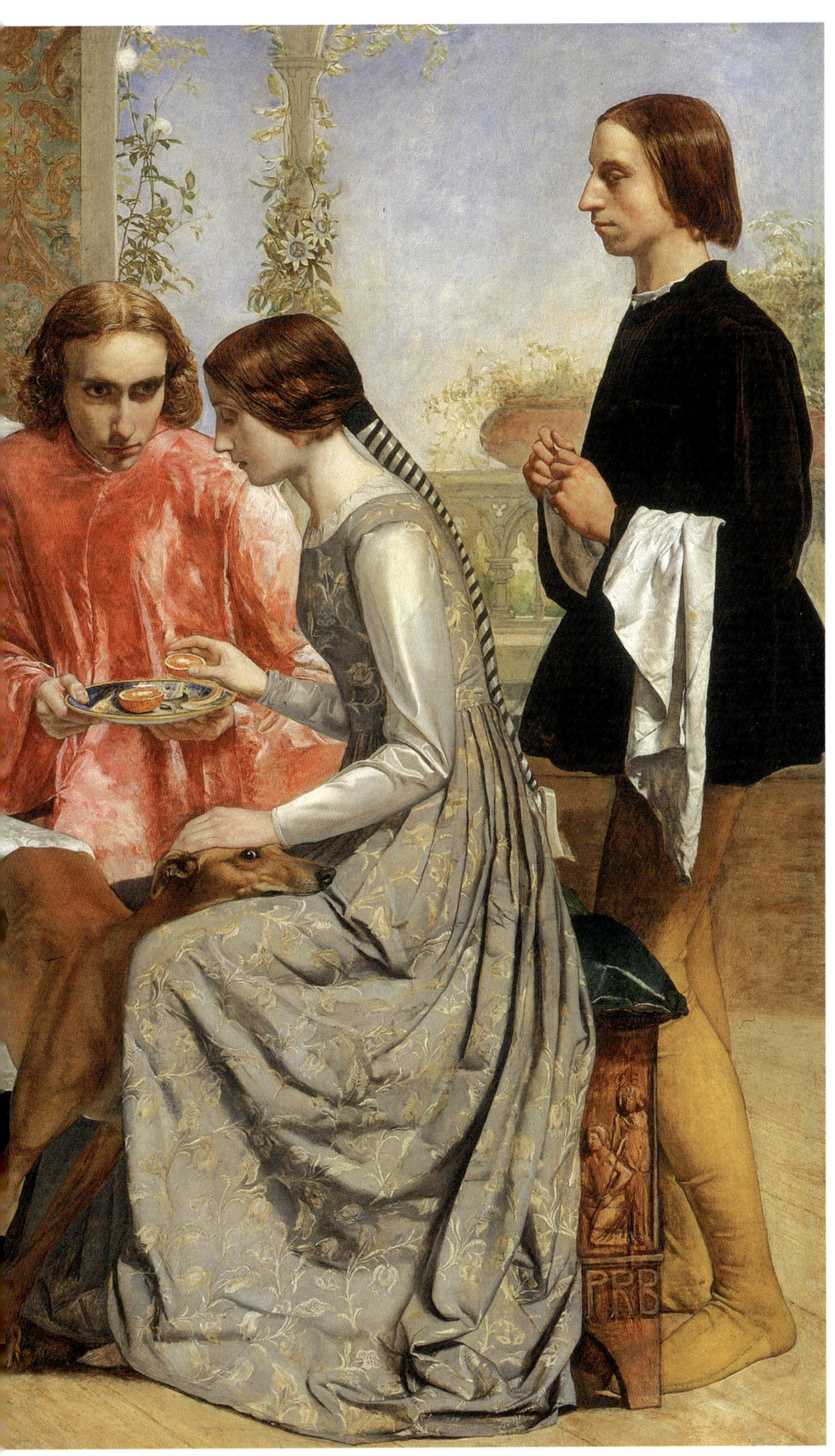

John Everett Millais (1829–96)

Isabella, 1848–9

Oil on canvas, 103 × 142.8 cm
Purchased in 1884; inv. no. WAG 1637

This is a painted manifesto of the aims of the Pre-Raphaelite Brotherhood. It was the first picture painted by Millais after he joined the group. The awkward poses of the figures, unbalanced composition and deliberate flatness echo the paintings by the early Italian masters admired by the Brotherhood. Millais has rejected the dramatic contrast of light and dark that he had been taught at art school and has used a more natural, even light. Every part of the picture has been painted with minute attention to detail, resolutely sticking to the group's aims to depict nature exactly as they found it. Millais includes many symbols to add layers of meaning to the scene, notably the roses and passion flowers above the doomed lovers Lorenzo and Isabella to indicate their feelings; the violent scenes painted on the family's plates which allude to a later section of the poem when Lorenzo is murdered by Isabella's brothers; and the pot of herbs which hints at the pot of basil in which Isabella buries her lover's head after finding his body. Millais uses the Brotherhood's palette of bright, jewel-like colours and has signalled his membership of the group by adding the initials PRB on the side of the stool upon which Isabella sits.

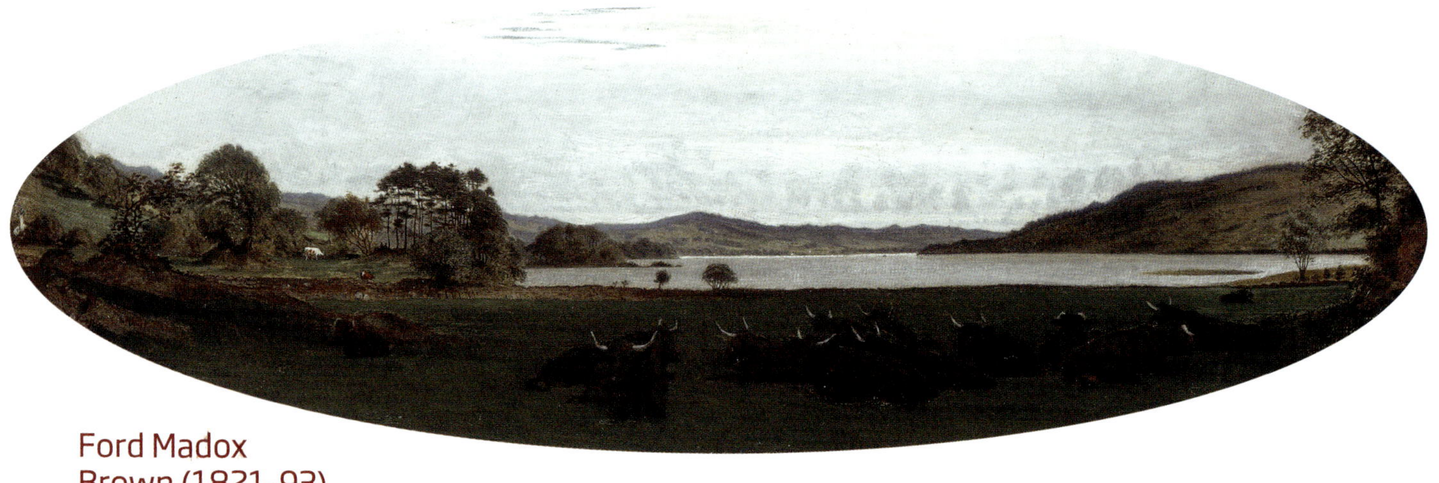

Ford Madox Brown (1821–93)

Windermere, 1848–55

Oil on canvas, 17.5 × 49.2 cm

Purchased by William Hesketh Lever in 1917; inv. no. LL 3638

Brown visited the Lake District with the artist Charles Lucy (1814–73) in September 1848. In this painting he captures the view of Windermere from the north of the lake, looking south. He worked on it for six days despite encountering typical Lakeland weather which meant that on the last day he had to paint 'in the rain under an umbrella'. After this the two friends hiked to Patterdale, Keswick, Borrowdale and Eskdale before catching the train to Liverpool to see one of Brown's paintings on show in an exhibition at the Liverpool Academy. Brown's delight in painting unassuming landscapes such as *Windermere* was one of the many reasons that he and Ruskin, who coached many Pre-Raphaelite painters, did not get on. Ruskin preferred dramatic landscapes that radiated the mystery and glory of nature like those painted by his hero JMW Turner (1775–1851). Despite this Brown's landscapes inspired many Pre-Raphaelite artists, particularly those in Liverpool, to find beauty in quieter landscapes which others might pass over.

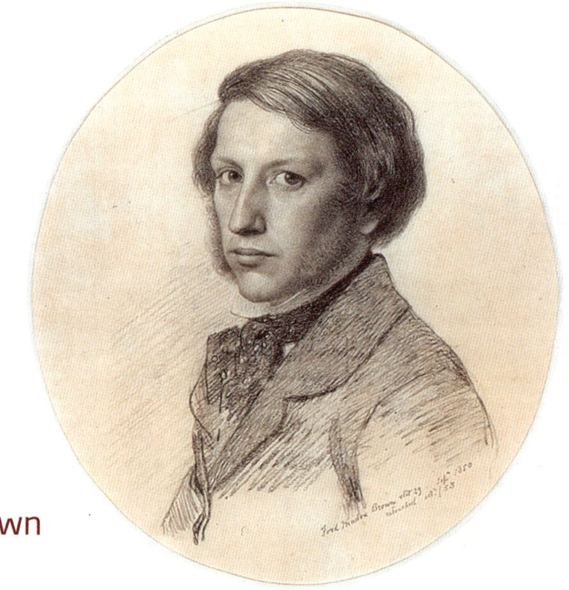

Ford Madox Brown (1821–93)

Self-portrait, 1850–3

Black chalk on paper, 25 × 23 cm

Purchased with the assistance of the Art Fund in 1984; inv. no. WAG 10505

By 1850, following years of sadness after the death of his wife, Brown had finally found hope with a new love, Emma Hill, a wide circle of artistic friends, and some positive recognition of his talent. This confidence is reflected in this self-assured portrait. It was painted while he was completing his enormous painting *Chaucer and the Court of Edward III* (1845–51, Art Gallery of New South Wales, Sydney) for the 1851 Royal Academy Summer Exhibition. Brown was 29 years old, and by this time, although not an official member of the Pre-Raphaelite Brotherhood, he had made lasting friendships with its leaders Rossetti, Holman Hunt and Millais.

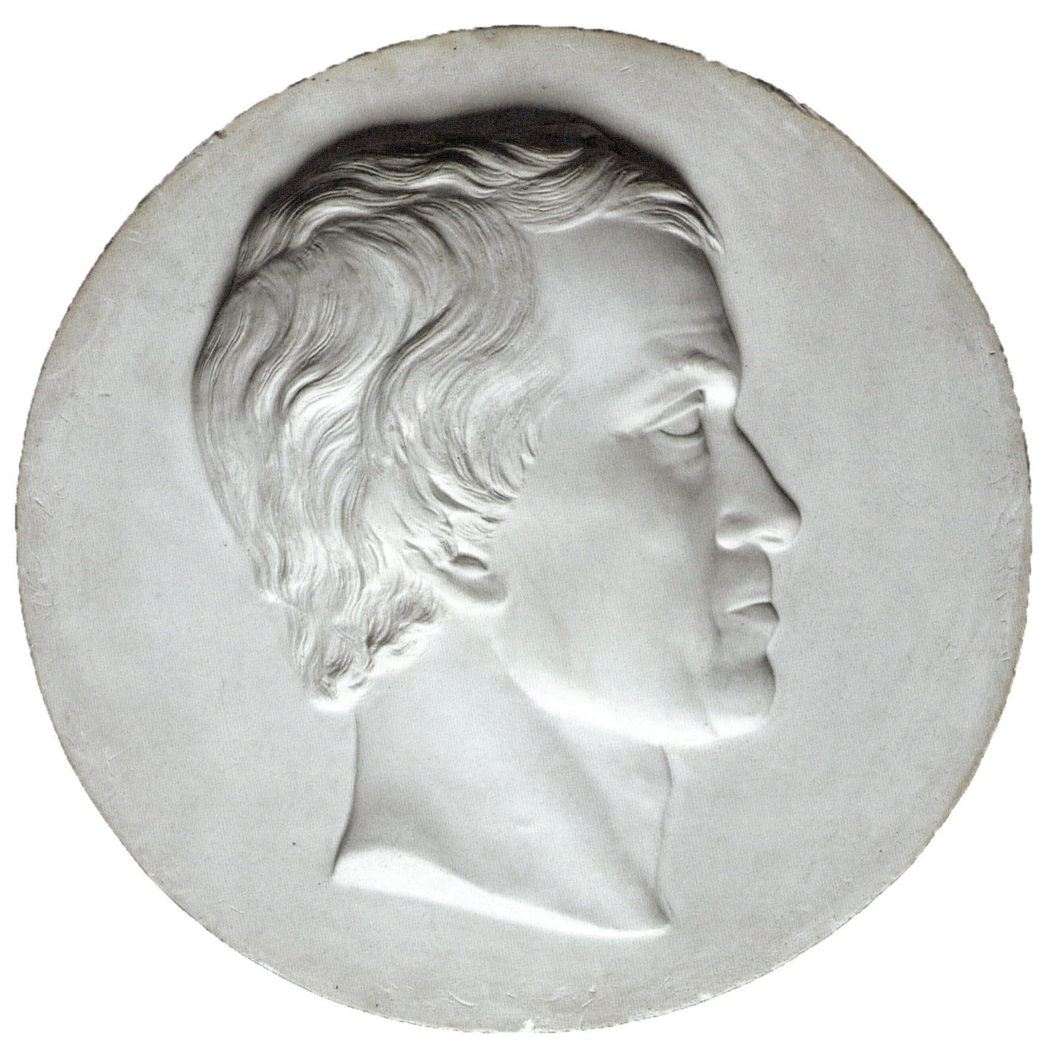

Thomas Woolner
(1825–92)

Thomas Carlyle, about 1851–5

Plaster, diameter 22.5cm

Presented by Miss Helen Martineau in 1942; inv. no. WAG 4110

Thomas Carlyle (1795–1881) was one of the most influential essayists and historians of the 19th century. Through the poet Coventry Patmore, Woolner arranged for Carlyle to sit for him in January 1851. This led to two bronze medallions being made in 1851 and 1855. It is not clear to which of the two bronzes this plaster medallion relates.

Woolner was a founding member of the Pre-Raphaelite Brotherhood and the only sculptor in the group. He left England to join the Australian gold rush in 1852 and his emigration inspired Ford Madox Brown's large painting *The Last of England* (1852–1855, Birmingham Museums and Art Gallery). Finding gold prospecting unprofitable Woolner returned to England in 1854 to continue working as a sculptor after completing several Australian commissions.

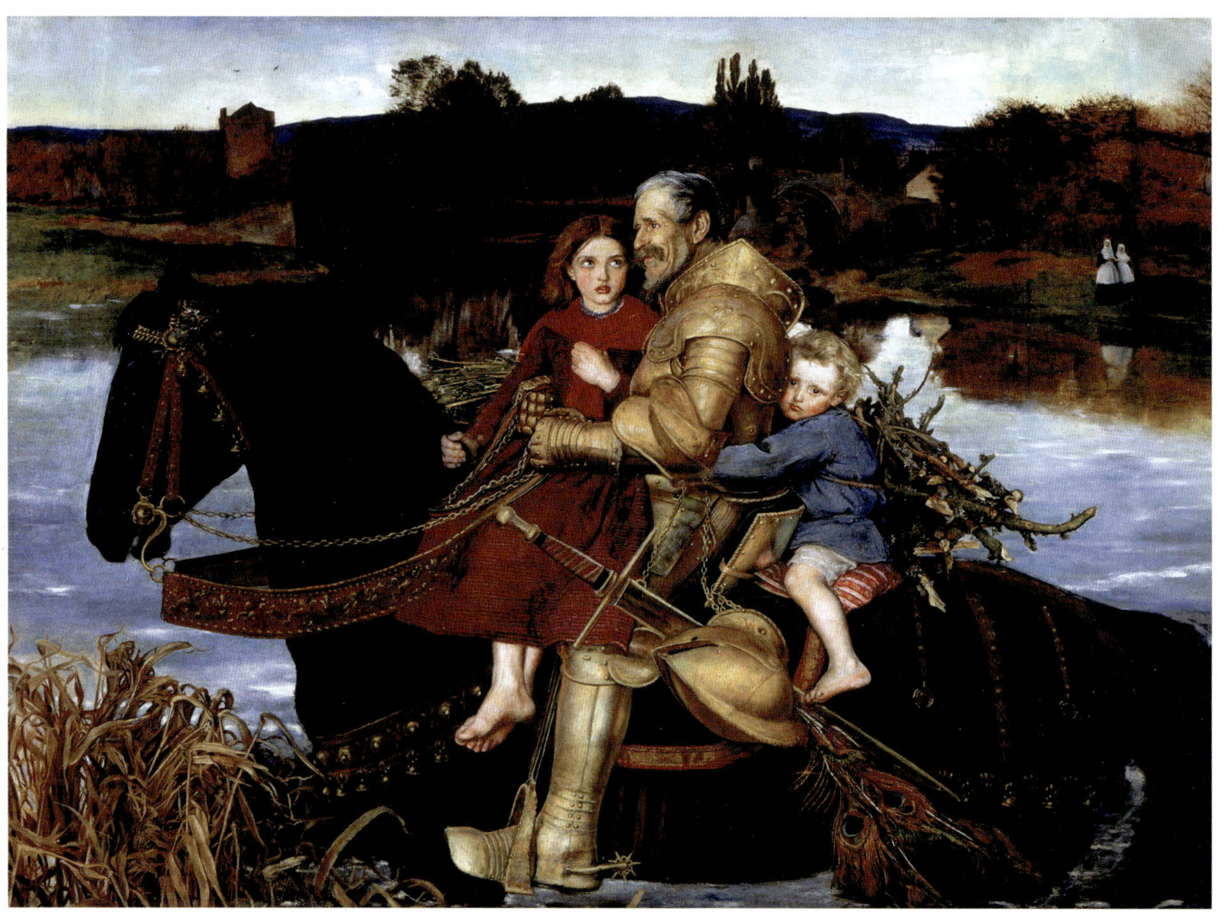

John Everett Millais (1829–96)

A Dream of the Past: Sir Isumbras at the Ford, 1857

Oil on canvas, 125.5 × 171.5 cm

Purchased by William Hesketh Lever in 1913; inv. no. LL 3625

The Pre-Raphaelite Brotherhood was drawn to medieval subjects and themes of chivalry. This painting shows Sir Isumbras, an ancient knight, carrying the children of a poor woodcutter across a river. Isumbras was a character from a 14th-century English Romance but this scene does not appear in the poem.

Although the landscape background with its fidelity to nature was much admired, the horse was heavily criticised for being too big, and Millais repainted it several times. In order to explain the painting Millais' friend, the art critic Tom Taylor, wrote a medieval-style verse to accompany the picture:

The goode hors that the knyghte bestrode,
I trow his backe it was full brode,
And wighte and warie still he yode,
  Noght reckinge of rivere:
He was so mickle and so stronge,
And thereto so wonderliche longe
  In londe was none his peer.
N'as hors but by him seemed smalle,
The knyghte him cleped Launcival;
But lords at borde and groomes in stalle
            Cleped him Graund Destrere.

(Extract from *Metrical Romance of Sir Ysumbras*)*

---

*   *Artists of the Pre-Raphaelite Circle: The First Generation. Catalogue of Works in the Walker Art Gallery, Lady Lever Art Gallery and Sudley Art Gallery*, Mary Bennett, National Museums & Galleries on Merseyside, 1988.

Frederick Sandys (1829–1904)

A Nightmare, 1857

Zincotype print on paper, 33.8 × 48.6 cm

Presented by HE Kidson in 1917; inv. no. WAG 5620

Sandys anonymously published this caricature of Millais' picture *A Dream of the Past: Sir Isumbras at the Ford* [see p.24] shortly after the painting appeared at the Royal Academy. This playful print pokes fun at the leaders of the Pre-Raphaelite Brotherhood and their champion, John Ruskin. Sandys replaced the knight's face with the head of Millais, the little girl became Rossetti and the little boy became Hunt. The horse has been turned into Ruskin who is depicted as a braying donkey with his initials burnt into his rump. Sandys was an emerging artist and despite the satirical nature of the caricature he became good friends with the Pre-Raphaelites, particularly Rossetti, whom he may have first met in order to memorise his likeness for the caricature.

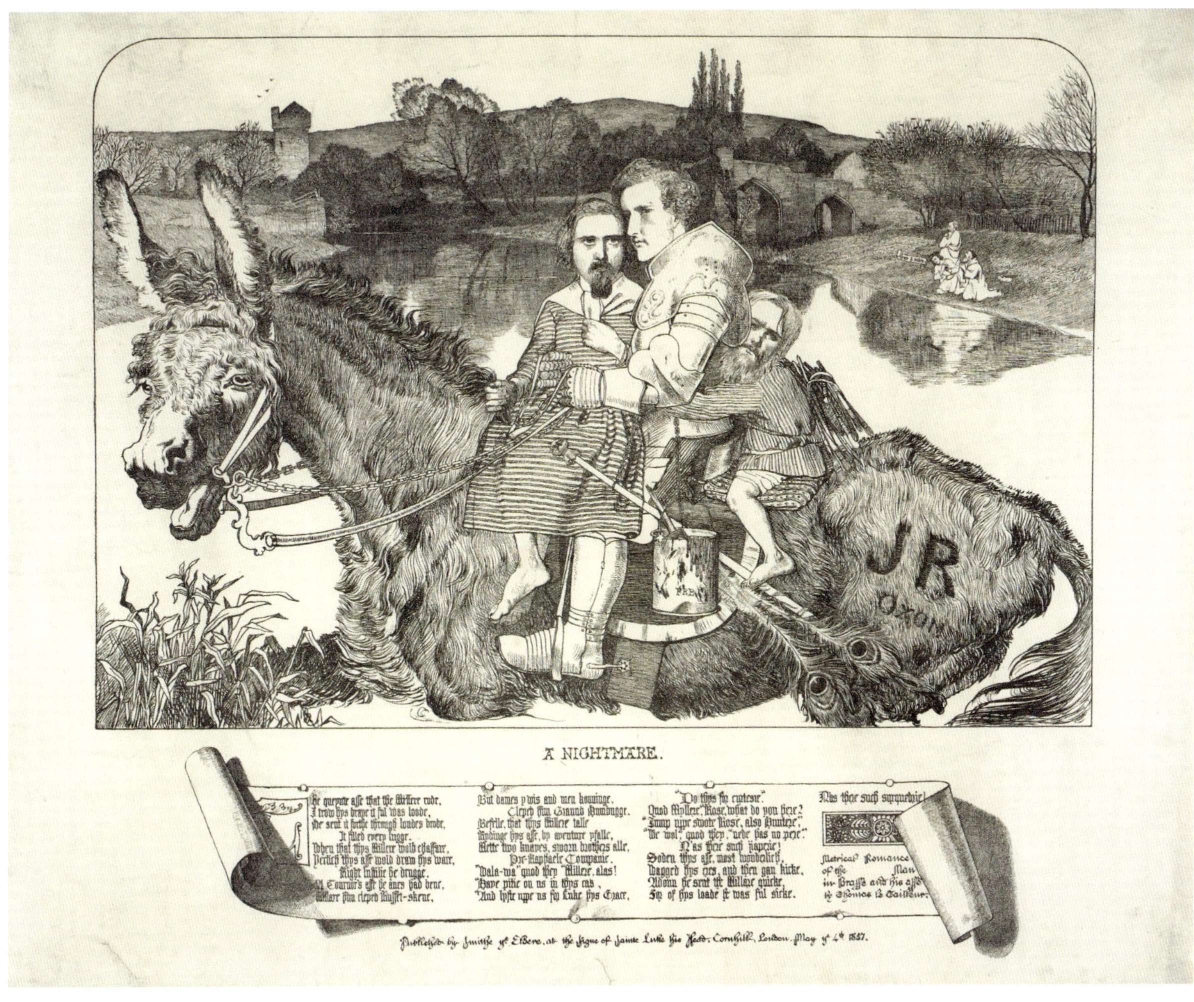

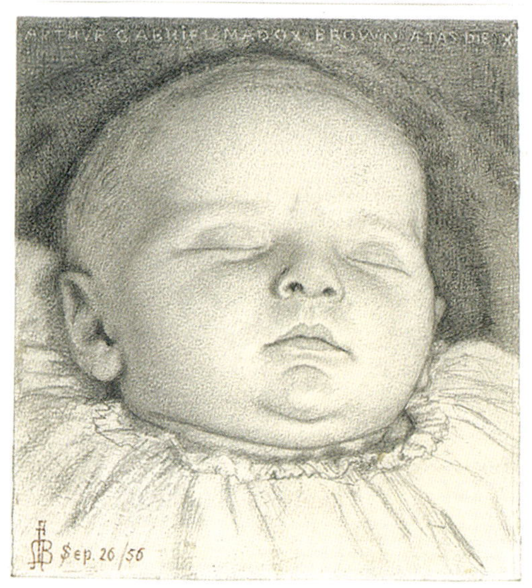

Ford Madox Brown (1821–93)

Arthur Gabriel Madox Brown as a Baby, 1856

Pencil on paper, 15.5 × 14 cm
Purchased with the assistance of the Art Fund in 1984; inv. no. WAG 10509

Arthur Gabriel Madox Brown, 1857

Black and red chalk on paper, 12 × 9.8 cm
Purchased with the assistance of the Art Fund in 1984; inv. no. WAG 10510

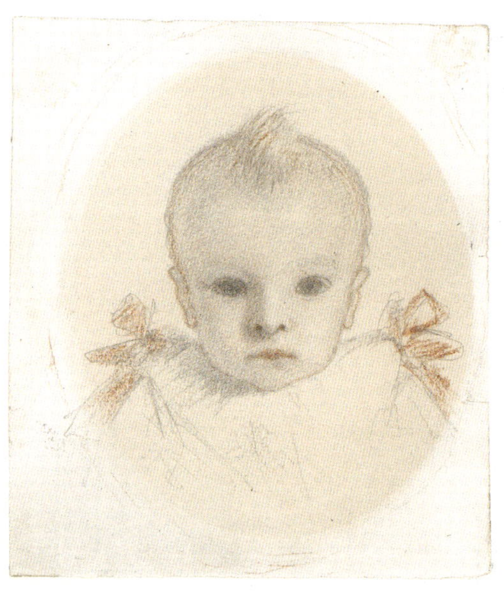

National Museums Liverpool's Pre-Raphaelite collection contains a number of drawings of Brown's four children made between 1847 and 1857. These two portraits are particularly poignant as they are of Brown's third son, Arthur Gabriel, who died aged 10 months. The drawings record his short life but also his father's pride in his new son. The first portrait of Arthur sleeping was completed when he was 10 days old. In this tender study Brown has captured the delicacy of the newborn's skin and his soft downy hair.

Brown liked to use his family as models in his paintings and this included even its youngest members. The second portrait of Arthur is a study for his painting *Work* (1852-65, Manchester City Art Gallery), an allegory of modern labour set in a contemporary London street.

John Brett (1831–1902)

The Stonebreaker, 1857–8

Oil on canvas, 51.3 × 68.5 cm

Bequeathed by Sarah Anne Barrow in 1918; inv. no. WAG 1632

Brett's painting of a boy breaking up flint for road repairs reflects his deep interest in geology, John Ruskin's ideas about the depiction of nature, and the art of the Pre-Raphaelite Brotherhood. Each element of the landscape is painted with minute attention to detail, including each individual rock, the dead tree and the foliage surrounding the boy and his dog. In the background is a view of the Mole Valley towards Box Hill, Surrey. The majority of the picture was painted outdoors on location. Brett wrote to his sister that: 'I can only work on it in sunny days - I hope it will look sunny. If it does not there will be no excuse for it for nothing has been done without the sun... I am gypsyish sun-tanned all over now.' Stone-breaking was a job given by local parishes to the destitute. Children were often among these impoverished workers. Although this boy looks well-clothed and appears to be enjoying his job in the sunny outdoors, Brett's painting nonetheless highlights the plight of child labour. He presents it in a form, however, that was more palatable to its middle- and upper-class Victorian viewers.

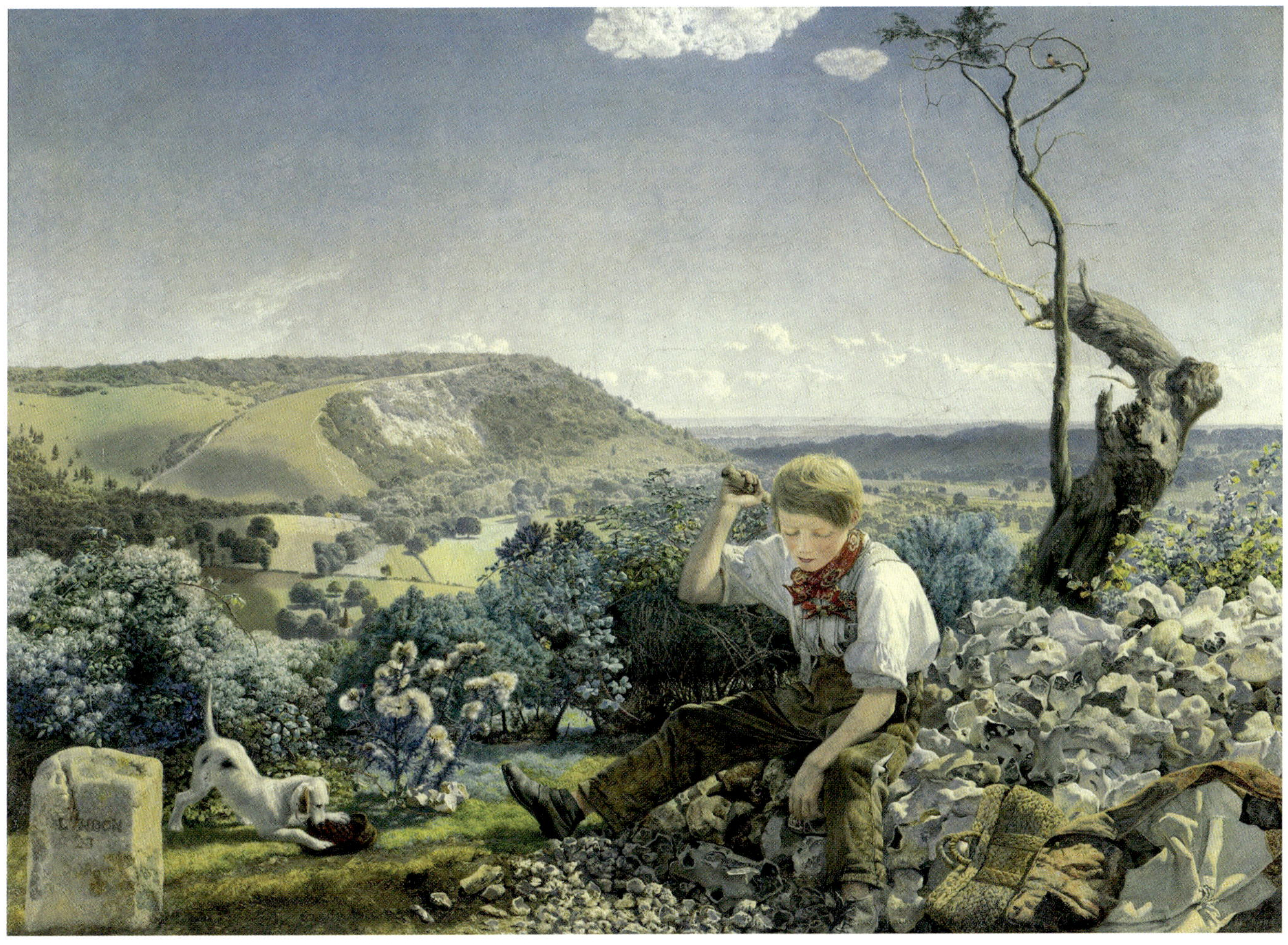

William Holman Hunt (1827–1910)

The Scapegoat, 1854–5

Oil on canvas, 87 × 139.8 cm
Purchased by William Hesketh Lever in 1923; inv. no. LL3623

In 1854 Hunt travelled to the Holy Land for the first time and stayed for almost two years. Fuelled by the Brotherhood's principles of 'truth to nature' and his own desire to revitalise Christian art, he was intent on finding authentic backgrounds for his biblical paintings. Before he departed Hunt read about a ritual in the Old Testament in which a goat, with scarlet cloth between its horns, was driven out of the temple into the wilderness carrying with it the sins of the congregation. If the sins were forgiven the cloth would turn white. For Hunt the goat symbolised Christ carrying the sins of the world. On seeing the Dead Sea for the first time he was inspired to paint *The Scapegoat*. He spent two weeks painting in the landscape and making notes. The beautiful but desolate wilderness is rendered with an intense attention to detail. Hunt showcases the vivid colours of the sunset which will soon leave the wretched goat alone in the darkness.

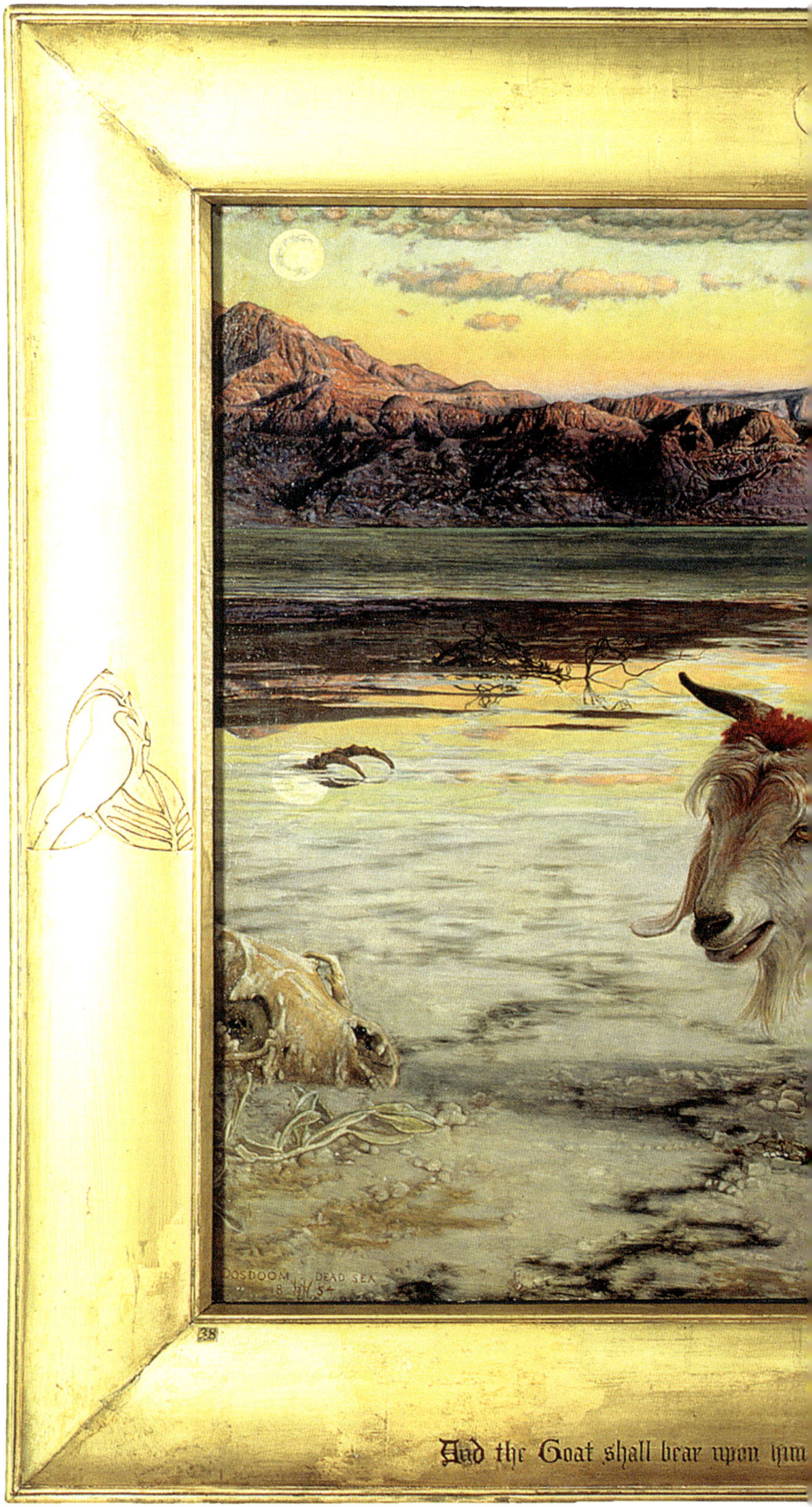

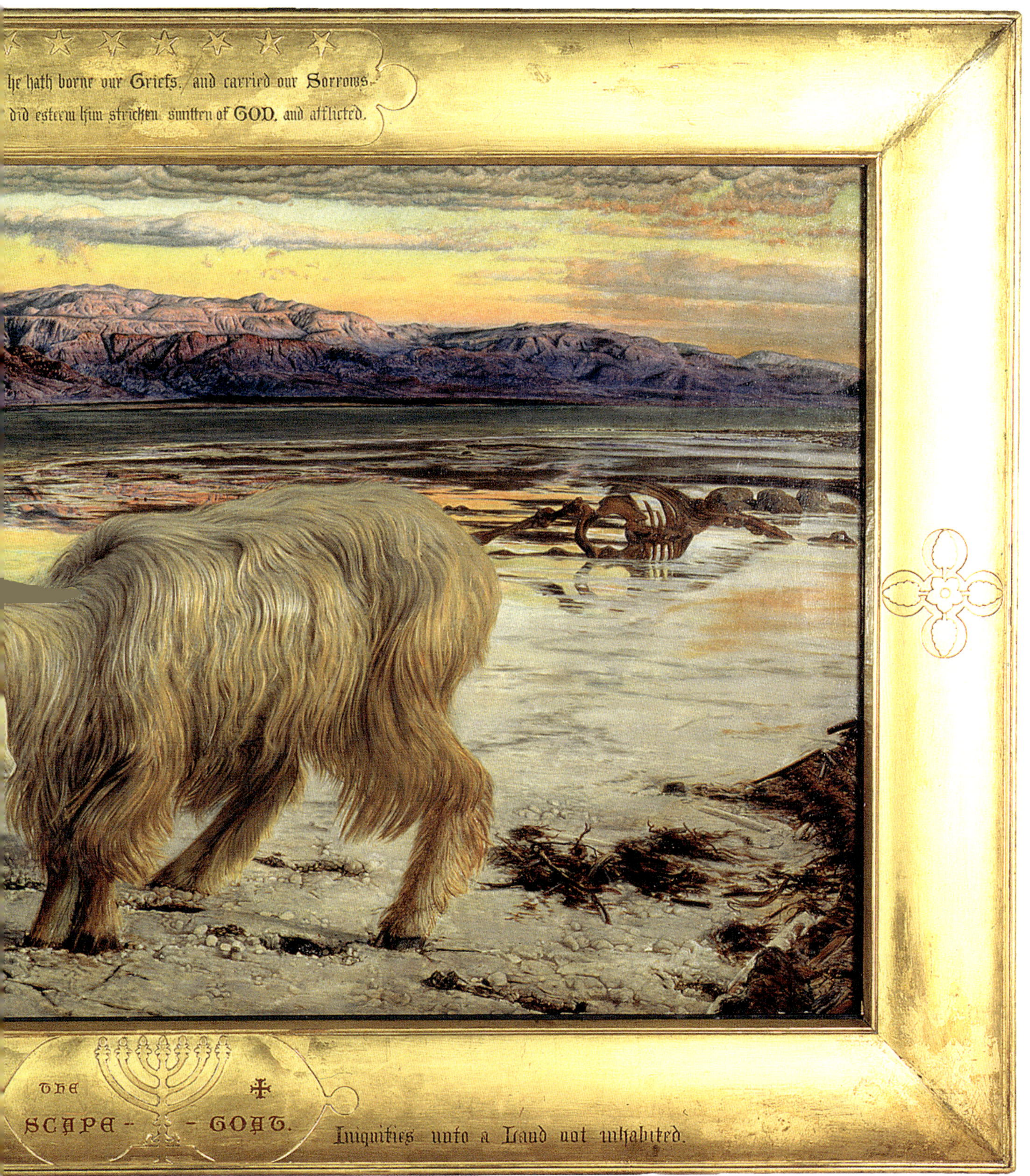
he hath borne our Griefs, and carried our Sorrows
did esteem him stricken, smitten of GOD, and afflicted.
THE
SCAPE - GOAT.
Iniquities unto a Land not inhabited.

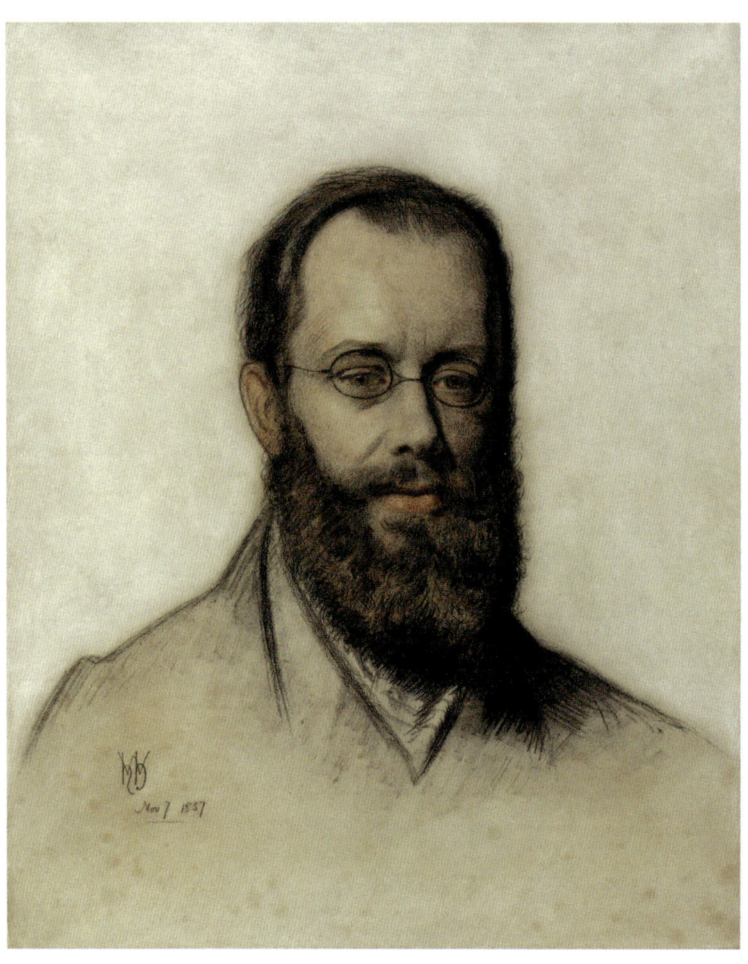

William Holman Hunt (1827–1910)

Edward Lear, 1857

Crayon and chalk on paper, 61.3 × 48.8 cm

Presented by William Holman Hunt in 1907; inv. no. WAG 1251

Lear gained fame as the author of *A Book of Nonsense* which he wrote in 1846 for the children and grandchildren of the 13th Earl of Derby. As well as an author Lear was a skilled zoological draughtsman who was commissioned by the Earl to draw the exotic birds in the menagerie at his estate in Knowsley. For the sake of his health Lear wintered abroad and used his skills to paint watercolours of the landscapes he saw on his travels in the Mediterranean and Egypt. Hunt met Lear in 1852 and gave him painting advice in return for Italian lessons. This led to a lifelong friendship which is recorded in this portrait of Lear, aged 45. Hunt liked to make chalk drawings of his friends to hang in his home and the Walker's collection also contains a portrait of his pupil Robert Braithwaite Martineau, another token of friendship.

Ford Madox Brown (1821–93)

Waiting: An English Fireside in the Winter of 1854–5, 1851–55

Oil on oak panel, 30.5 × 20 cm

Purchased with the assistance of the National Heritage Memorial Fund, the V&A Purchase Grant Fund, the Pilgrim Trust and the Friends of Merseyside Museums and Art Galleries in 1985; inv. no. WAG 10533

This small picture was Brown's first completed work to focus on a contemporary scene. His belief that modern life was a fit subject for serious painting led others in the Pre-Raphaelite circle to look to the everyday for inspiration. Family was extremely important to Brown. In this painting he celebrates motherhood but also his own family as he used his second wife, Emma, and their baby, Catherine, as models. The artist met Emma in 1848 and Catherine was born in 1850 but they did not marry until 1853. Like his other works from the 1850s and '60s this picture exemplifies Brown's obsessive attention to detail. He records each object in minute faithfulness; from the reflection of the fire on the handle of the poker to the single thread Emma is using to sew. He also insisted on painting his models in the actual light to be depicted in the picture. Here the glow from the lamp and the fire cast a large shadow behind Emma while the flames reflect brightly on Cathy's nightgown. This is the second version of the painting. The first was simply titled *Waiting* but Brown made this version more topical. He added a letter and a miniature portrait of an officer to the composition and changed the title to include the date of 1854–5 to suggest that the dutiful wife is waiting for her husband to return from the Crimean War.

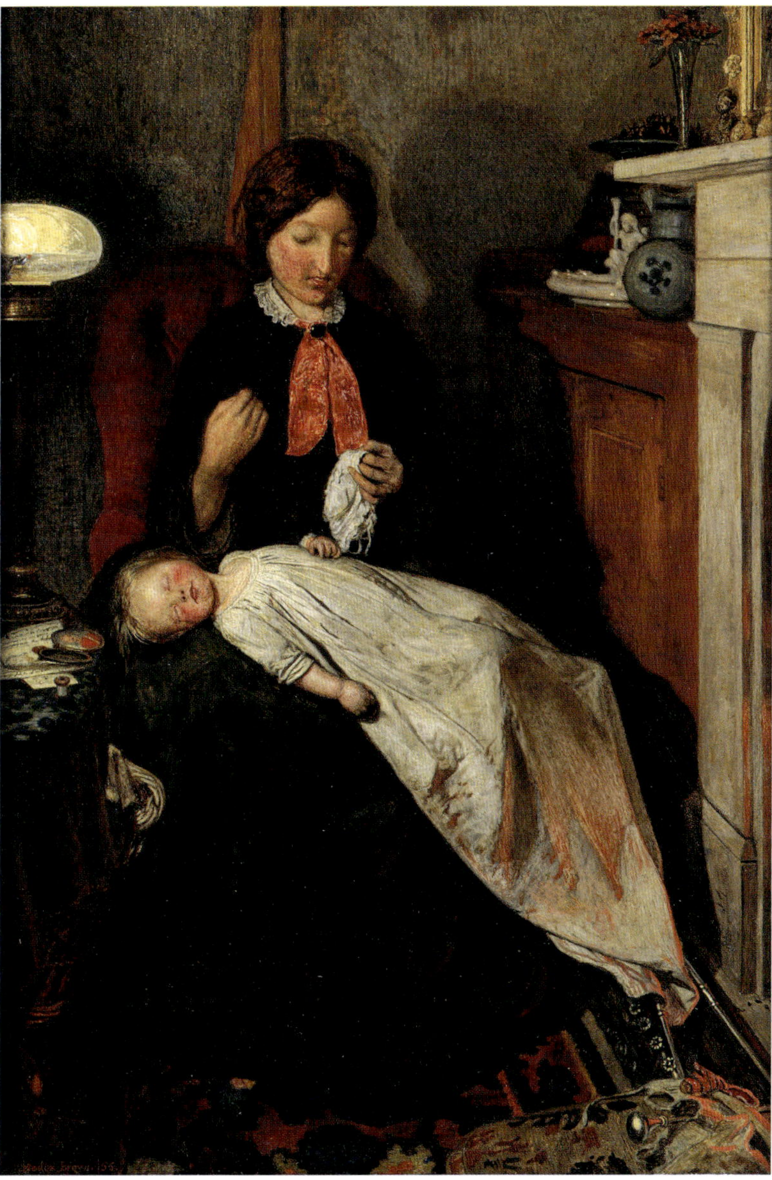

Henry Wallis (1830–1916)

A Coastal Scene, Sunset, Seaford, 1859

Oil on board, 22.5 × 35.5 cm

Purchased in 1954; inv. no. WAG 1640

This painting was a gift from Wallis to the landscape artist George Price Boyce (1826–97). The two friends socialised with many of the Pre-Raphaelite artists and Wallis is mentioned repeatedly in Boyce's diary in the company of Dante Gabriel Rossetti and Edward Burne-Jones.

Wallis was drawn to the beauty of melancholic twilight scenes. The view in this picture is the coastline at Seaford, near Newhaven in Sussex. Wallis got to know this area well in the mid-1850s when visiting his friend, the novelist and poet George Meredith (1828–1909) and his wife at their summer lodgings in Seaford. Wallis used Meredith as a model for the face of the dying poet in his masterpiece *The Death of Chatterton* (1856, Tate). The painting brought him overnight success when it was shown at the Royal Academy in 1856. A year later, Wallis and Meredith's wife, Mary Ellen (1821–61), became lovers. She left her husband and had a son with Wallis before the couple separated in 1859. Mary Ellen stayed in Seaford every year from 1857 until 1859 and this picture, which was painted the year they parted, may have been inspired by the bittersweet emotions of their love affair.

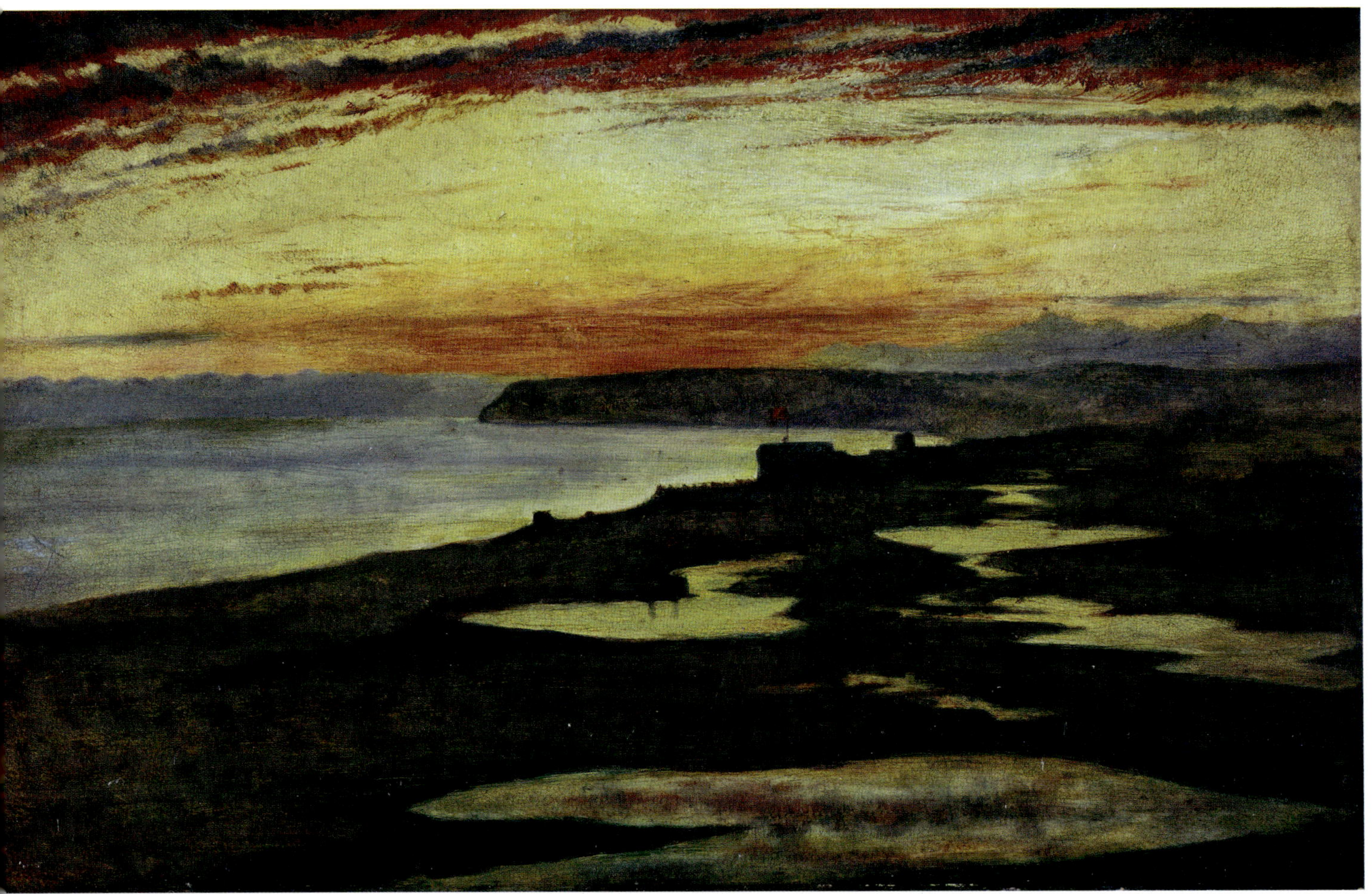

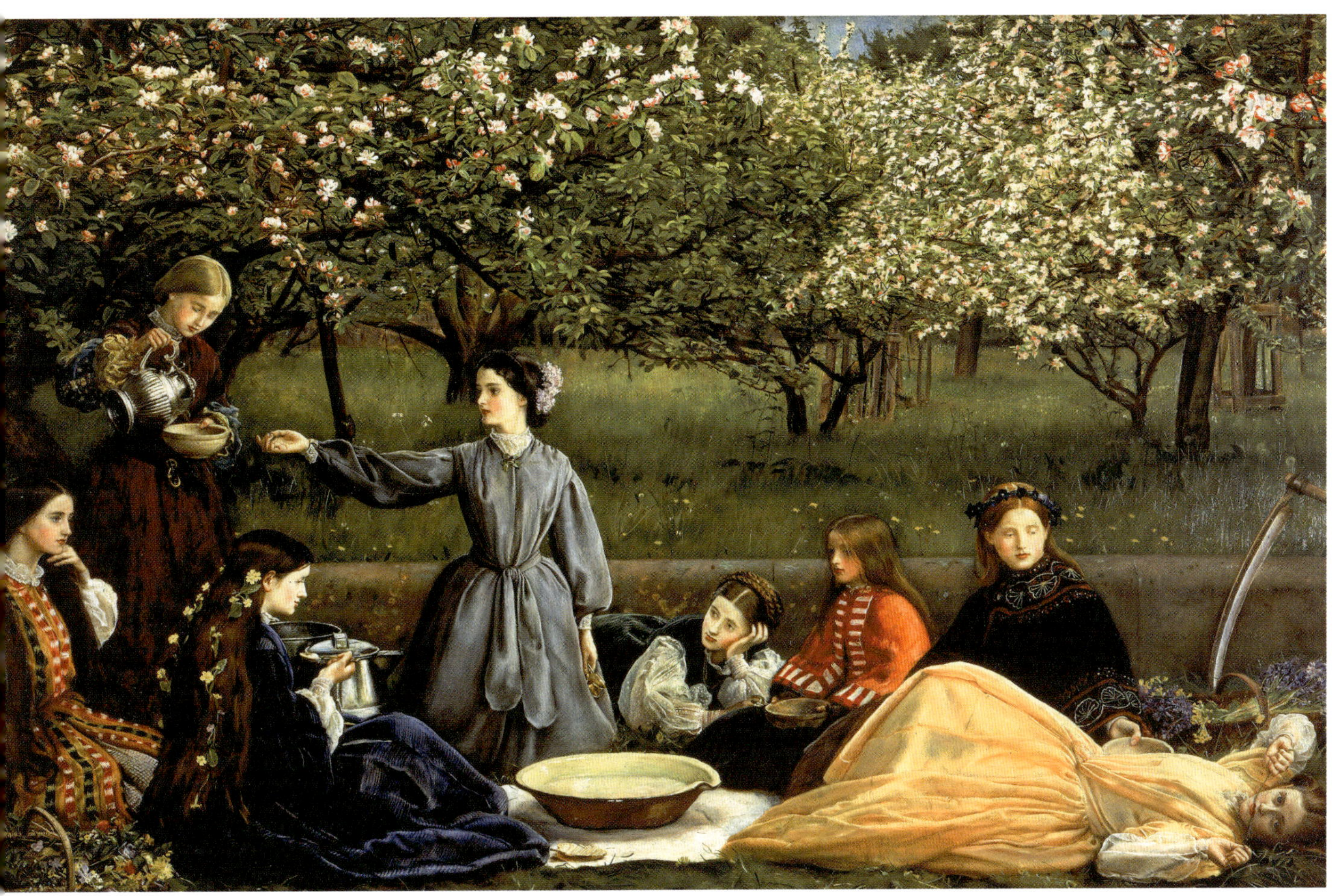

John Everett Millais (1829–96)

Spring (Apple Blossoms), 1859

Oil on canvas, 113 × 176.3 cm

Purchased with the assistance of the National Heritage Memorial Fund in 1986; inv. no. LL3624

This painting of young women in modern dress received negative comments from the art critics when it was exhibited in 1859. Reviewers felt Millais' paint handling was heavy-handed in comparison to the delicate, detailed pictures he had previously painted. The painting marks a change in the style and subject of Millais' work. It was very different from most of his previous pictures of subjects taken from history, literature and the Bible. Rather than creating a narrative he sought to evoke a particular mood and move the viewer to contemplation. The young women in the scene are enjoying a spring picnic, eating curds and whey. Only one girl gazes out of the picture, drawing the viewer's eye to the scythe above her. This discarded farm tool symbolises death and reminds the viewer that even these pretty girls, like the apple blossom in the orchard, will lose their youthful vitality and succumb to life's natural ending.

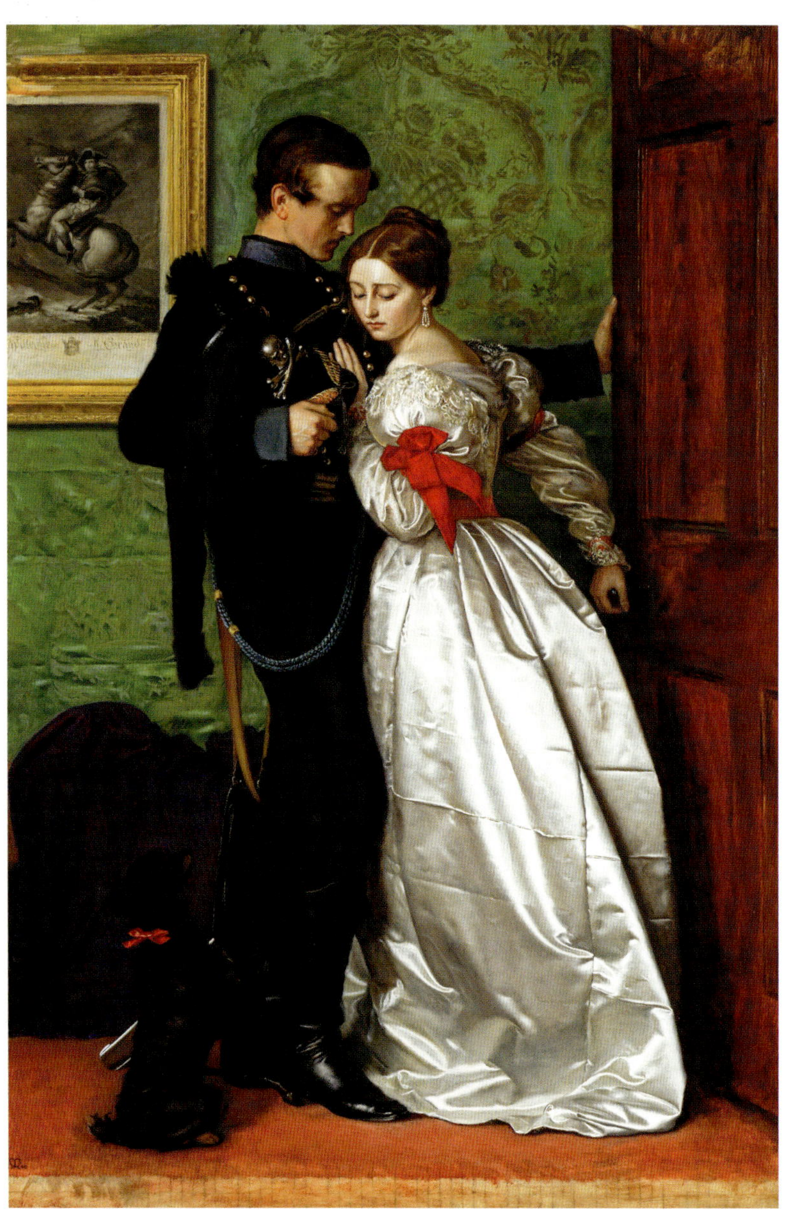

John Everett Millais (1829–96)

The Black Brunswickers, 1860

Oil on canvas, 104 × 68.5 cm

Purchased by William Hesketh Lever in 1898; inv. no. LL 3643

The Black Brunswickers were formed in 1809 by Frederick William, Duke of Brunswick (1771–1815), nephew of George III. They were known for their black uniforms and distinctive death's-head cap badge. On 16 June 1815 they fought Napoleon's troops in the battle of Quatre Bras at Waterloo and suffered severe losses, including the death of their Commander-in-Chief, the Duke of Brunswick. Two days later they fought in the Battle of Waterloo. Millais gives a taste of the drama to come by adding a framed print of Napoleon in the top left corner of the painting.

For this picture of a young German officer and his English sweetheart parting on the eve of the momentous battle Millais used the author Charles Dickens' daughter Kate as a model. To maintain her respectability Kate, and the private from the Life Guards who sat for the officer, modelled for Millais at separate times, using an artist's dummy to stand in for the other figure.

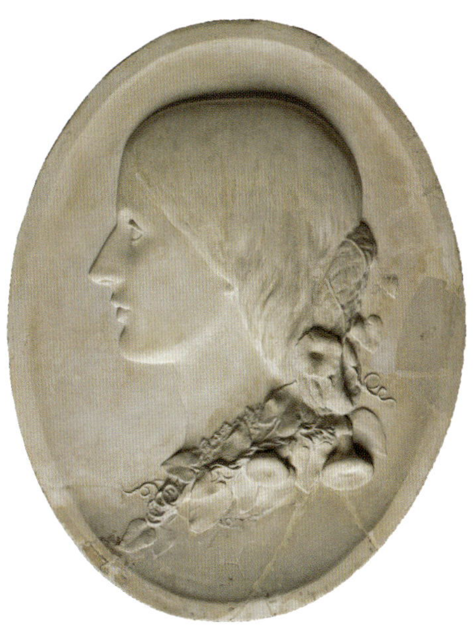

Josephine Butler (Mrs George Butler), by 1857

Marble, (h) 69 cm

Presented by the Diocese of Liverpool in 1975;
inv. no. WAG 8782

The woman immortalised by these two sculptures is Josephine Butler (née Grey, 1828–1906). Butler was a social reformer and women's activist who was known for her charisma as a leader. She moved to Liverpool in 1864 with her husband and young family. During her time in this port city she worked tirelessly to improve the lives of poverty-stricken and downtrodden women. She nursed many destitute women in her own house, founded a home of rest for the dying, and established a small envelope factory to provide employment and lodgings for girls with no other means of supporting themselves. In 1869 she successfully led the campaign to repeal the Contagious Diseases Act. This act had allowed police and doctors forcibly to inspect those suspected of being prostitutes in garrison towns and ports for contagious diseases, brutally infringing upon the women's human rights.

The Butlers met Munro in around 1855 when they lived in Oxford and he was working on sculptures to decorate the Oxford Museum. In both sculptures the artist has captured the beauty for which Josephine was well known. His inclusion of *convolvulus*, or morning glory, in the relief portrait may well symbolise humility, an appropriate sentiment in connection with this remarkable woman.

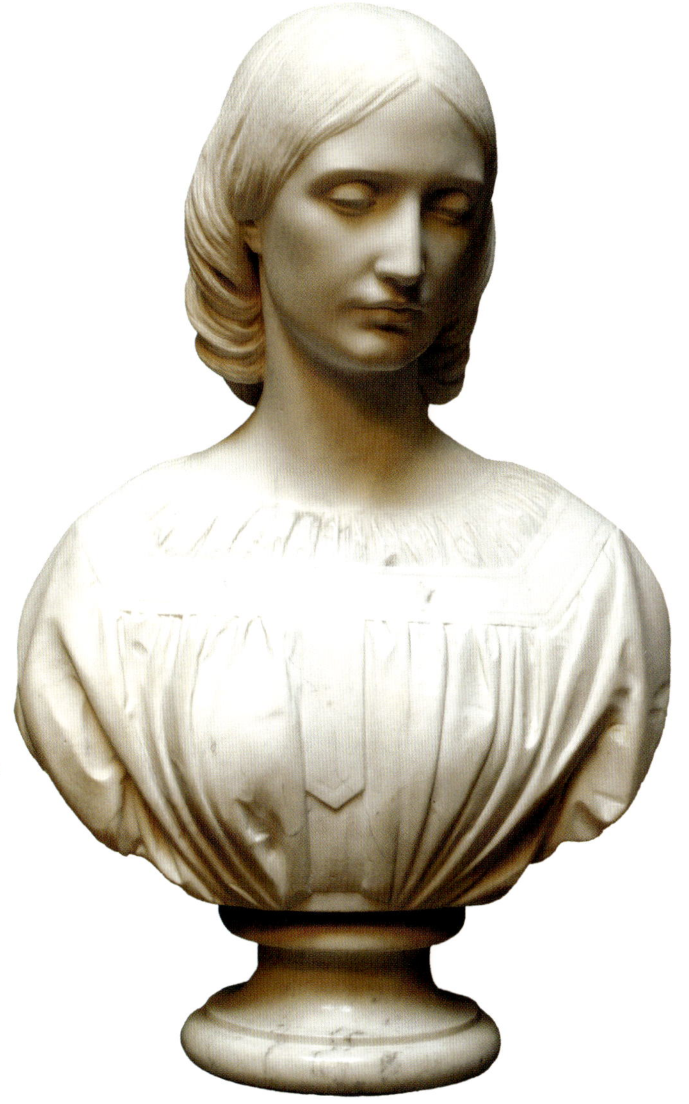

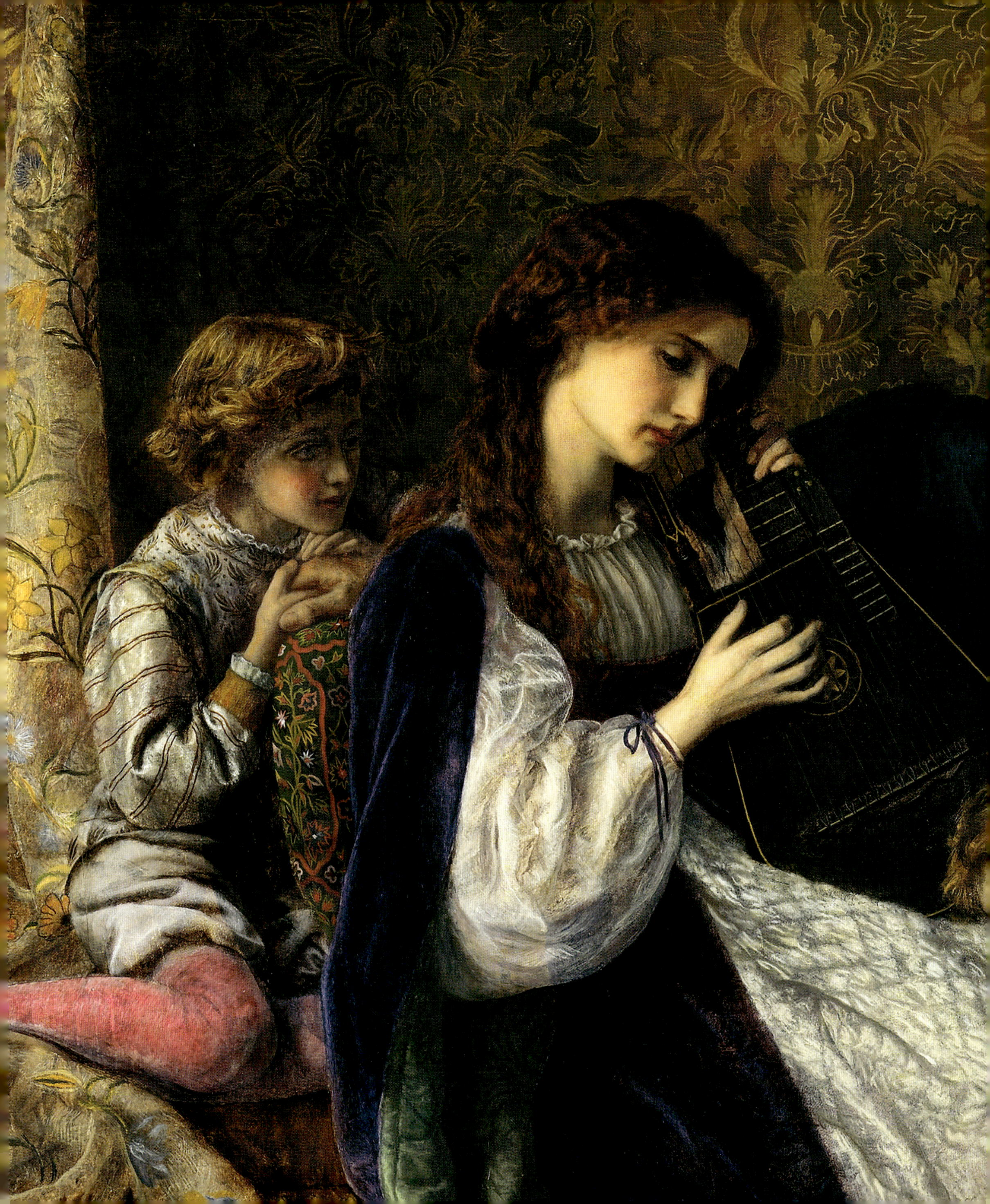

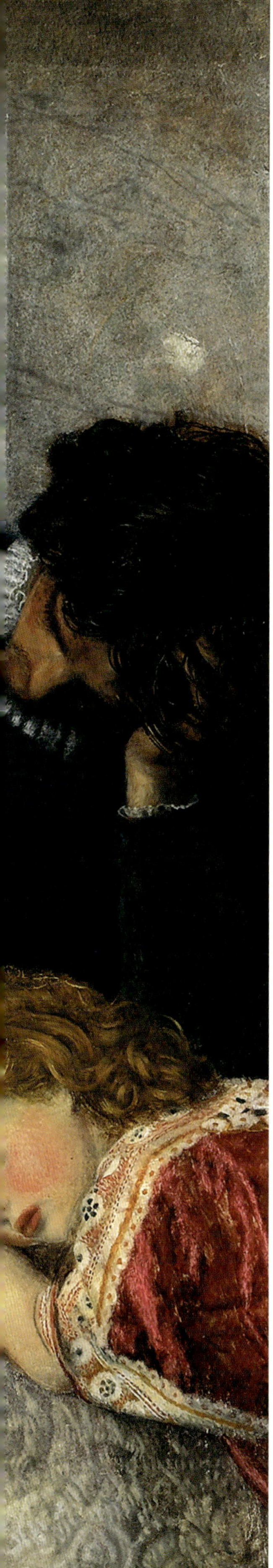

The Later Pre-Raphaelites

A second generation of Pre-Raphaelite artists emerged in the late 1850s, led initially by Dante Gabriel Rossetti, one of the founders of the original Pre-Raphaelite Brotherhood. In 1857 he gathered together a new group of young artists to decorate the ceiling of the Oxford Union Debating Hall. Like the original Brotherhood, Rossetti created a group of seven, asking William Morris (1834-96), Edward Burne-Jones (1833-98), Arthur Hughes (1832-1915), John Roddam Spencer Stanhope (1829-1908), John Hungerford Pollen (1820-1902) and Valentine Cameron Prinsep (1838-1904) to join him. Rossetti had not exhibited in public since his early biblical work *Ecce Ancilla Domini!* (1849-50, Tate) was heavily criticised when it was shown at the Royal Academy in 1850. Instead he had focused on making watercolours of archaic medieval subjects involving chivalry and romance. Despite his reluctance to exhibit his work, Rossetti found ready patrons. They eagerly purchased his painstakingly painted works whose jewel-like colours radiated luminosity. The younger artists were drawn to Rossetti's medieval subjects, and a scheme of decoration for the Hall based on Sir Thomas Malory's *Morte d'Arthur* (completed 1469-70) was designed. The walls were painted using fresco but owing to

the artists' lack of experience in the medium, they rapidly faded and within ten years were barely discernable.

The Oxford mural project, despite its unsatisfactory results, kick-started a second phase of the Pre-Raphaelite movement with Edward Burne-Jones and William Morris at the forefront. They had met Rossetti in 1856, and when they moved from Oxford the two bachelors rented the house in Red Lion Square, London, which had had previously been leased by him. The house soon became the centre of social gatherings for the new wave of Pre-Raphaelites. With the help of their artistic friends, Burne-Jones and Morris created a whole medieval scheme of decoration and furniture for their rooms.

Burne-Jones, who received some informal tutoring from Rossetti, focused initially on medieval subjects, painting watercolours in soft, muted colours. He impressed John Ruskin (1819-1900), the Pre-Raphaelite champion, who took him to Italy to paint copies of Old Master paintings. Burne-Jones came back inspired by the works of 15th-century Venetian artists, notably Giorgione (active 1506, died 1510), whose lush green canvases influenced his style in the 1860s. Like the other late Pre-Raphaelites Burne-Jones shared interests with the artists of the Aesthetic Movement. This circle of artists

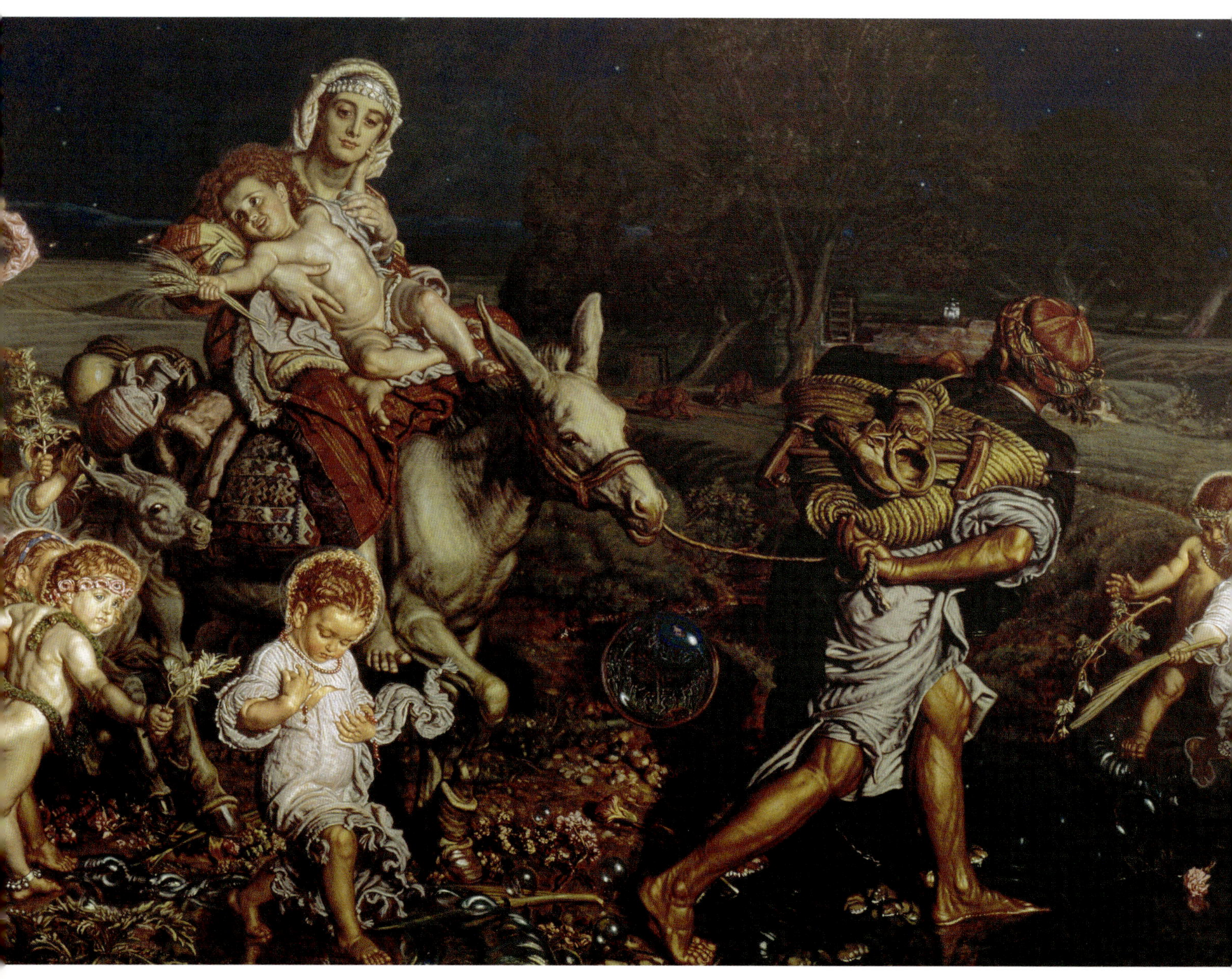

and writers believed that art needed no purpose other than to be beautiful. Painters such as James Abbot McNeill Whistler (1834–1903) and Albert Moore (1841–93) experimented with colour, creating harmonies that affected the eyes just as music affects the ears. Burne-Jones' works often had a loose medieval, mythological or biblical narrative but their primary focus was the beauty of the figures and the colour harmonies created by his choice of palette. His style influenced a number of painters including John Melhuish Strudwick (1849–1937), Marie Stillman (1844–1927) and Evelyn de Morgan (1855–1919), all of whom are represented in National Museums Liverpool's collection.

Morris, following an unsatisfying attempt at painting, turned to the decorative arts. Shortly after marrying Jane Burden in 1859, he and his bride moved to the newly built Red House in Kent. As with his London lodgings Morris enlisted his artistic friends to design the furniture and decorations for his new home. By 1861, inspired by furnishing the Red House, Morris and other members of the Pre-Raphaelite circle established Morris, Marshall, Faulkner & Co, a furnishing and decorative arts manufacturer and retailer. Rossetti, Madox Brown and Burne-Jones were founding partners and supplied the company with designs. The firm produced a huge range of goods from tiles, embroideries and wallpaper to furniture and stained glass. Following Morris' belief that factories stifled personal creativity, all pieces were handmade by individual craftsmen and women. In 1875 Morris reorganised the firm and renamed it Morris & Co, upsetting Brown, the chief stained-glass designer, by replacing him with Burne-Jones. Brown and Morris did not speak for more than ten years but were reconciled when they met again in old age.

Like that of Burne-Jones, Rossetti's late work was influenced by Venetian Renaissance painters, particularly Titian (about 1485/90-1576). His earlier preoccupation with medieval watercolours, painted using tiny brushstrokes and depicting figures in awkward poses, metamorphosed into large oil paintings of sensuous women, with long necks and full Cupid's bow lips. His personal life was marred by drama: his wife Lizzie Siddal (1829-62), a promising artist, died from a suspected overdose of the drug laudanum brought on by depression over their stillborn child and perhaps his infidelity. Having buried her with the only copy of his new poems, he later had her coffin exhumed to retrieve the script. After her death Rossetti moved to Tudor House in London's fashionable Chelsea with his one-time mistress, model and housekeeper, Fanny Cornforth. He developed a collecting mania for Chinese and Japanese blue and white porcelain, Japanese woodblock prints and musical instruments. He also had a menagerie of animals including two short-lived wombats. His obsessions may well have been symptomatic of the depression to which he succumbed in the 1870s. Rossetti fell in love with William Morris' wife Jane, who became the model for many of his later works, but even this romance was unable to cure his melancholy and he became addicted to chloral hydrate in order to alleviate his symptoms. This ultimately led to his early death in 1882 at the age of 54.

Of the original members of the Pre-Raphaelite Brotherhood, William Holman Hunt remained closest to their original ideals. He continued to produce religious paintings loaded with symbolism but his mature style favoured rounded figures and acidly bright colours such as those evident in *The Triumph of the Innocents*. Millais became an associate member of the Royal Academy in 1853 and a full member ten years later. To many this seemed as if he had joined ranks with the very institution that the Brotherhood had fought against. However, Millais had consistently exhibited there even while a member of the Brotherhood and through him the Pre-Raphaelite style had transformed British art. In his later work his dedication to minute attention to detail waned, his painting style became looser and his subjects more popular, often focusing on the delight of childhood. In 1885 he became a baronet and in 1896, the year he died, he became President of the Royal Academy.

Although the founders of the Brotherhood had died by the early 1900s the Pre-Raphaelite movement continued well into the 20th century with Eleanor Fortescue-Brickdale becoming the last disciple. A number of her later works brought the style into the fully mechanised age by taking as their subject matter the modern technology of the aeroplane and fusing it with Pre-Raphaelite symbolism and colour.

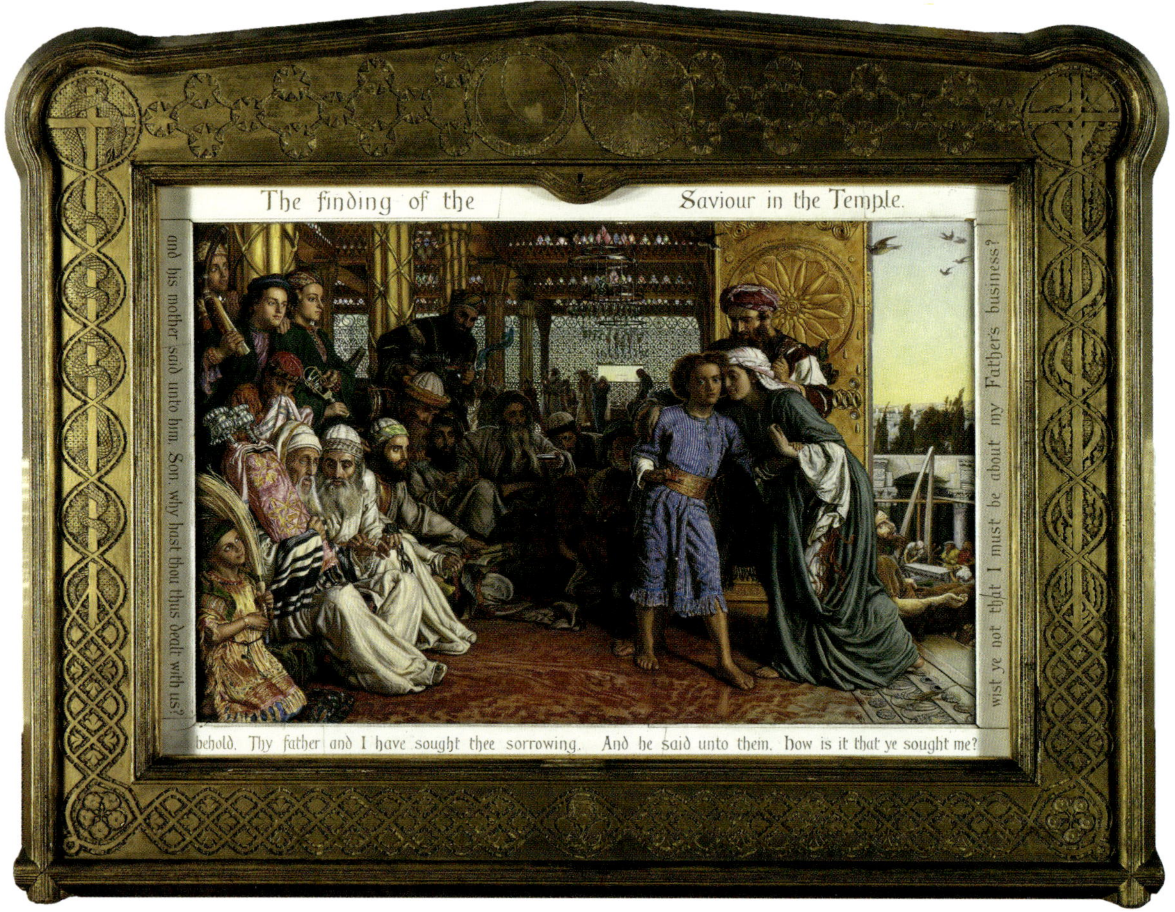

William Holman Hunt (1827–1910)

The Finding of the Saviour in the Temple, 1862

Oil on canvas, 45.5 × 70.2 cm

Bequeathed by Emma Holt in 1944; inv. no. WAG 246

Hunt began work on a painting of this scene on his first trip to Palestine in 1854. He used local models for the figures of Joseph and most of the Rabbis and elders. He made sketches of the landscape in the background showing north-east Jerusalem and the Mount of Olives before he returned to England. Once back in London, Hunt completed the picture, asking Mary Ada Mocatta, the wife of Frederic Mocatta, a wealthy philanthropist from one of the leading Anglo-Jewish families, to sit for Mary. He used a pupil from a nearby Jewish school to sit for Jesus. The interior of the temple was based on the Alhambra Court at Crystal Palace in Sydenham. Hunt undertook a great deal of research into Old Testament customs so that his evocation of the biblical past would be as accurate as possible and would bring Christ to life for his contemporary audience. The painting and its frame are brimming with religious symbols, giving added meaning to Hunt's narrative. The original painting was completed in 1860 and sold to the dealer Ernest Gambart. In 1861 he produced an engraving of the work, greatly increasing its fame and popularity. This half-sized version was bought by the Liverpool-based ship-owner George Holt in 1888 for 1,200 guineas.

Designed by Edward Burne-Jones (1833–98) and Philip Webb (1831–1915) for Morris, Marshall, Faulkner & Co

Cinderella tile panel, 1863

Painted tin-glazed earthenware, 56 × 137.8 cm

Purchased with the assistance of the Art Fund in 1989;
inv. no. WAG 1989.210

These tiles represent some of the earliest designs Burne-Jones made for Morris, Marshall, Faulkner & Co of which he was a founding partner. They were commissioned by the artist Myles Birket Foster (1825–99) to be placed above the fireplace in one of the bedrooms at The Hill, the house he designed for himself in Witley, Surrey. The house was a triumph of the Arts and Crafts movement, with artistic friends and craftsmen filling the rooms with unique pieces of furniture, decoration and textiles.

Unlike the 19th-century art market, the firm offered female artists more equality with their male contemporaries and welcomed their talents. The Cinderella tiles were painted by Lucy Faulkner Orrinsmith (1839–1910), sister of Charles Faulkner, another founding member of the firm. Both she and her sister Kate were skilled craftswomen, and Lucy worked for the firm from about 1861 until her marriage in 1870. The swan tiles were designed by the architect Philip Webb and became one of the firm's most iconic patterns.

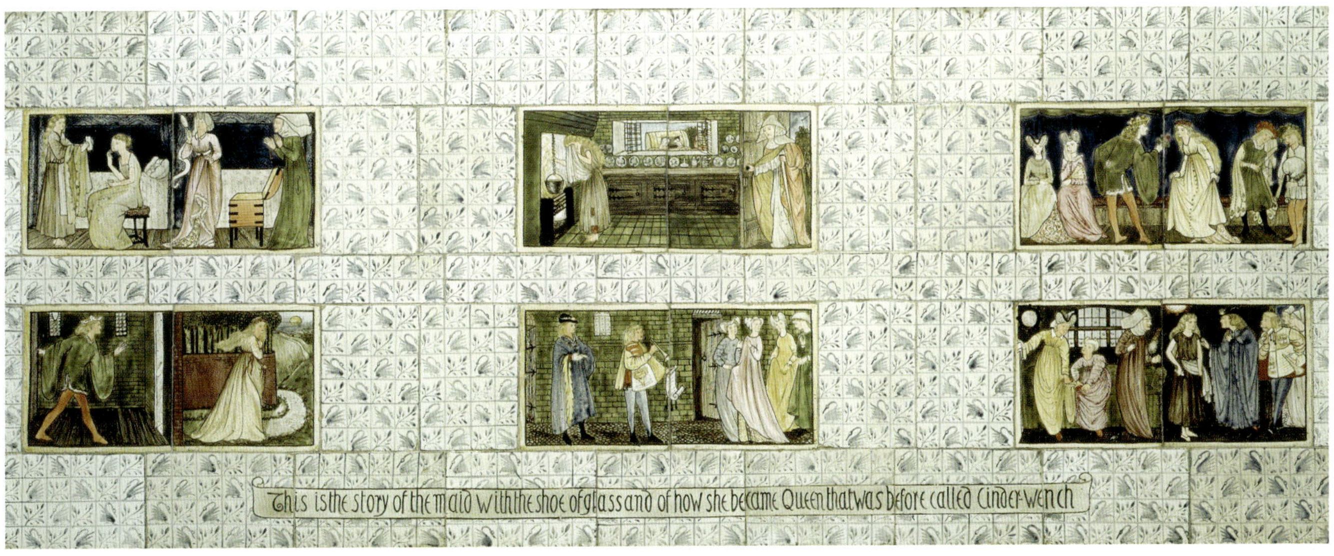

Arthur Hughes (1832–1915)

A Music Party, 1864

Oil on canvas, 58 × 76 cm

Purchased by William Hesketh Lever in 1917; inv. no. LL 3642

In 1862 Hughes visited Italy. He was particularly struck by Venice, and this picture highlights his enthusiasm for all things Venetian. The young family sits in a luxuriously furnished room wearing Renaissance costumes based on those found in paintings by the Venetian masters, Titian and Veronese. The composition focuses on the mother who plays an archaic music instrument. Her husband has put down his sword, and like his children, he is lost in the music played by his wife. Music-making is a theme often found in Venetian paintings from the 15th and 16th centuries, but in these historic works it is more likely to be in connection with a romantic or erotic scene. Here, Hughes uses the idea of a beautiful woman playing music but sets it in the context of a family scene. This was much more in keeping with the tastes of his middle-class Victorian buyers who cherished family values and saw the wife as the angel of the house. The happiness of this family is highlighted by their physical closeness and the tender way in which the father holds his son's hand as they listen to the music.

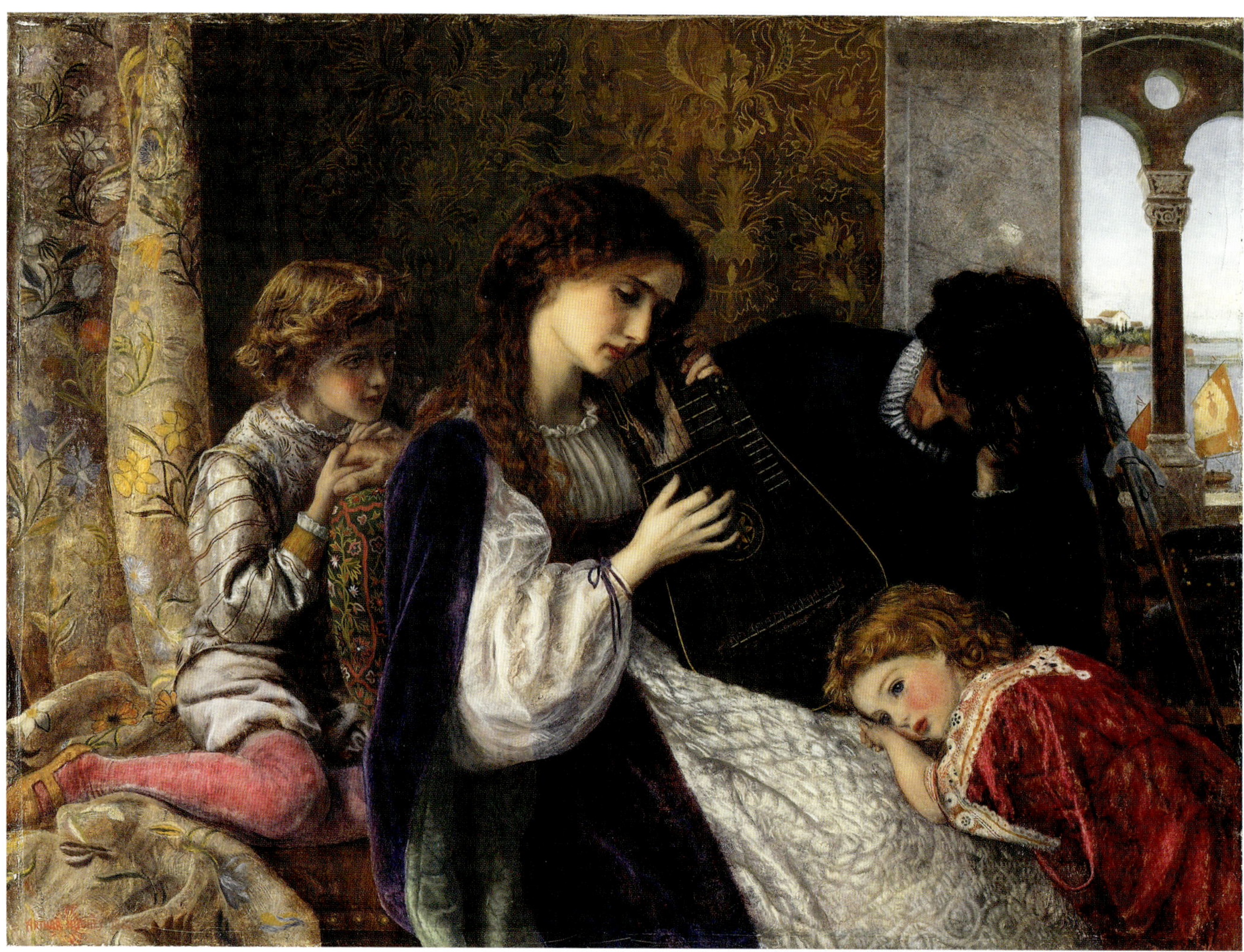

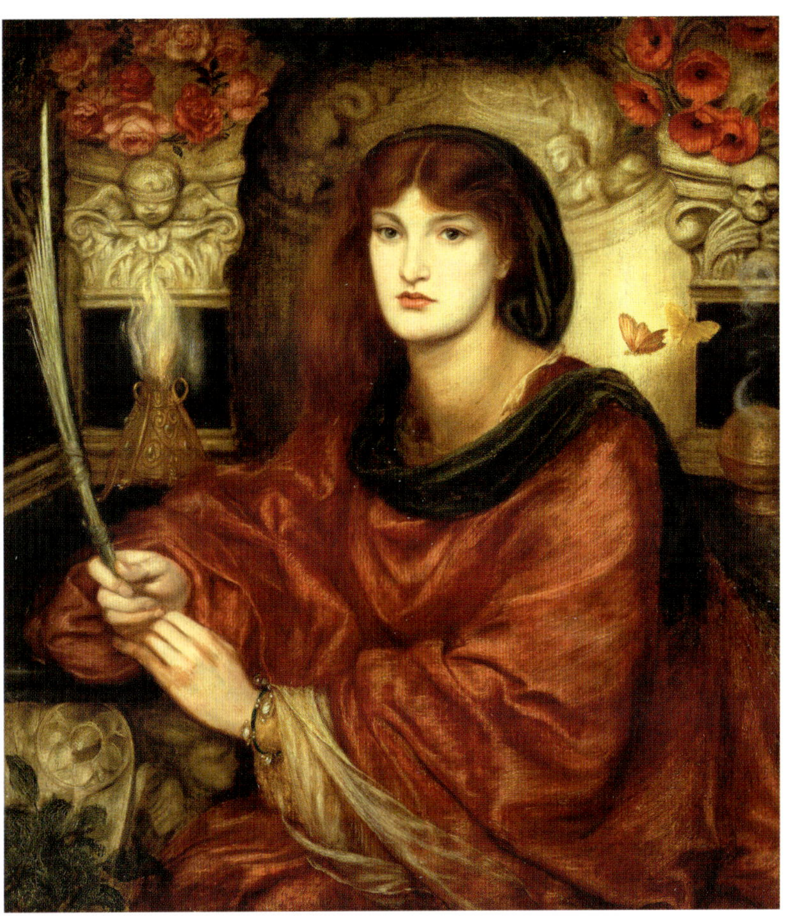

Dante Gabriel Rossetti (1828–82)

Sibylla Palmifera, 1865–70

Oil on canvas, 98.4 × 85 cm

Purchased by William Hesketh Lever in 1917; inv. no. LL 3628

Rossetti's admiration of the 16th-century Venetian painter Titian is highlighted by this half-length portrait personifying Beauty. Titian's works portray beautiful, fleshy women, draped in luxurious fabrics and often accompanied by allegorical symbols. Compared to the fragile heroines in medieval dress on whom Rossetti focused in the 1850s, the woman in this painting is far more robust and alluring. This portrait highlights his new preoccupation with painting beautiful pictures with no narrative. It can be considered an early work of the Aesthetic Movement, whose motto 'Art for Art's sake' argued that art could be beautiful in its own right without needing to be didactic or tell a story.

The woman in this portrait is Alexa Wilding, a professional artist's model who became one of Rossetti's favourite sitters after he discovered her in 1865. She holds a palm sceptre to symbolise her status as a sibyl, an ancient female priestess or prophet. In the background is her marble shrine with a blindfolded cupid on the left and a skull on the right alluding to Beauty's power over love and death. By her shoulder flutter two butterflies signifying the human soul.

Emma Sandys (1843–77)

Viola, about 1865/77

Oil on canvas, 53 × 40.2 cm

Bequeathed by Mrs Constance Emily Warr on behalf of her husband, the late Professor George Warr, in 1908; inv. no. WAG 674

Sandys was taught by her father, a jobbing painter, but her chief advisor was her brother, the Pre-Raphaelite artist Frederick Sandys (1829–1904). Emma spent time in his London studio and, like her brother, focused on painting portraits and female heads, often inspired by literature.

Viola is a character in Shakespeare's *Twelfth Night*. Disguised as a male servant she falls in love with her employer, Orsino, the Duke. Here, however, Sandys depicts Viola in female clothes. This emphasises her inner turmoil to which, like her real identity, the Duke is oblivious.

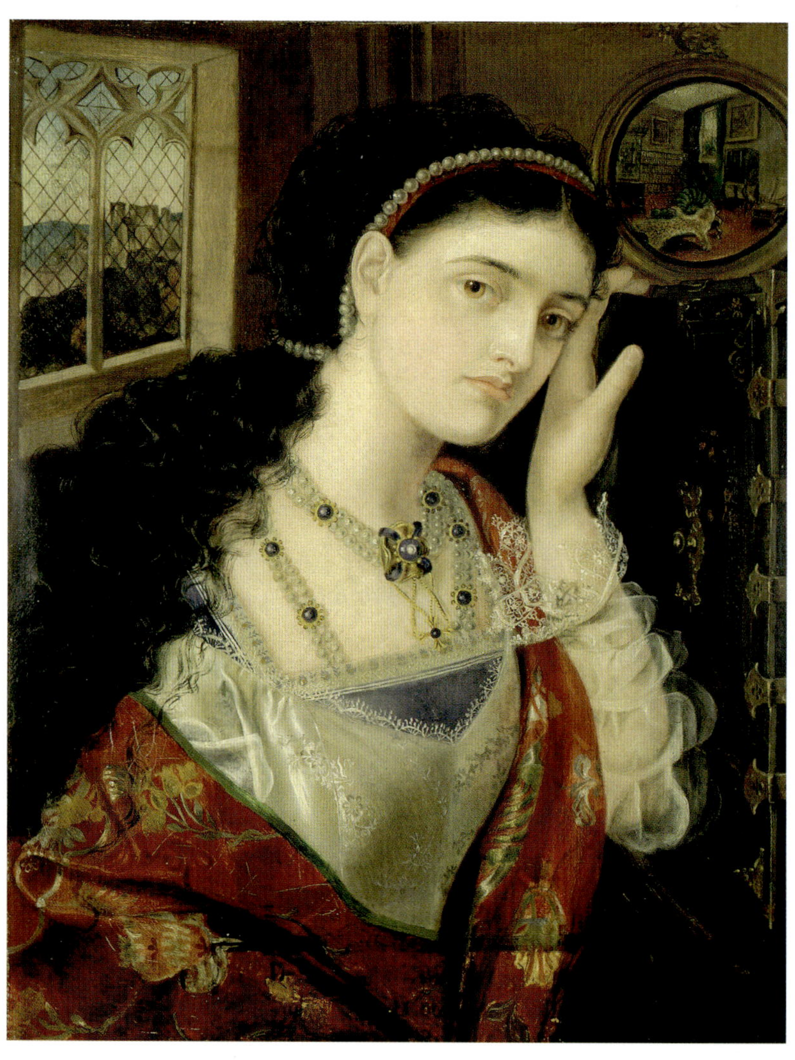

Ford Madox Brown (1821–93)

The Coat of Many Colours (Jacob and Joseph's Coat), 1866

Oil on canvas, 108 × 103.2 cm
Presented by Eleanor Coltart in 1904;
inv. no. WAG 1633

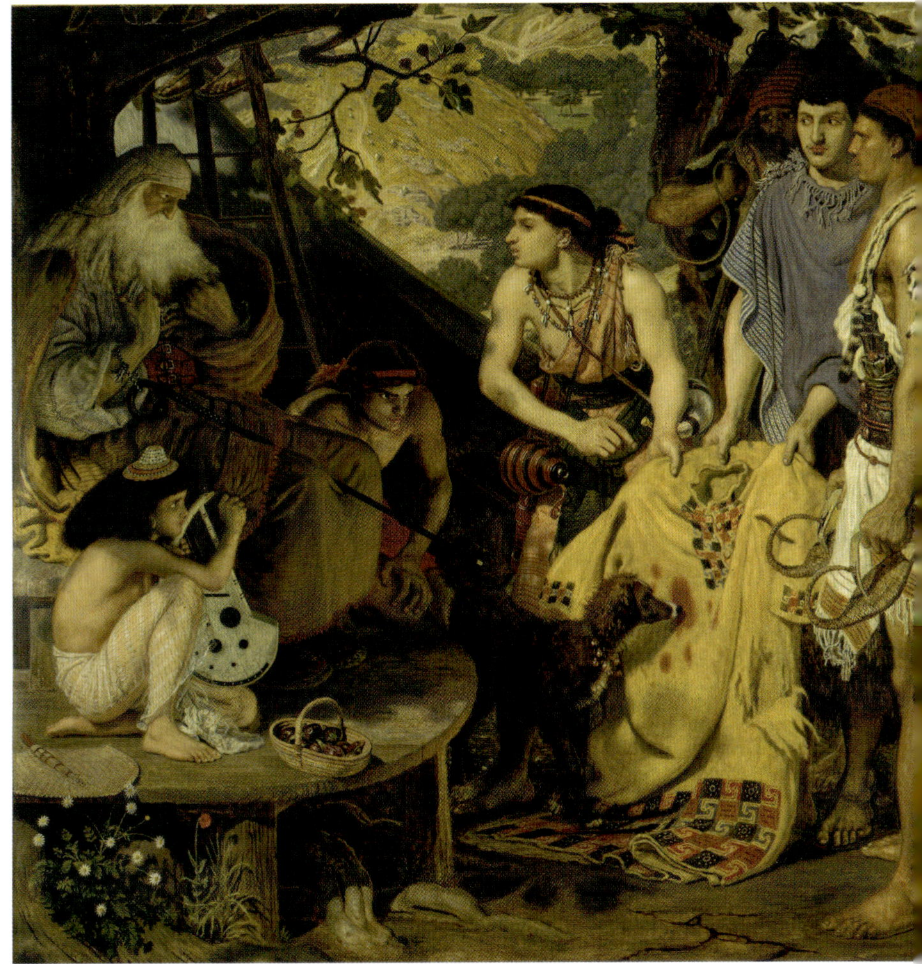

This painting began as an illustration in the *Dalziels' Bible Gallery*. Dalziel Brothers was one of the leading wood-engraving firms in the 19th century, producing images for newspapers, magazines and books using wooden printing blocks, hand carved by skilled engravers. The Dalziels worked on a number of high-end books including the Moxon edition of Tennyson's poems (1857). For these editions they approached leading artists to design the illustrations. Initially, the brothers secured Brown, along with other artists including William Holman Hunt and Simeon Solomon, to work on an illustrated Bible in 1863. Brown got to work on three designs including this one of Joseph's father, Jacob, being told of the death of his son and shown his bloodstained coat by his deceitful brothers.

The project dragged on and eventually the idea of illustrating an entire Bible was abandoned for a large format illustrated book of scenes from the Old Testament. Brown undertook a large amount of historical research for his illustrations of the biblical past. He took advantage of the new archaeological finds that were entering the British Museum, the research published by those excavating them, as well as new knowledge of the culture of the Holy Land, which friends such as William Holman Hunt had experienced first hand. Even before completing the drawing for the Dalziel Brothers, Brown began using the design as the basis for this painting. It was commissioned by his extremely wealthy Birkenhead patron, George Rae, who had a large collection of Pre-Raphaelite art.

Ford Madox Brown (1821–93)

Cordelia's Portion, 1866–72

Watercolour, gouache and pastel on paper,
70.5 × 107.3 cm

Purchased by the Trustees of the Lady Lever Art
Gallery in 1925; inv. no. LL 3640

Shakespeare's play *King Lear* fascinated Brown
throughout his life. It was as a young man living
in Paris that he first made a series of pen and ink
drawings narrating scenes from the play. Brown
repeatedly returned to these wild, expressive
drawings, using them as the basis of his first
printed illustration as well as for oil paintings and
watercolours. It was while working on his oil
painting *Lear and Cordelia* that Brown first met
his second wife, Emma, who modelled for the
figure of Cordelia. She is also the model for
Cordelia in this watercolour, which is based on a
much earlier drawing.

In this scene Lear demands that his youngest
daughter pay deference to him in order to secure
her portion of his kingdom. She refuses to
pander to him, saying that she honours him as
her father and can offer him no higher
admiration than her filial love and respect. This
outrages proud Lear and Cordelia is banished –
an act that leaves him in the hands of his two
other scheming daughters and ultimately leads
to his tragic demise.

This late watercolour highlights the
development of Brown's mature style,
exemplified by his use of curvaceous lines and
his move away from minute attention to detail.

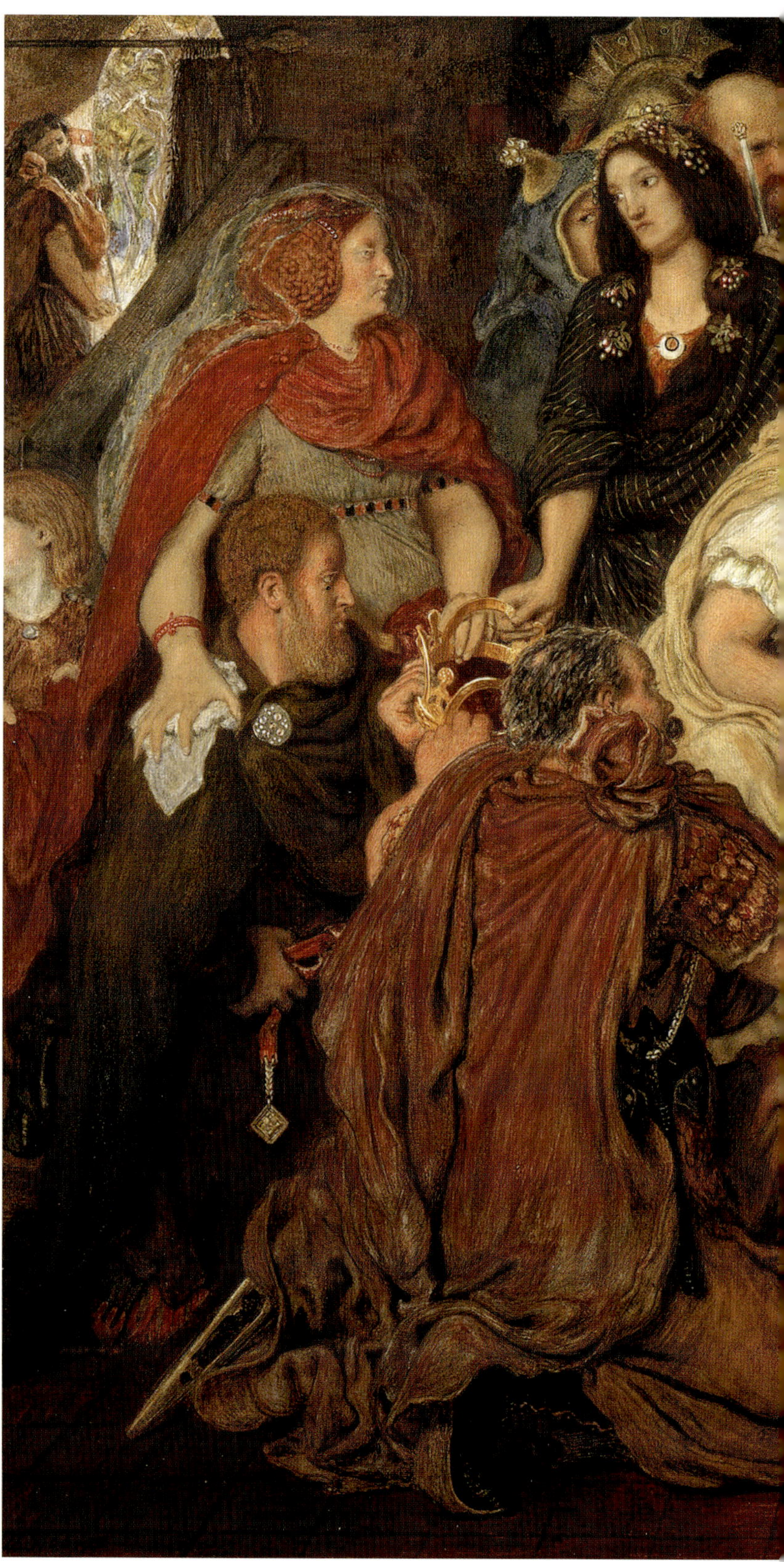

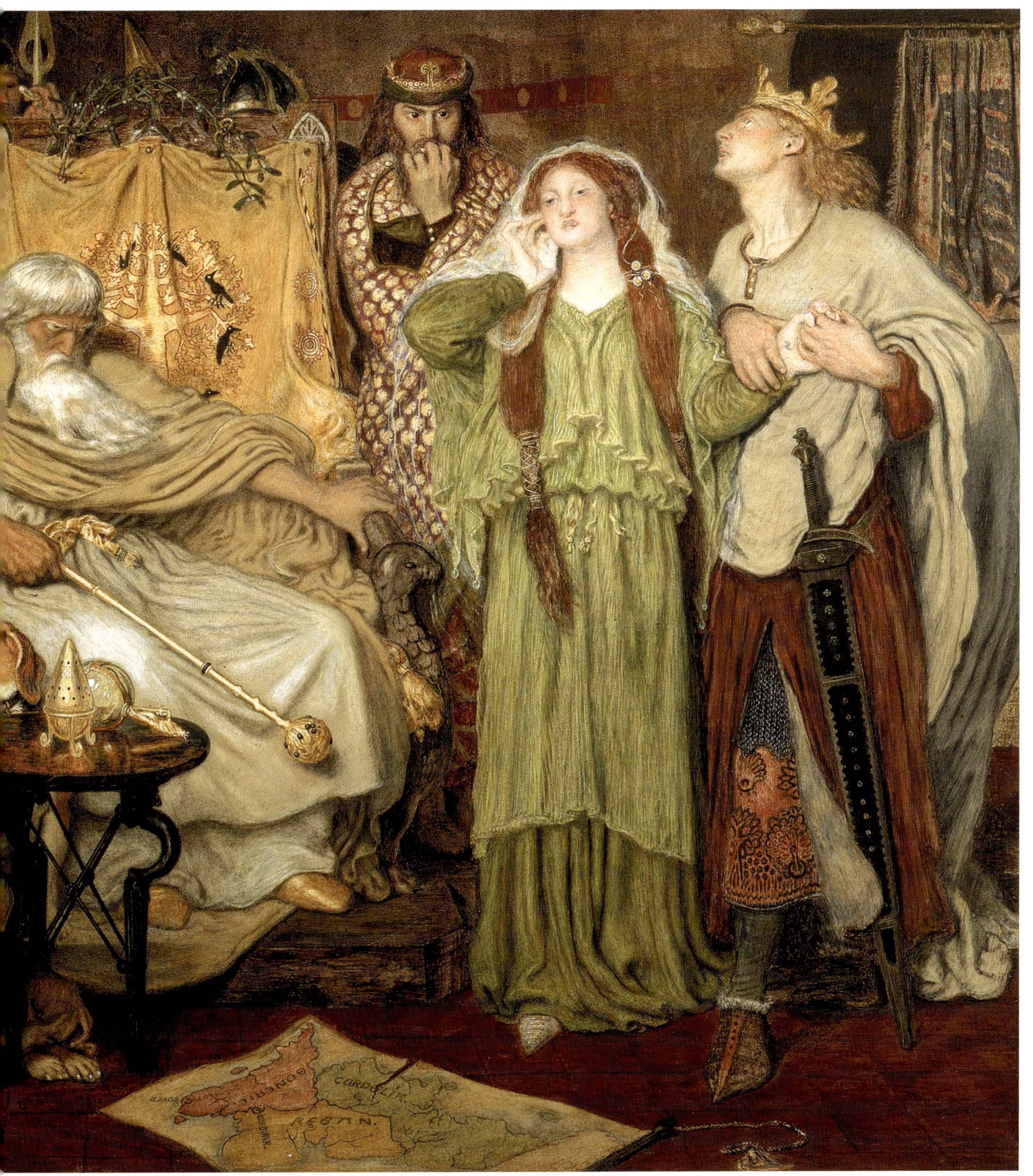
GONERIL
CORDELIA
REGAN

Frederick Sandys (1829-1904)

Helen of Troy, about 1867

Oil on panel, 38.4 × 30.5 cm

Bequeathed by Mrs Constance Emily Warr
on behalf of Professor George Warr in 1908;
inv. no. WAG 2633

Helen of Troy was a particularly appealing
subject for both Sandys and Rossetti. As the
most beautiful woman in the world and the
adulteress whose elopement brought about
the Trojan War, choosing her as their subject
allowed them to paint pictures of beautiful,
sensuous women. The two artists painted
portraits of Helen using models who
exemplified their ideas about beauty. Their
muses had masses of wavy, auburn hair and
full lips, and both men adorned them with
exotic jewellery. It was these similarities
that fuelled a quarrel between the two
friends. Rossetti accused Sandys of
copying his ideas and this created a
permanent rift. Sandys used the actress
Mary Clive as his model and she became his
mistress. Having left an unsuccessful
marriage, but never divorced, Sandys could
not marry Mary though she bore him nine
children.

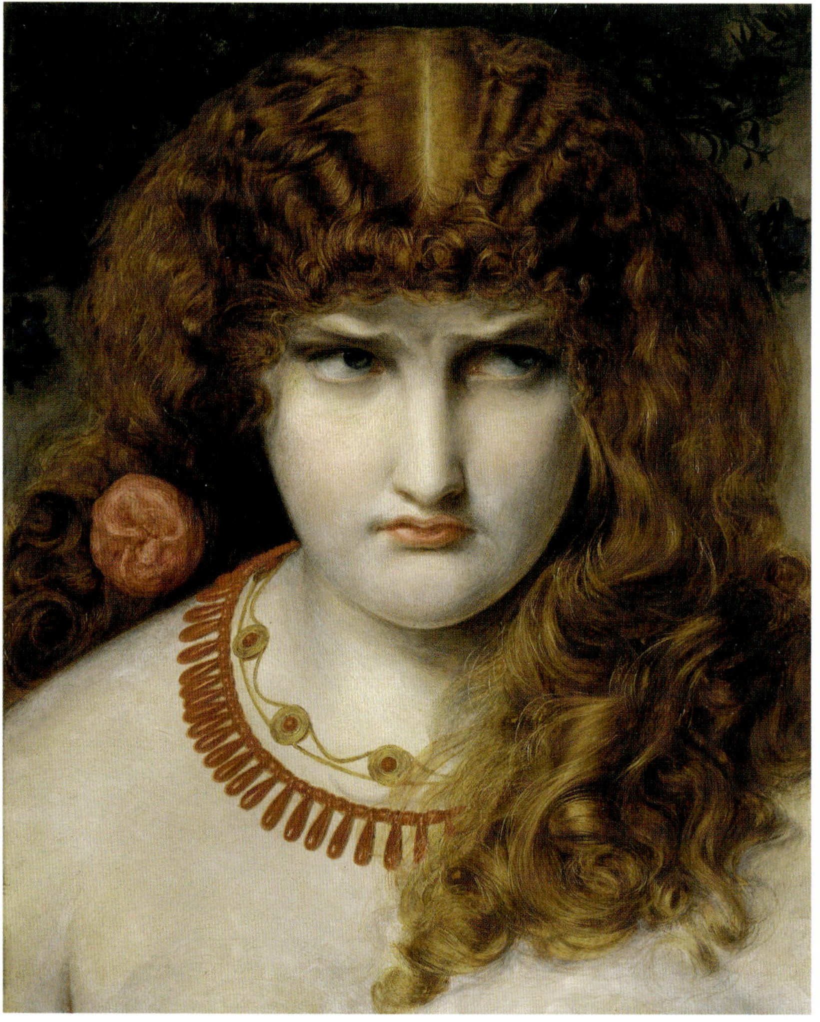

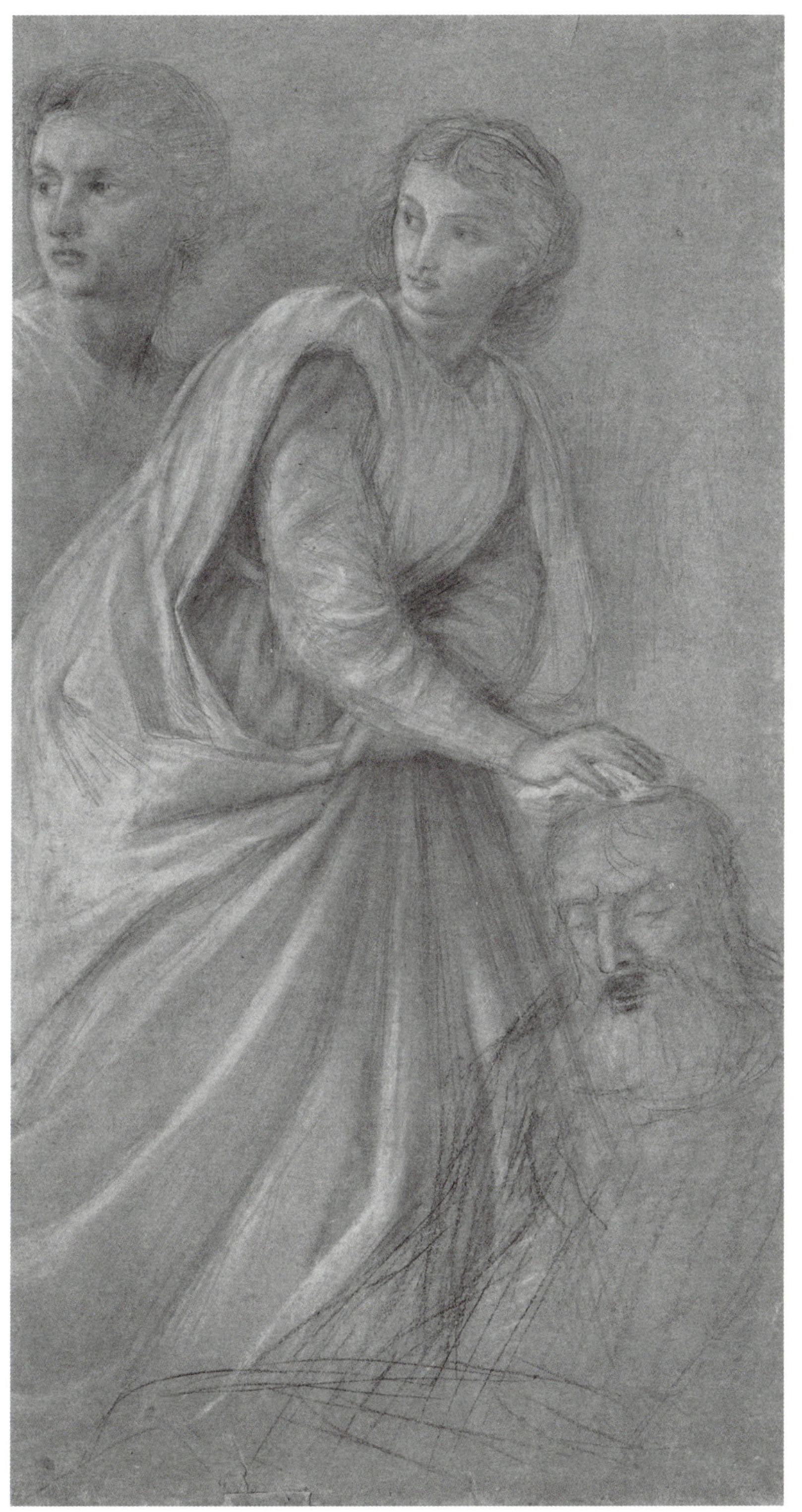

Robert Braithwaite Martineau (1826–69)

Study for the Young Woman and the Jew for 'Christians and Christians', about 1869

Pencil, black and white chalk on paper, 55.3 × 28.9 cm

Presented by Miss Helen Martineau in 1942; inv. no. WAG 1616

Martineau became William Holman Hunt's pupil in 1851 having given up studying law to attend art school. He was an active member of the Pre-Raphaelite circle, exhibiting with them and gaining a good reputation for his works. This delicate and detailed study is for the painting *Christians and Christians* that Martineau was working on when he died of rheumatic fever aged only 43. The picture was to portray a scene from the 13th century when Jews were expelled from England. In his composition, Martineau contrasts the behaviour of a true Christian woman who comes to the aid of an elderly Jewish man, with the Christian attackers who have been hounding him. This drawing focuses on the woman's clothing and the tilt of her head. Like his Pre-Raphaelite colleagues, Martineau made numerous drapery and figure studies in order to ensure each detail in the finished picture would be correct.

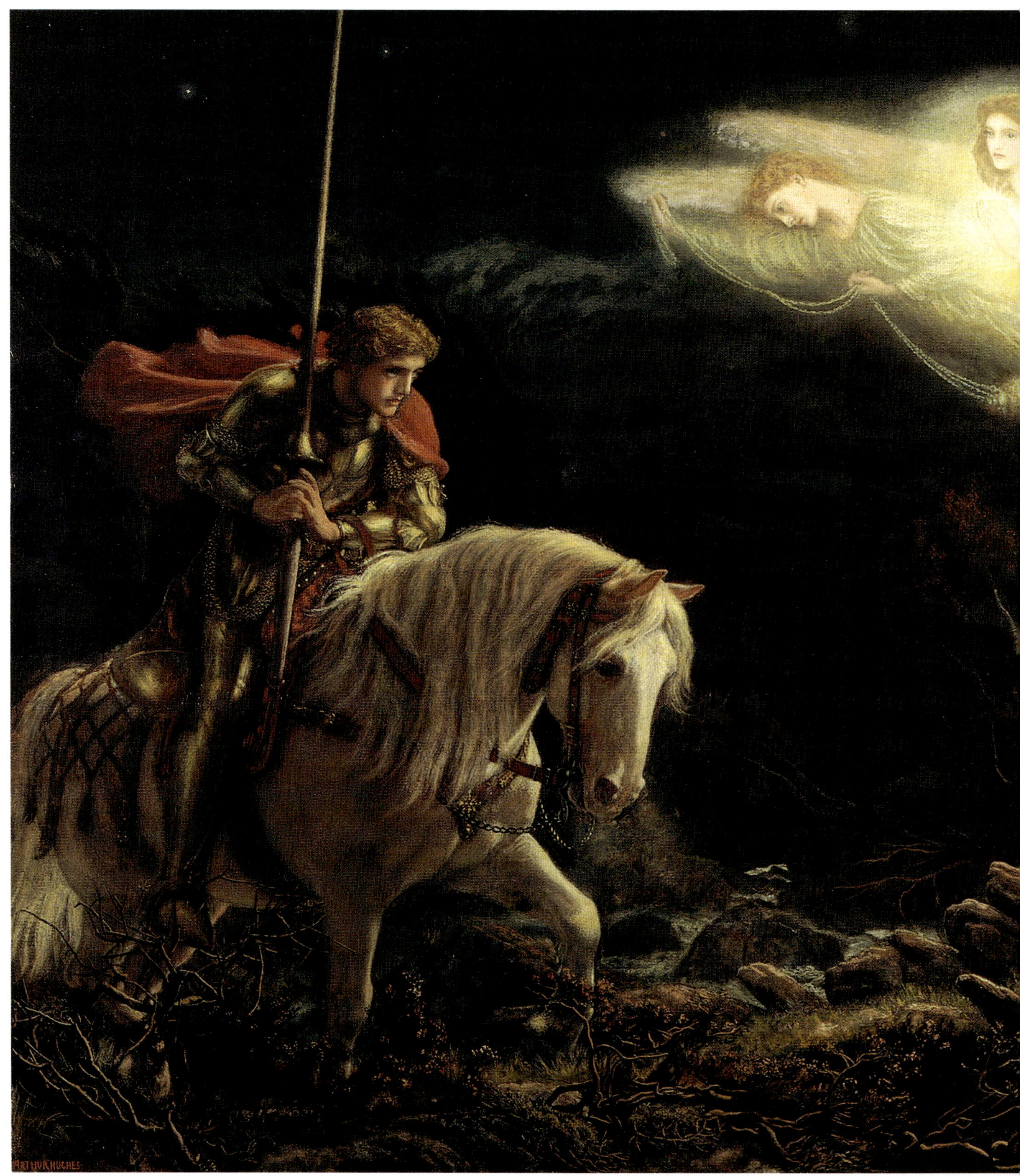

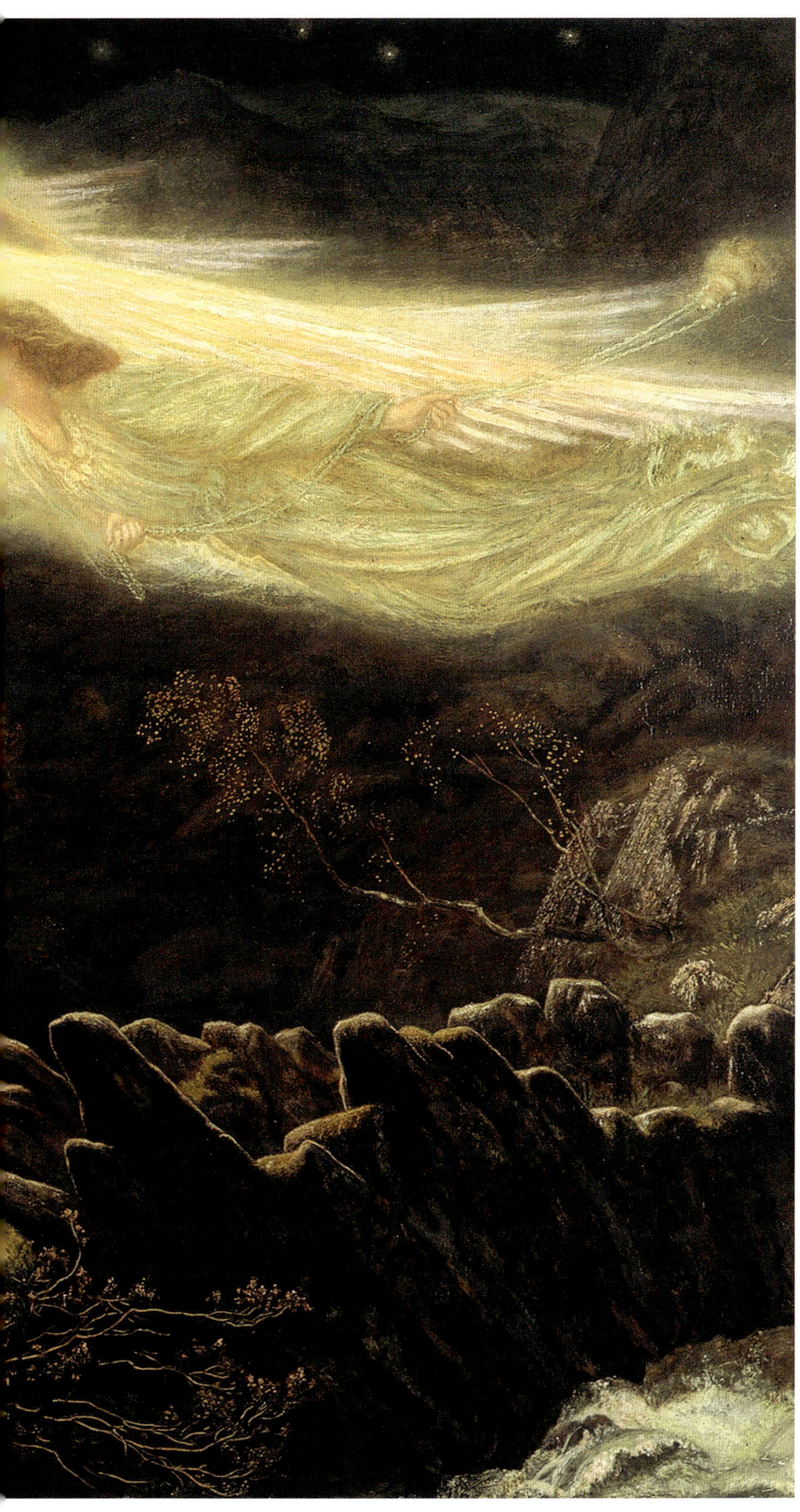

Arthur Hughes (1832–1915)

Sir Galahad – The Quest of the Holy Grail, about 1870

Oil on canvas, 113 × 167.6 cm

Presented by Mrs Alexander M Synge in 1925; inv. no. WAG 2936

Hughes was one of the young painters gathered together by Rossetti to paint murals of the Arthurian legends on the walls of the Oxford Union in 1857. The stories surrounding King Arthur and the Knights of the Round Table continued to inspire Hughes after the murals were finished. In this painting he focuses on Sir Galahad, the only knight to find the Holy Grail – the chalice used by Christ at the Last Supper. Sir Galahad is the virgin knight, son of Sir Lancelot and descended from Joseph of Arimathea, the original custodian of the cup. It is his purity which allows Galahad to succeed in his task. On finding the Holy Grail, his soul attains complete communion with Christ and he dies. Hughes used the landscape around Ashness Bridge, near Derwent Water, Cumbria, as the bleak, mountainous setting for Sir Galahad's journey.

Simeon Solomon (1840–1905)

The Mystery of Faith, 1870

Watercolour with gum Arabic and gouache on paper laid down on board, 51.3 × 38.8 cm

Bequeathed by Clyde Birkmyre Coltart of Chester in 1950; inv. no. LL 3997

Born into a Jewish family, Solomon's works often explored the rituals and traditions surrounding religion, both Jewish and Christian. In this luminous watercolour, a young Roman Catholic or High Anglican priest carries the monstrance containing the consecrated Eucharistic 'host'. The 'host' is a wafer that, for believers, literally becomes the body of Christ through the act of consecration. This ritual may be the mystery to which the title refers. Solomon captures the intensity of the religious experience and highlights its magnificence by painting almost entirely in white and gold.

Solomon counted Rossetti and Burne-Jones as close friends, and his works were widely bought by Pre-Raphaelite collectors. In 1871 this watercolour received good reviews when it was exhibited at the Dudley Gallery in London, a progressive venue that had shown works by Solomon since the 1860s. By 1873 Solomon's reputation was in tatters following his arrest for homosexual activity, and he died in 1905 in a London workhouse.

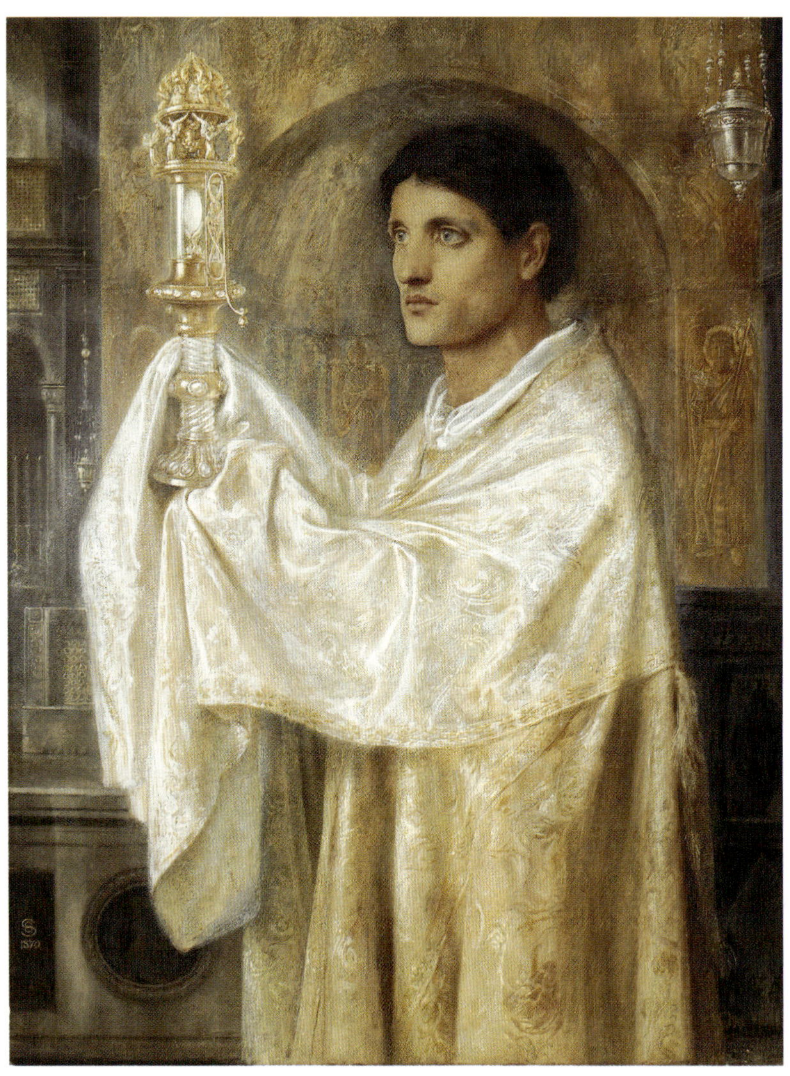

Dante Gabriel Rossetti (1828-82)

Pandora, 1878

Pastel on paper, 100.8 × 66.7 cm

Purchased by William Hesketh Lever in 1919; inv. no. LL 3647

Rossetti first met Jane Morris (1840–1914) when he and his protégé, Edward Burne-Jones, discovered her in Oxford in 1857 and asked her to model for them. She was a Pre-Raphaelite 'stunner' with masses of dark, wavy hair, a long neck, Cupid's bow lips and large melancholy eyes. It was William Morris who first fell in love with her and the couple were married by 1860.

Following the death of his wife Elizabeth Siddal, Rossetti and Jane began an affair. She became his comforter and artistic muse. He spent increasing amounts of time with Jane at Kelmscott Manor, a country house in Oxfordshire, which he leased jointly with William Morris. Jane became one of his favourite models, whether for small personal drawings as in the black and white chalk portrait of her reclining on a sofa, or larger finished drawings such as *Pandora*. In this striking pastel he portrays Jane as Pandora, from whose box escape all the ills of the world.

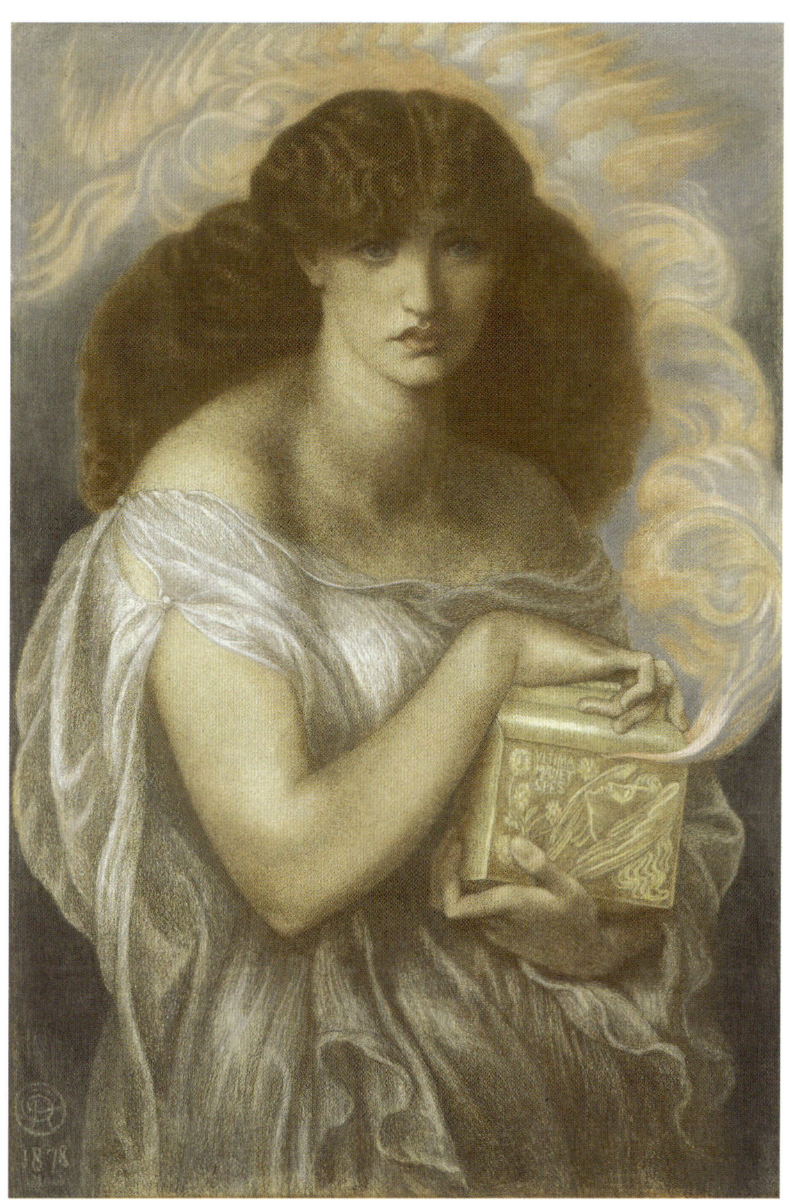

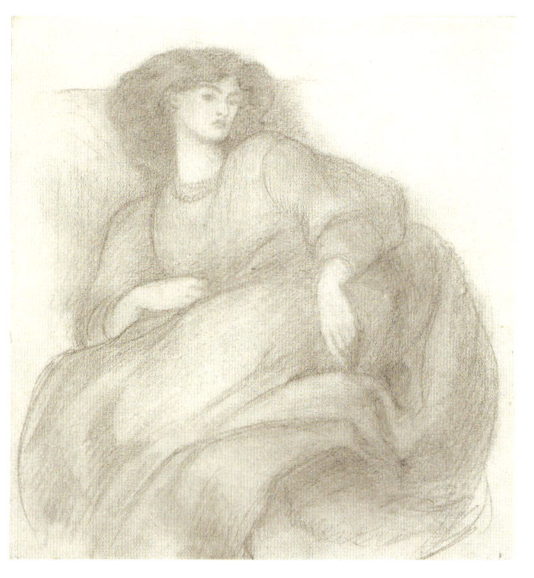

Jane Morris Reclining, about 1870

Pencil on paper, 25.4 × 23.8 cm

Purchased for the Walker Art Gallery by PH Rathbone in 1883; inv. no. WAG 3207

Dante Gabriel Rossetti (1828–82)

Dante's Dream, 1871

Oil on canvas, 216 × 312.4 cm
Purchased in 1881; inv. no. WAG 3091

This is Rossetti's largest painting and was bought for Liverpool following its first public display in the Liverpool Autumn Exhibition held at the Walker Art Gallery in 1881. The picture was inspired by an episode from *Vita Nuova* written in 1295 by Rossetti's lifelong hero, the medieval Italian poet Dante Alighieri (1265–1321). The scene represented is Dante's dream in which he is led by Love to the deathbed of Beatrice, the object of his unrequited passion.

In the centre of the composition is Beatrice, modelled on Jane Morris, Rossetti's real life lover. Either side of her are two beautiful women in medieval dress, modelled on Alexa Wilding, one of Rossetti's favourite professional models, and Maria Spartali Stillman, a pupil of Ford Madox Brown who was considered a Pre-Raphaelite beauty. The dreamlike world that Rossetti creates is full of symbolism. Poppies refer to the sleep of the dreamer and the sleep of death, doves symbolise love, and the apple blossom, violets and roses signify Beatrice's purity.

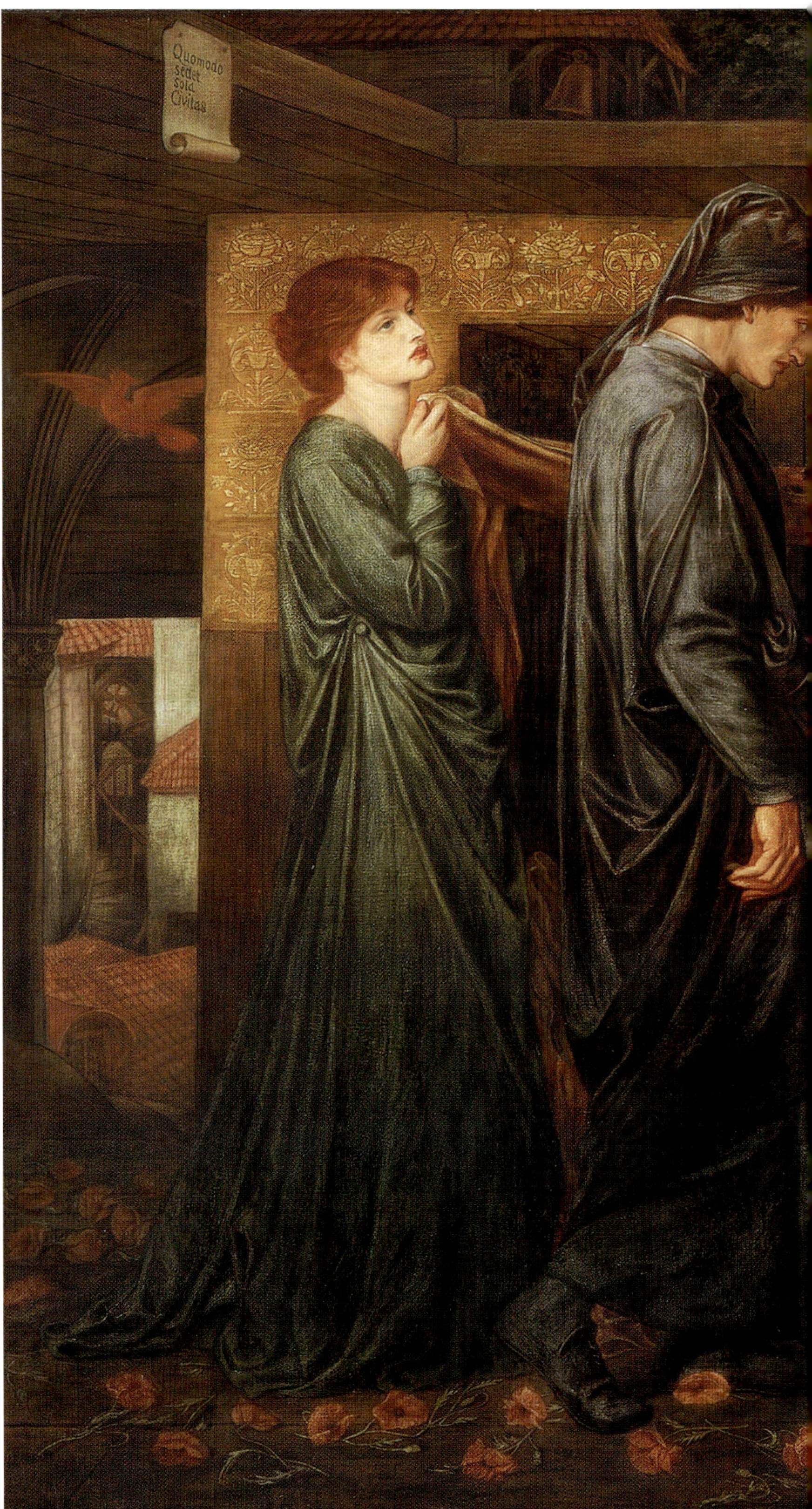

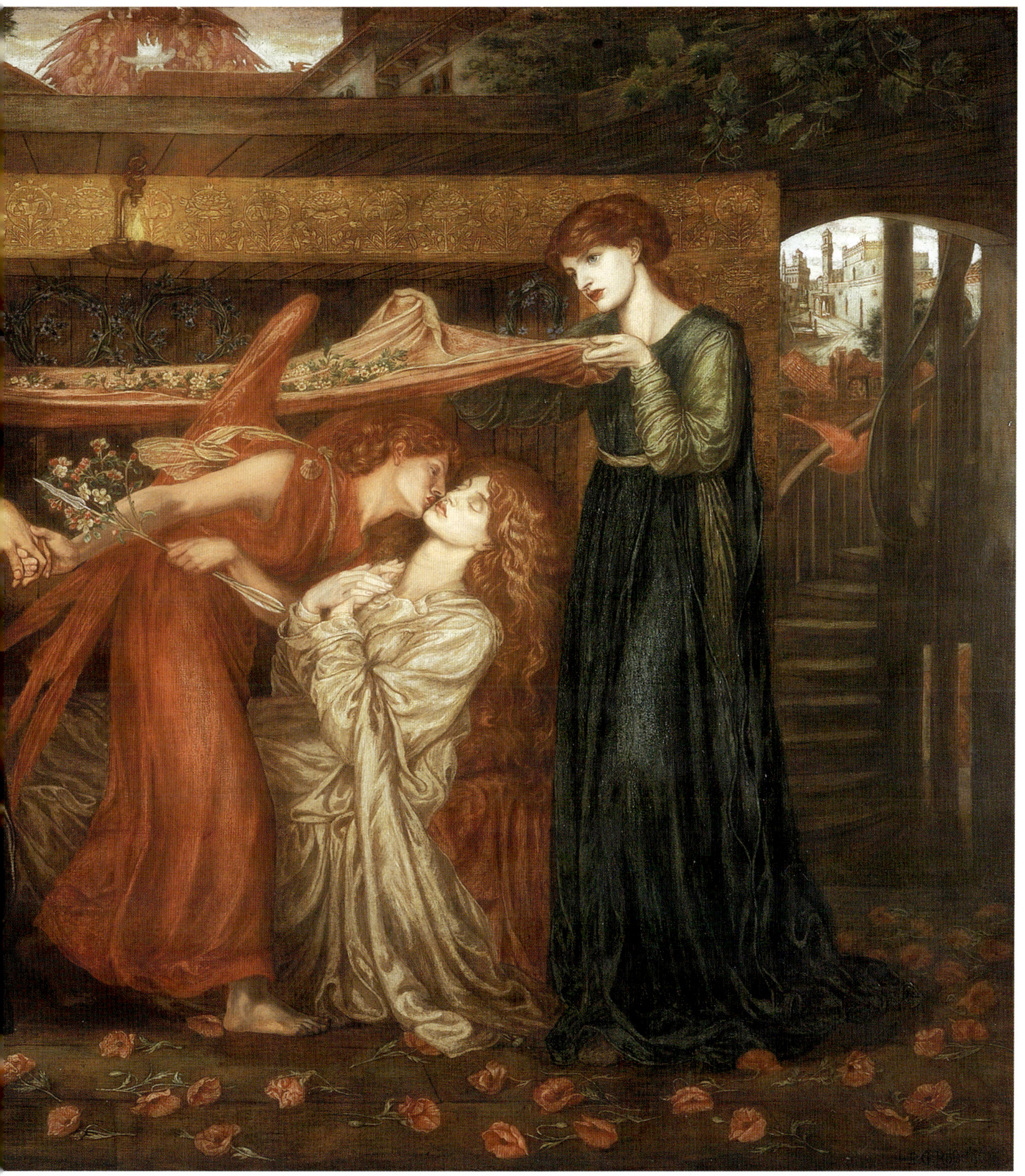

Edward Burne-Jones (1833–98)

The Beguiling of Merlin, 1873–7

Oil on canvas, 186 × 111 cm

Purchased by William Hesketh Lever in 1918;
inv. no. LL 3121

In this scene from the Arthurian legends, the infatuated Merlin is enchanted into a deep sleep by the Lady of the Lake, Nimue. With Merlin under her power she reads his book of spells to gain the secrets of his magic for herself. As a young man Burne-Jones was enthralled by Thomas Malory's *Morte d'Arthur* (published 1485) with its tales of chivalry, romance and heroism. His passion for these medieval stories remained with him throughout his career. It fuelled his friendship with William Morris and led the pair to give up their academic studies to become artists with the help of Dante Gabriel Rossetti. Later, Burne-Jones continued to turn to the legends for inspiration. The model for Nimue is Maria Zambaco (1843–1914), a medallist and sculptor but also Burne-Jones' mistress. They met in 1866 when her mother commissioned Burne-Jones to paint a portrait of Maria. From the late 1860s to the mid-1870s Maria's likeness appeared in almost all his works in the faces of both female and male figures. Like Merlin, Burne-Jones was enchanted by his lover.

Dante Gabriel Rossetti (1828–82)

The Blessed Damozel,
about 1875–81

Oil on canvas, 36.5 × 82.8 cm

Purchased by William Hesketh Lever in 1922;
inv. no. LL 3148

This painting shows Rossetti's late sensuous style. The picture is dominated by the damozel, a long-necked beauty with Cupid's bow lips and stars in her hair. Having died in the fullness of youth she is shown in Heaven, pining for her lover, as he looks up towards her. The picture was based on a poem Rossetti wrote in 1850 for 'The Germ', a short-lived magazine published by the Pre-Raphaelite Brotherhood and their associates. The unusual composition, with a small *predella*, or decorated base, under the main picture, was suggested by Rossetti's patron, William Graham, who bought the original, larger version of this painting. This version was commissioned by the Pre-Raphaelite patron FR Leyland who hung it in his house with his significant collection of works by Rossetti.

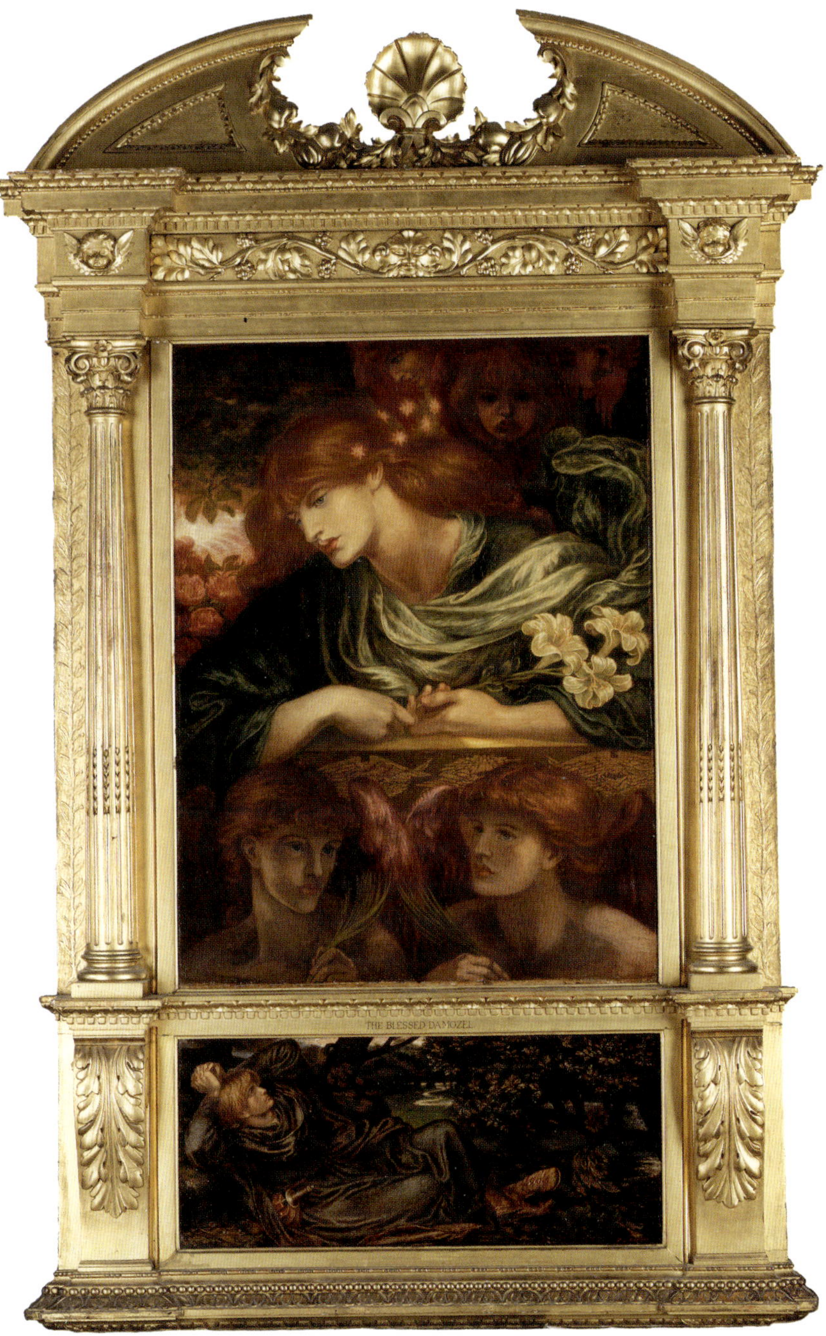

William Holman Hunt (1827–1910)

Study for the Christ Child in the Virgin's Arms for 'The Triumph of the Innocents', 1876

Pen and black chalk on paper, 50.3 × 35.5 cm
Purchased in 1967; inv. no. WAG 6595

The Flight into Egypt was a traditional subject for painters, but Hunt's imagining of the scene in this painting is highly unusual. He includes the familiar figures of Mary holding the infant Jesus, and Joseph leading the ass, but unconventionally surrounds the Holy Family with the spirits of the recently deceased baby boys who have been murdered by Herod's soldiers. At the top left, one little boy clutches a bird, representing his soul, while in the centre another child examines his recently slashed clothing, his wound having already healed.

In August 1869 Hunt embarked on his second trip to Jerusalem and made landscape sketches for the background. The chalk drawing of a baby for the figure of Christ dates from 1876 when he began working on the painting properly during his third trip to Jerusalem. The picture's completion was fraught with difficulties and this original version was only completed in 1887. This was largely due to Hunt using a canvas made from local linen on which it became increasingly difficult to work. In 1891 the Walker Art Gallery bought the finished painting to hang alongside its other recently purchased pictures by the leaders of the Pre-Raphaelite Brotherhood: *Dante's Dream* by Rossetti and *Isabella* by Millais.

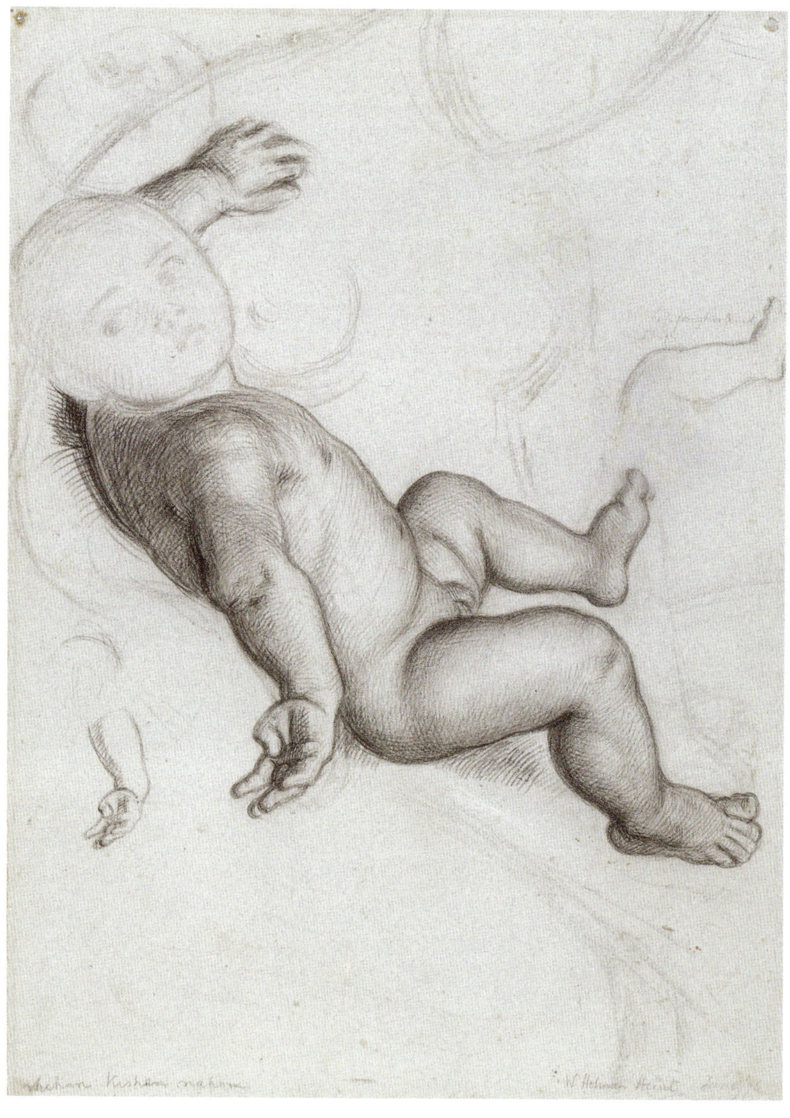

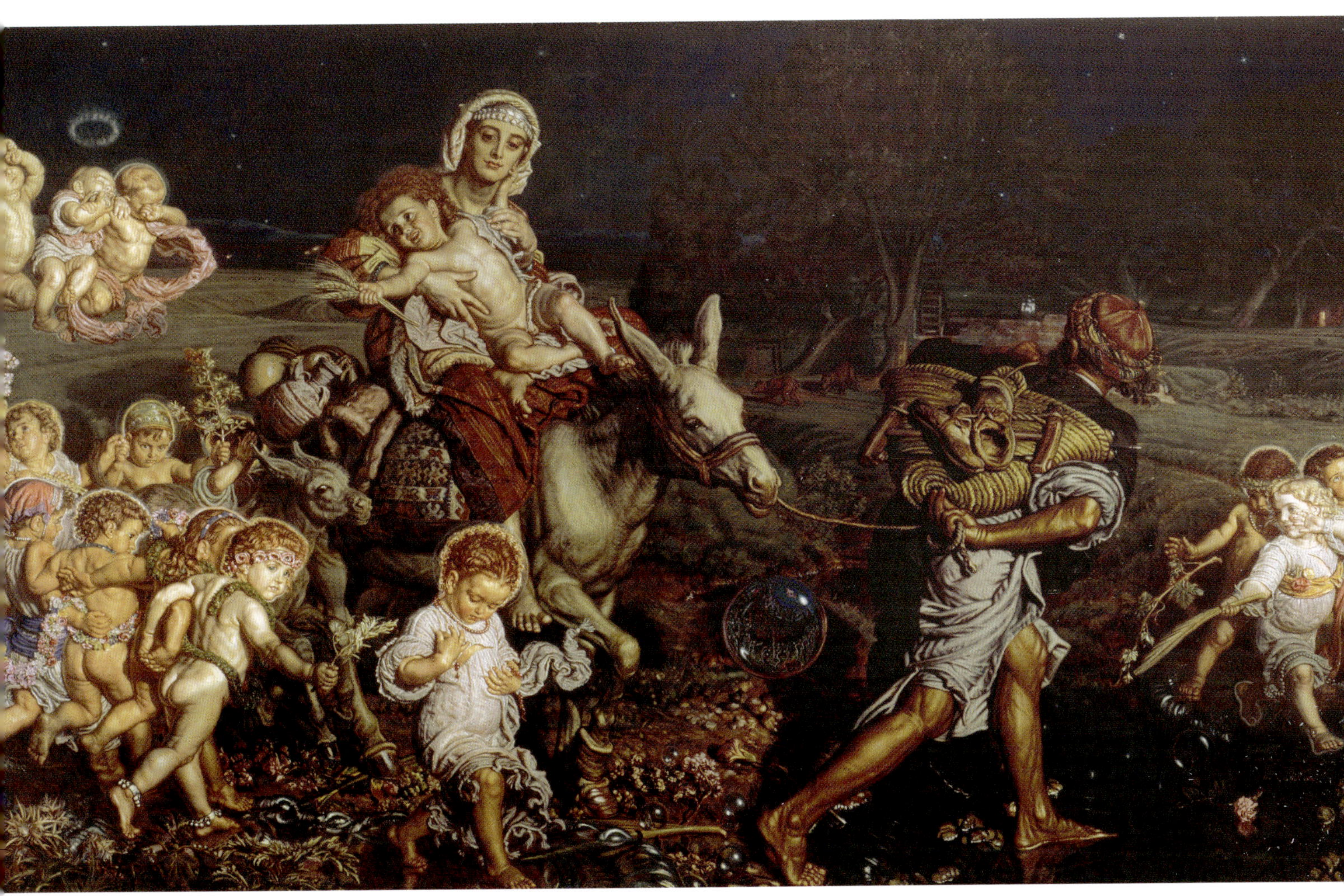

William Holman Hunt (1827–1910)

The Triumph of the Innocents,
1876–87

Oil on canvas, 157.5 × 247.7cm
Purchased in 1891; inv. no WAG 2115

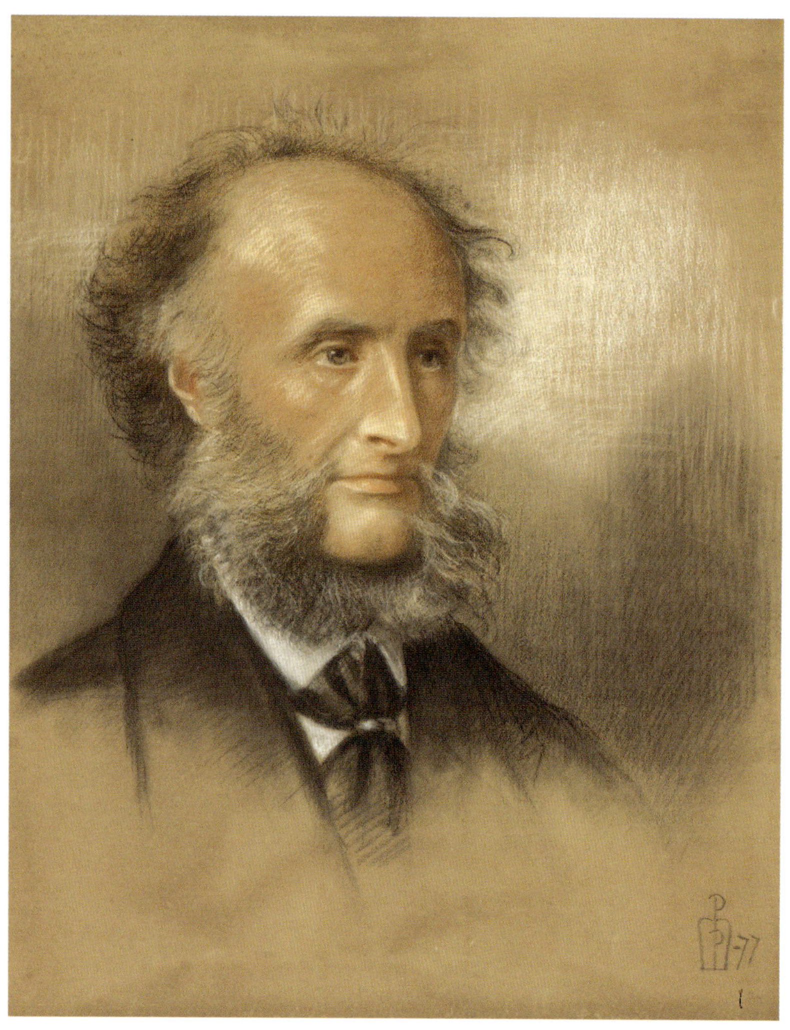

Peter Paul Marshall (1830–1900)

Donald Currie, 1877

Black, white and red chalk on paper,
60 × 44.5 cm

Purchased in 1970; inv. no. WAG 7396

According to Rossetti's brother William Michael, it was Peter Marshall who suggested founding the decorating firm of Morris, Marshall, Faulkner & Co in 1861. Although an engineer by profession, Marshall practised as an artist in his spare time, and had met the leaders of the Pre-Raphaelite movement through Ford Madox Brown. The subject of this drawing, Donald Currie, was the owner of the Union-Castle steamship company and the artist's brother-in-law. Both men married daughters of John Miller, a Liverpool merchant and major Pre-Raphaelite patron. This drawing shows great similarity to Ford Madox Brown's late chalk portraits, even down to the stylised monogram and date in the lower right corner.

Edward Burne-Jones (1833–98)

Angel Playing a Flageolet, 1878

Tempera and gold paint on paper, 46.1 × 68 × 4.3 cm

Bequeathed by Emma Holt in 1945; inv. no. WAG 192

Throughout his career Burne-Jones used music as a subject for his paintings. His interest in the theme increased in the 1870s when he painted this picture. For Burne-Jones and his contemporaries, representing the making of music had a dual purpose. It symbolised devotion in a religious work, but when musical instruments were included in a piece depicting a romance it suggested the idea of sexual love. In this devotional painting the viewer is invited to imagine the heavenly music being played by an ethereal angel.

Inspired by the art of the 14th and 15th centuries, Burne-Jones painted the work using tempera. This traditional technique was used by the artists Burne-Jones admired, such as Botticelli (about 1445–1510), working before the invention of oil paints. They used egg yolk rather than oil to bind the colour pigments. The medium allowed Burne-Jones to create vivid reds and blues and to use luxurious gold paint to enhance the splendour of the heavenly setting.

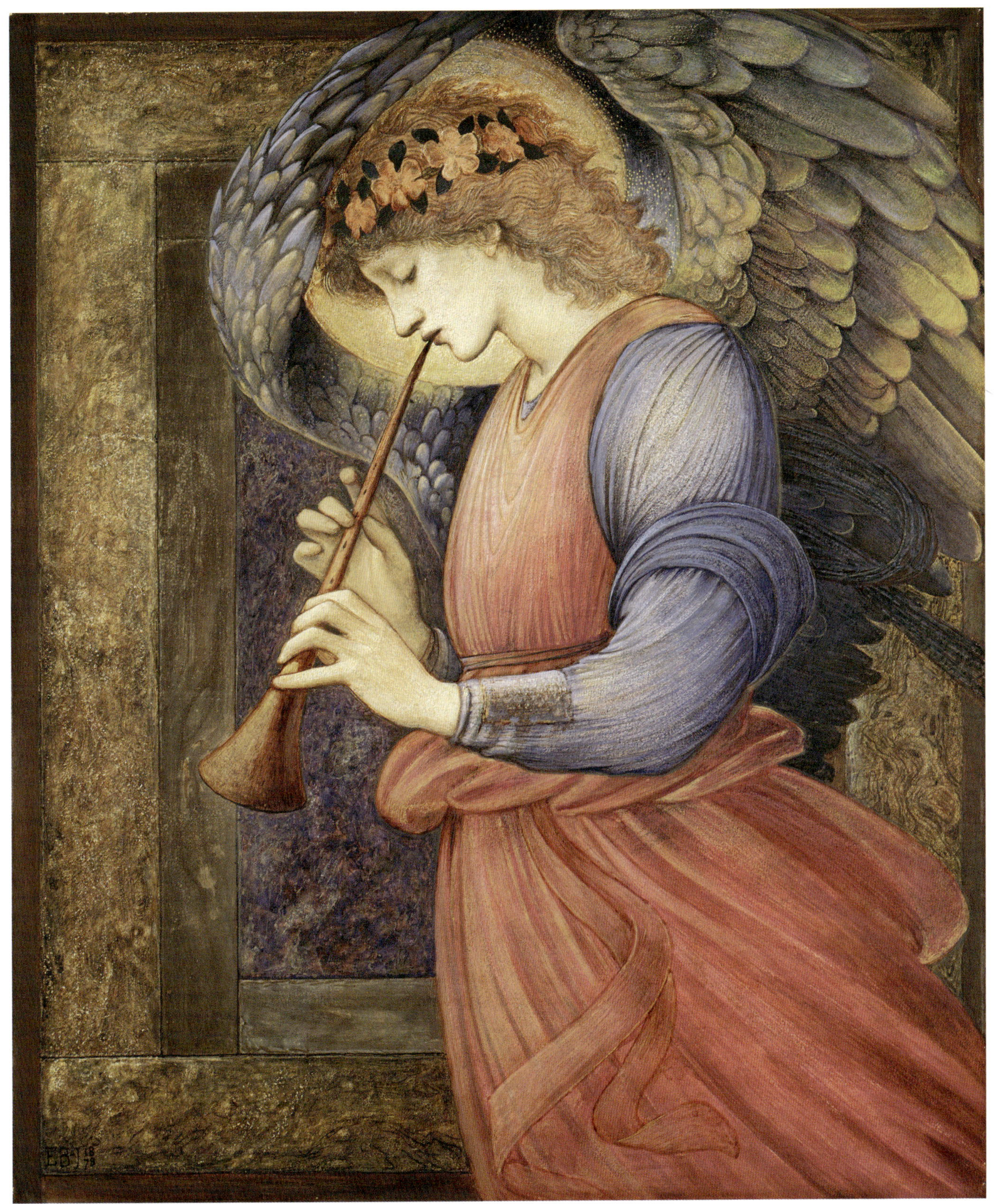

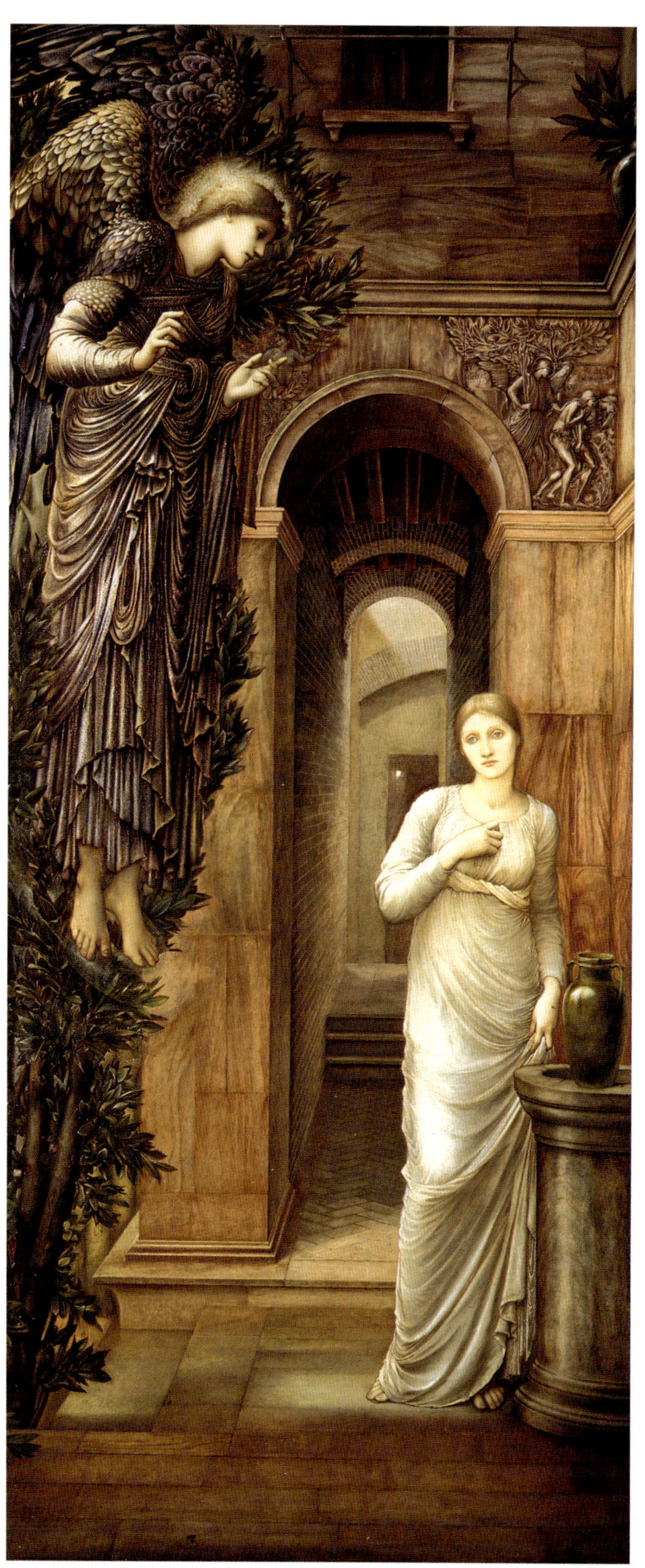

Edward Burne-Jones (1833–98)

The Annunciation, 1879

Oil on canvas, 250 × 104.5 cm

Purchased by William Hesketh Lever in 1923;
inv. no. LL 3634

Burne-Jones was inspired by the work of the 14th- and 15th-century Italian masters he saw on his visits to Italy. Their influence can be seen in this painting in the calm faces of the figures and in their statuesque drapery. Rather than using facial expression, Burne-Jones expresses the Virgin's surprise at the Angel Gabriel by using her hands; one is drawn to her chest while the other clutches at her skirts. The importance of her role in bearing a son who will save humanity is highlighted by the relief sculpture on the side of the arch which shows Adam and Eve being expelled from the Garden of Eden. The picture uses a limited range of colours, indicating Burne-Jones' affinity with the Aesthetic Movement and the works of Whistler (1834–1903), who believed in creating colour harmonies. Unlike early Pre-Raphaelite works, which showed the Holy Family as real people, the two figures are stylised and remain aloof from the viewer. They evoke contemplation rather than empathy.

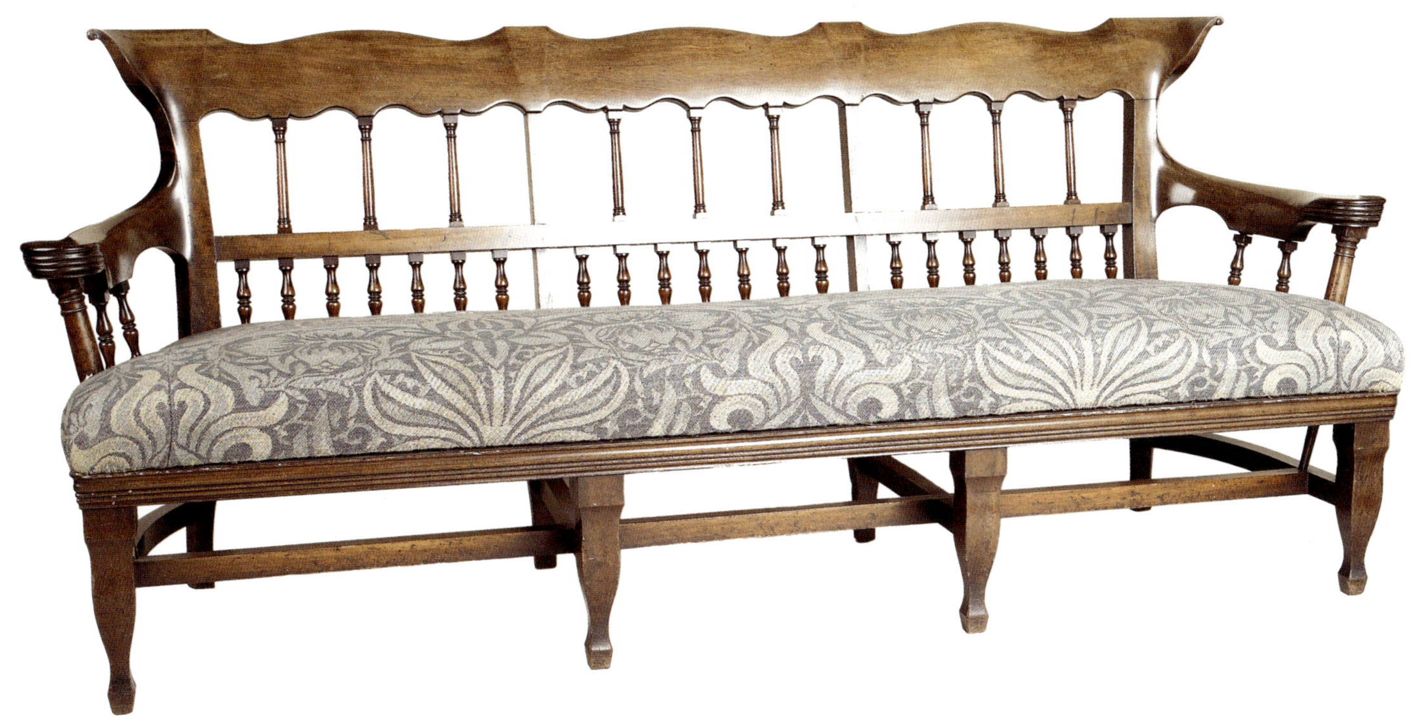

Designed by George Jack (1855–1932) for Morris & Co

Settee, about 1880

Walnut wood, upholstered in the *Peacock and Dragon* woven wool fabric designed by William Morris (1830–96) in 1878, 96.2 × 221 × 77.2 cm

Purchased in 1992; inv. no. WAG 1993.84

George Jack was an architect and designer who also taught wood-carving at the newly founded Central School of Arts and Crafts in London. His knowledge and love of wood-carving is apparent in the design of this curvaceous settee. The scalloped back and design of the arms are loosely based on humble 18th-century farmhouse furniture, but Jack has chosen to use walnut, an expensive wood that was more appealing to Morris and Co's wealthy customers. The seat is covered in Morris' *Peacock and Dragon* fabric. The pattern was inspired by 15th- and 16th-century Sicilian textiles and proved to be one of Morris' most popular designs. The fabric was hand-woven following Morris' belief in promoting the skills of individual craftspeople rather than mass producing items in factories.

Maria Spartali Stillman
(1843–1927)

Madonna Pietra degli Scrovigni, 1884

Watercolour and bodycolour on paper,
77.1 × 58.1 cm

Presented on behalf of subscribers by
Harold Rathbone in 1884; inv. no. WAG 923

The subject of this watercolour is a poem by
the medieval Italian poet Dante Alighieri
(1265–1321), which was translated by his
namesake Dante Gabriel Rossetti. It
describes the poet's love for a beautiful but
aloof lady, dressed in green. Stillman was a
pupil of Ford Madox Brown along with
Brown's two daughters and his son. As well
being a successful artist in her own right,
she also sat as a model for other members of
the Pre-Raphaelite circle including the
painters Edward Burne-Jones, Rossetti and
the photographer Julia Margaret Cameron
(1815–79).

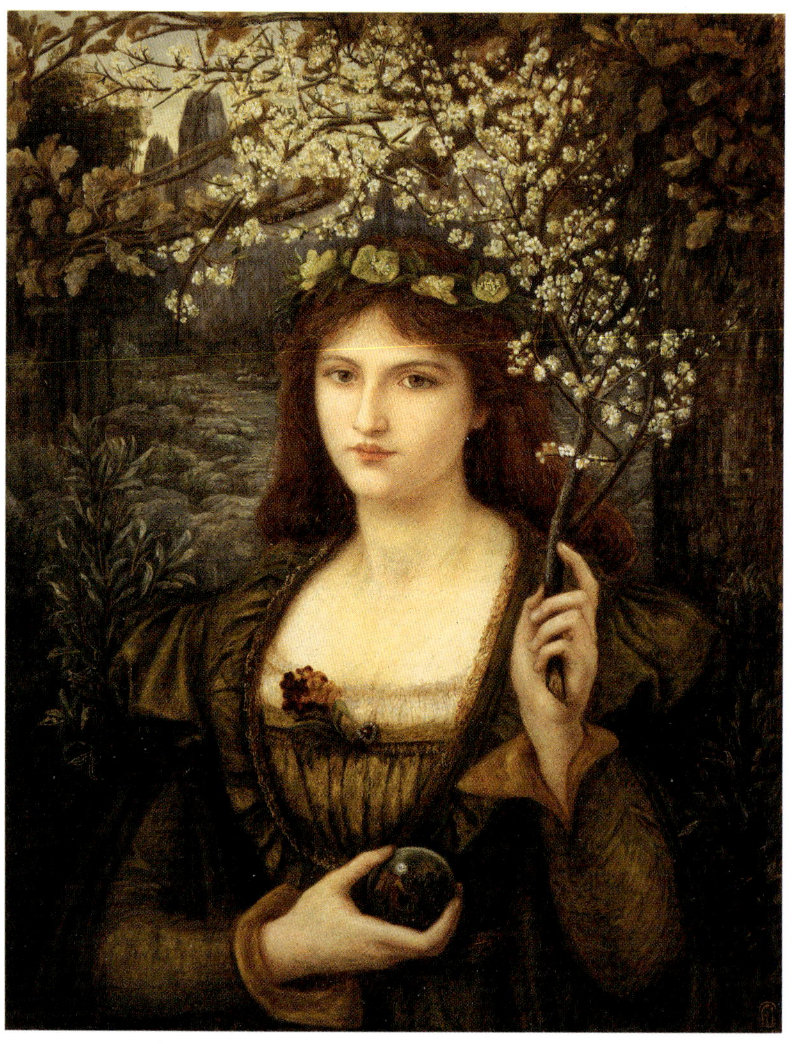

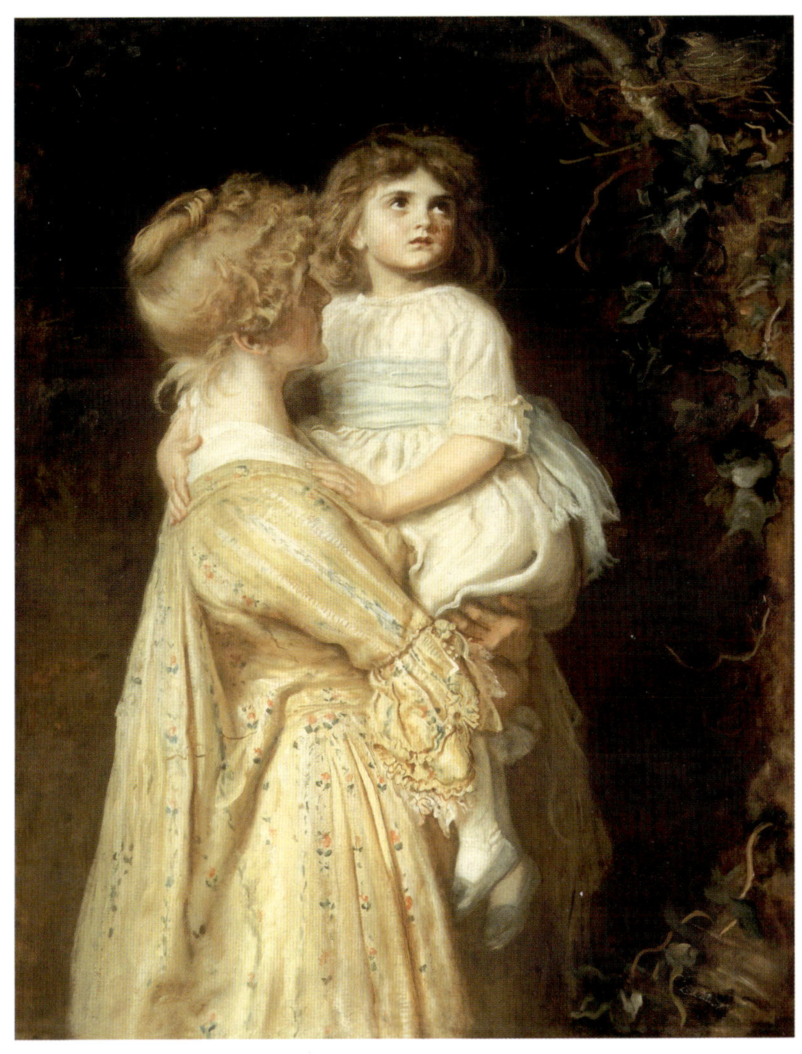

John Everett Millais (1829-96)

The Nest, about 1887

Oil on canvas, 129.5 × 99 cm

Purchased by William Hesketh Lever in 1896; inv. no. LL 3141

Children were the subject of many of Millais' later works. These often sentimental pictures may have been inspired by the exploits of his own children. He had four sons and four daughters, and the need to support such a large family meant that painting popular, saleable works must have become increasingly important to him. In parallel, his style also became looser, with broader brushstrokes, and he moved away from his earlier, painstakingly slow technique of painting every object in minute detail. This allowed him to keep up with the demand for his paintings and to provide for his growing family.

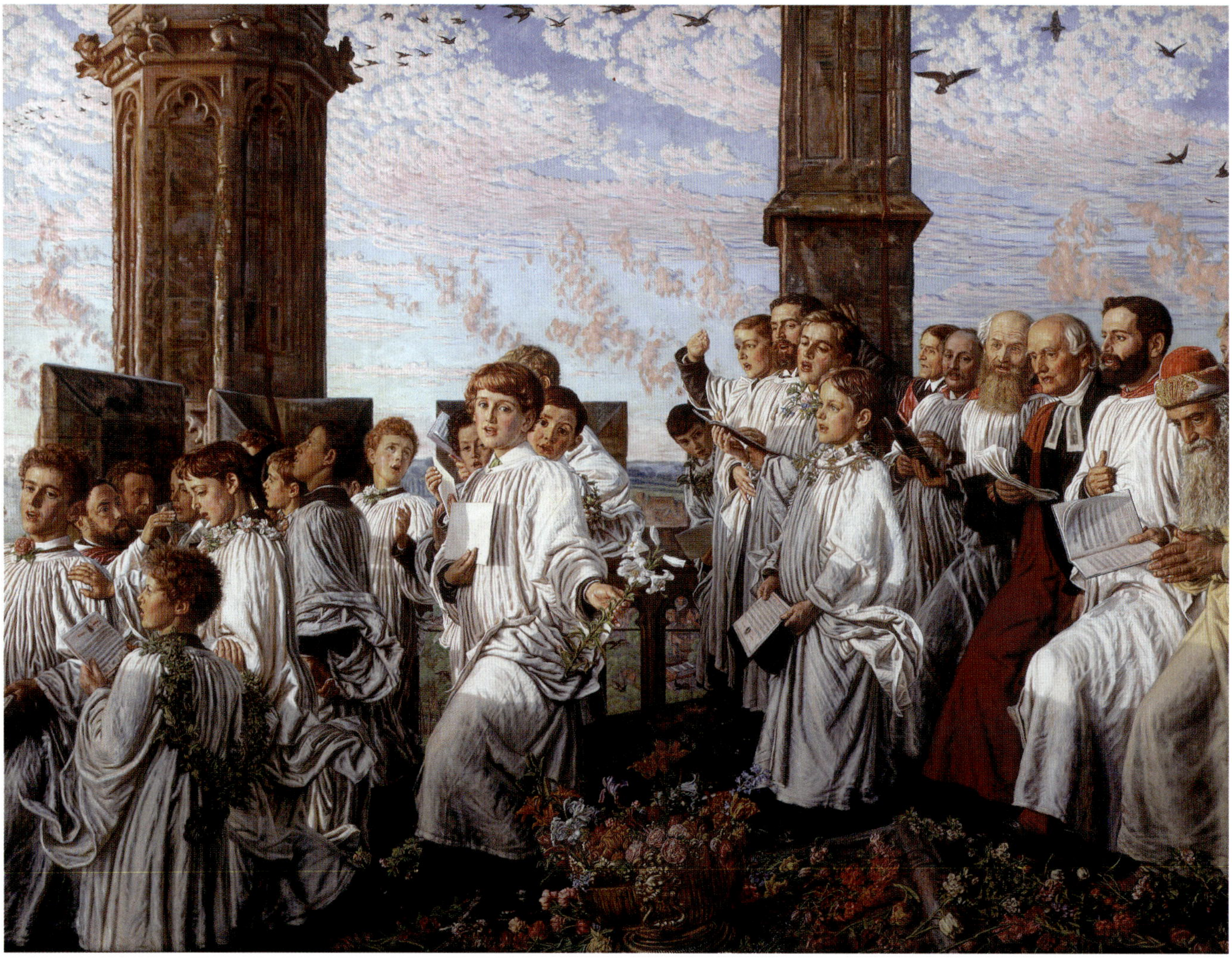

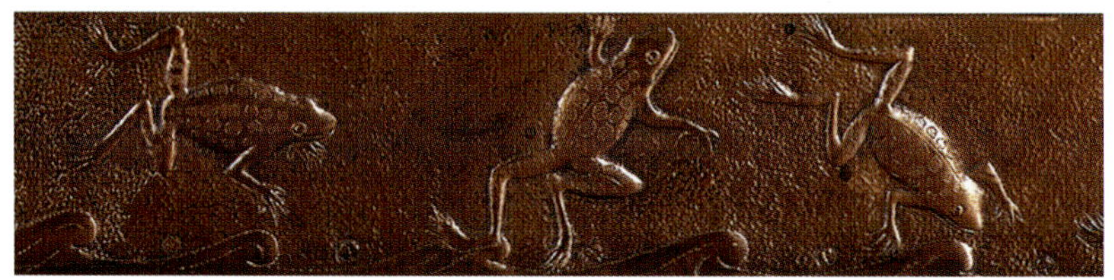

William Holman Hunt (1827–1910)

May Morning on Magdalen Tower,
1890

Oil on canvas, 154.5 × 200 cm

Purchased by William Hesketh Lever in 1919;
inv. no. LLAG 3599

William Holman Hunt (1827–1910)

Sheet of Studies for 'May Morning on Magdalen Tower', 1888

Pencil and watercolour over grey wash on paper, 25.3 × 35.4 cm

Purchased with the assistance of the Art Fund, the V&A Purchase Grant Fund and the Friends of Merseyside Museums and Art Galleries in 1985; inv. no. WAG 10537

Every year on the first day of May the choir of Magdalen College, Oxford climbs the chapel tower and sings the *Hymnus Eucharisticus* to greet the rising sun. This pre-Christian tradition was reintroduced in the 19th century. It fascinated Hunt who began making sketches for a painting of the event in May 1888. As the sheet of drawings shows he recorded the tower's architecture and the buildings below with Pre-Raphaelite accuracy, climbing the tower several times at 4am to study the sunrise. Despite including portraits of the choristers and staff he did not intend the painting (see opposite) to be a realistic record of the ritual. He added elements not found in the real festivities. These include the figure of a Parsee, or sun worshipper, in the far right to symbolise the common links between all religions. He also depicted the tower strewn with flowers to symbolise the coming of summer. The painting's copper frame (detail opposite) was made by the Guild of Handicrafts and enhances the symbolism of the scene. Frogs and fishes, both previously thought to be created by the warmth of the sun, leap about on the lower edge of the frame, and on the top edge a lark rises above a crescent moon.

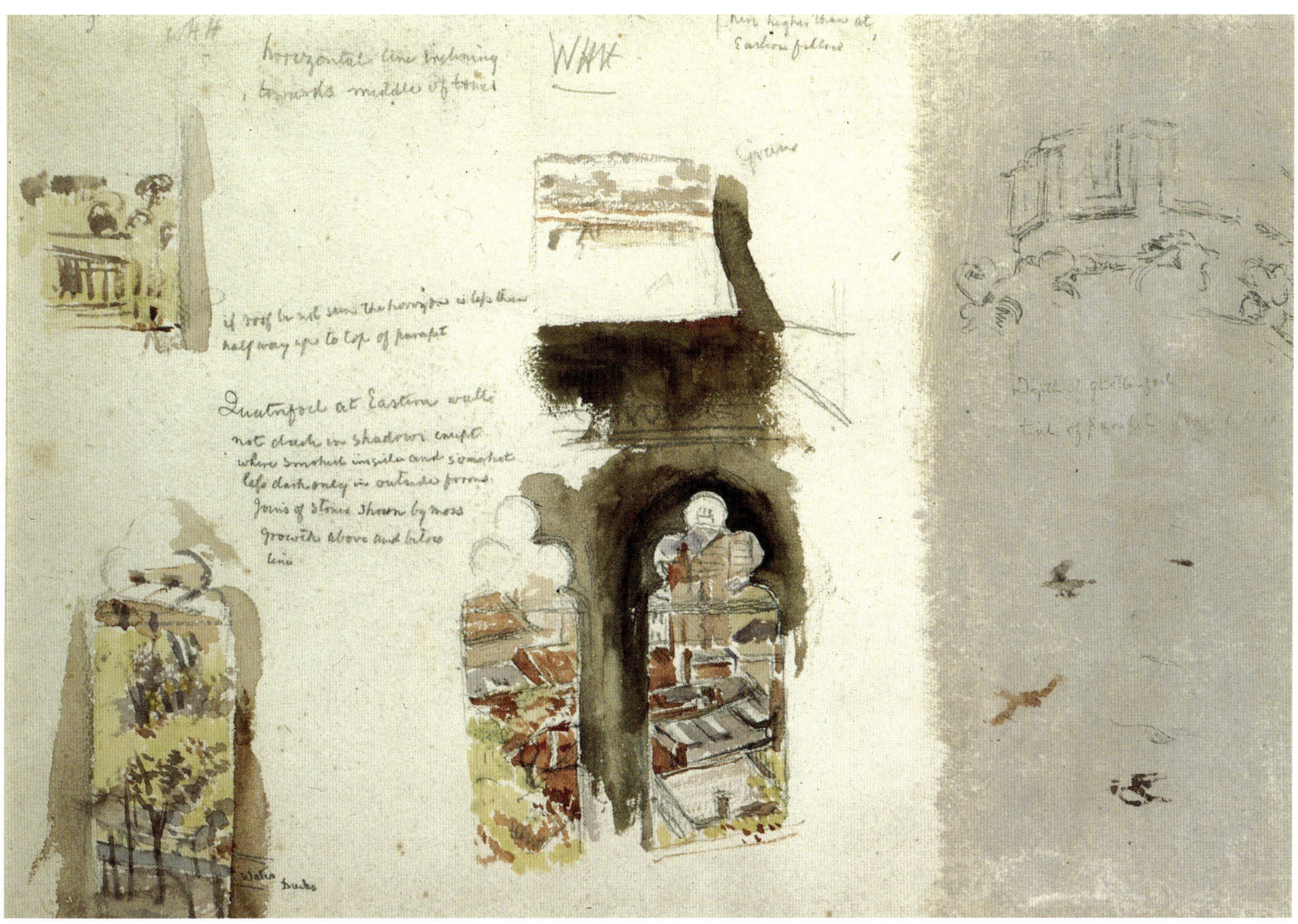

Edward Burne-Jones (1833–98)

Study of a female head for 'Sponsa de Libano', about 1891

Coloured chalks and watercolour on salmon-pink wove paper, 34.7 × 29 cm

Purchased by William Hesketh Lever in 1896; inv. no. LL 3788

In his later career Burne-Jones favoured making drawings in chalk, often signing them to give as gifts or to sell as finished works. This study shows his delight in the medium and the delicacy of his drawing skills. In the late 1870s Burne-Jones made a number of designs for works based on the biblical *Song of Solomon* including one inspired by the lines 'Awake O North Wind, and come thou South, blow upon my garden that the spices thereof may flow out'. He returned to the subject in 1891 and produced the watercolour *Sponsa de Libano* (Bride of Lebanon, Walker Art Gallery), featuring Solomon's bride and the two winds swirling above her. This drawing is a study for one of the winds. Burne-Jones recorded that the model was a Jewish girl from Houndsditch and described her as 'self-possessed, mature and worldly, and only about twelve years old'.

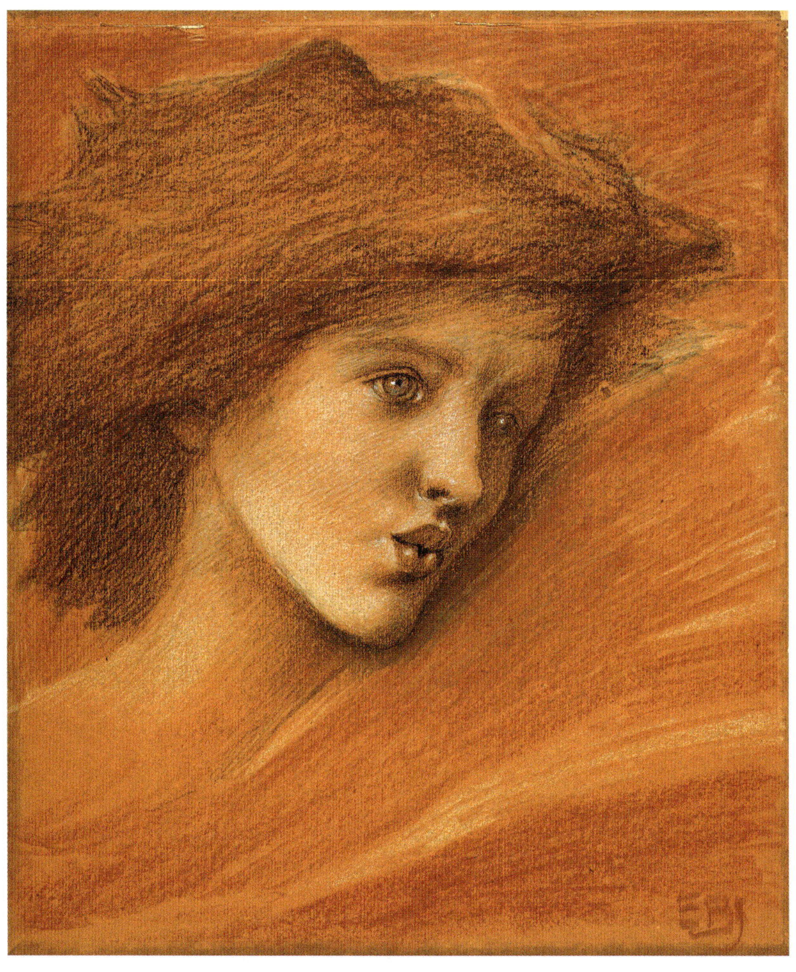

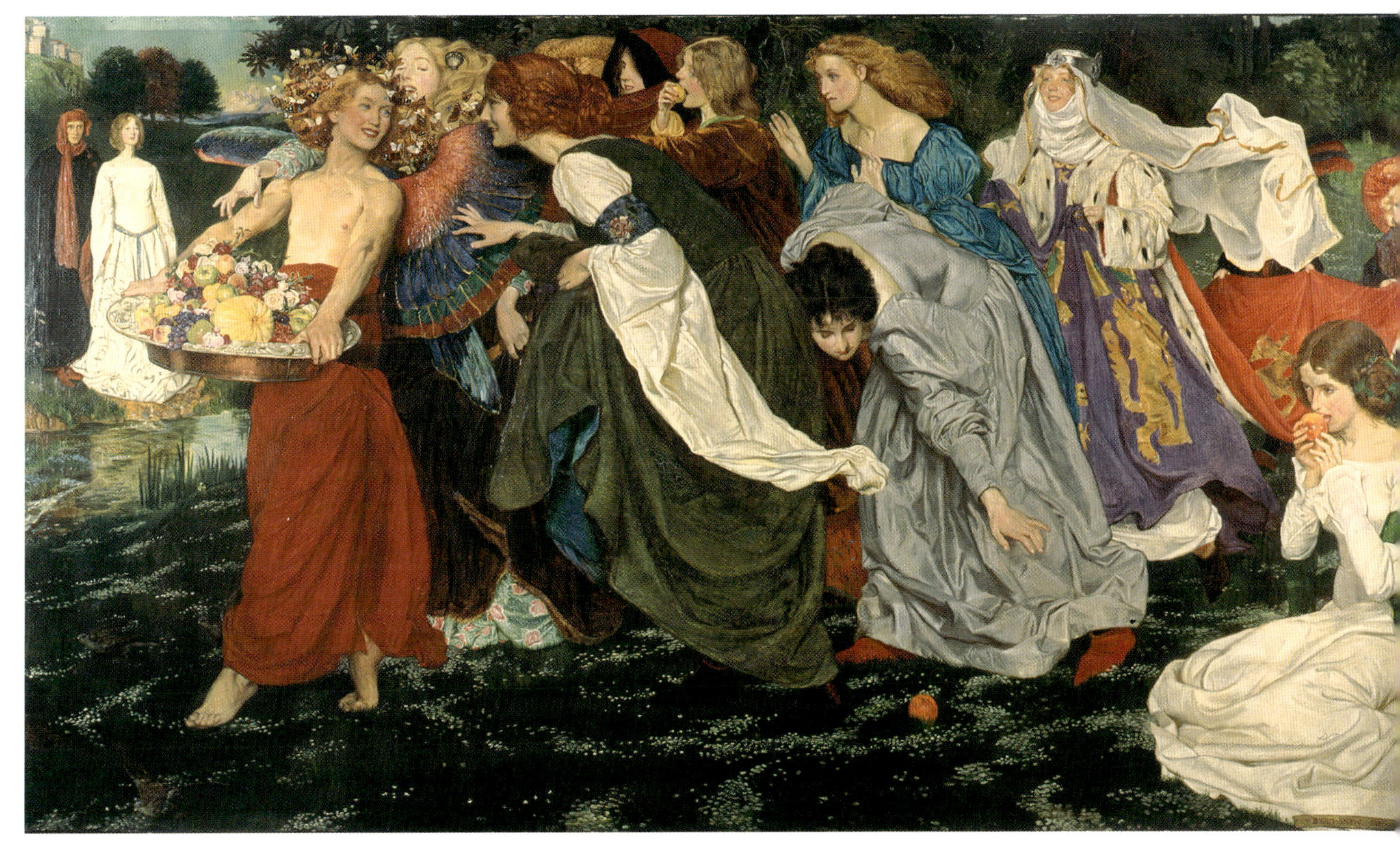

John Byam Shaw (1872–1919)

Love's Baubles, 1897

Oil on canvas, 104 × 180 cm

Purchased in 1897; inv. no. WAG 2650

In Shaw's startlingly colourful painting, Love leads young women in medieval dress on a frantic dance, luring them with fruits and flowers. Watching the frenzied excitement from the other side of the river are a poet and his lady, who have found true love and remain free from the snares of 'Love's baubles'. This strange allegorical painting was inspired by one of Dante Gabriel Rossetti's sonnets. Byam Shaw was a great admirer of Rossetti's poems and the art of the Pre-Raphaelite circle. Along with his friend Eleanor Fortescue-Brickdale he kept the flame of Pre-Raphaelitism burning well into the 20th century.

Evelyn de Morgan (1855–1919)

Life and Thought emerging from the Tomb, 1893

Oil on canvas, size 165 × 292.5 cm

Purchased in 1901; inv. no. WAG 3074

Evelyn de Morgan was the wife of the ceramicist William de Morgan (1839–1917) and the niece of the Pre-Raphaelite painter John Roddam Spencer Stanhope (1829–1908). When she was young her uncle introduced her to Italian Renaissance painting. It remained a source of inspiration throughout her career, as can be seen in this painting in which the draped figures resemble those in works by Botticelli (about 1445–1510).

The source for this allegorical painting is Alfred, Lord Tennyson's (1809–92) poem *The Deserted House* in which a lifeless body is symbolised by an empty home from which Life and Thought have fled to a 'great and distant city'. In the picture Life can be seen standing in armour next to Thought, who holds a book. Together they represent the immortality of the soul. The two figures emerge out of a mausoleum, rather than a house, and are being guided by a host of angels towards the far-off city representing Heaven. De Morgan fills the scene with symbols of life after death including a peacock, a butterfly and a bird emerging from an egg.

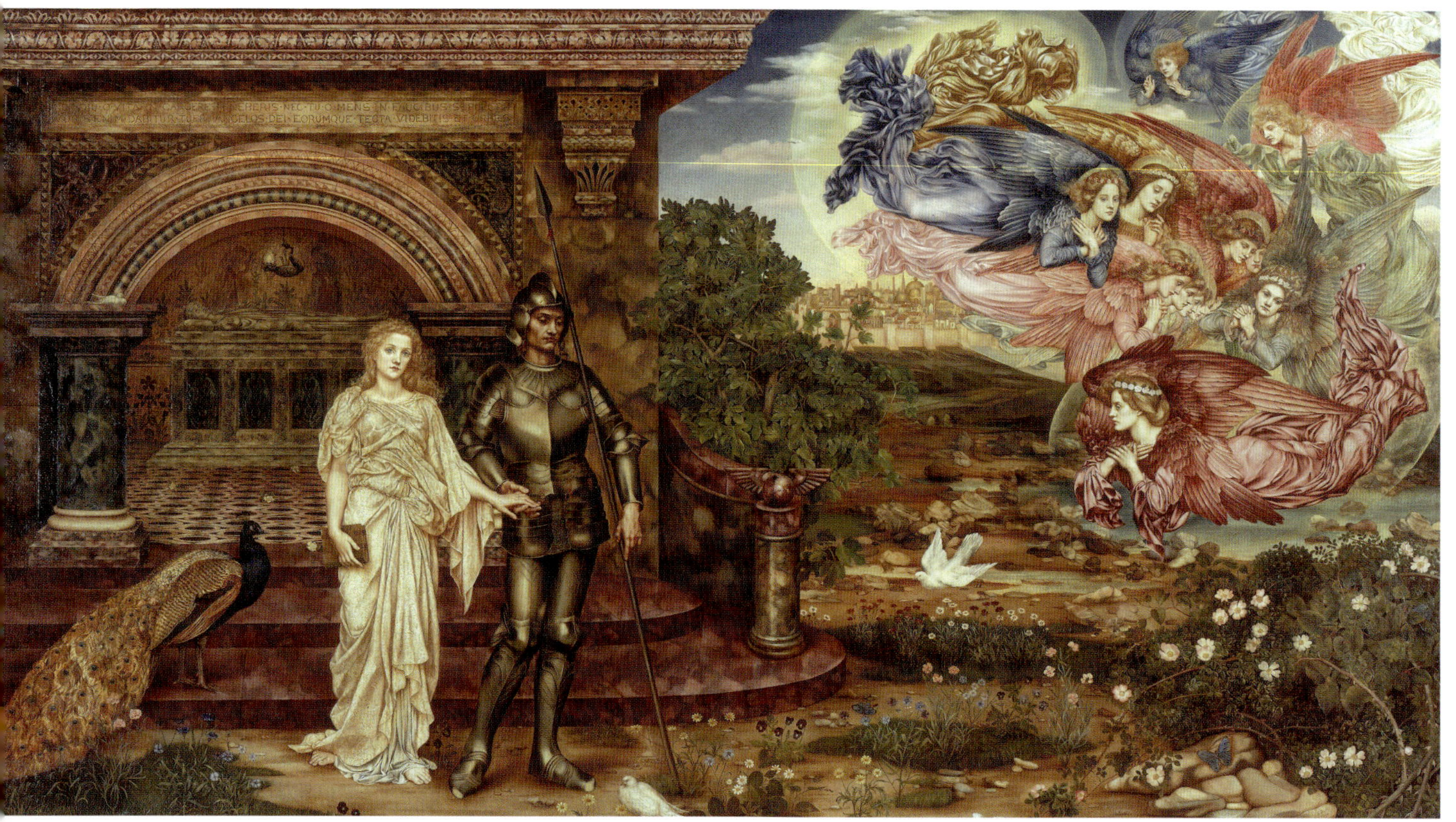

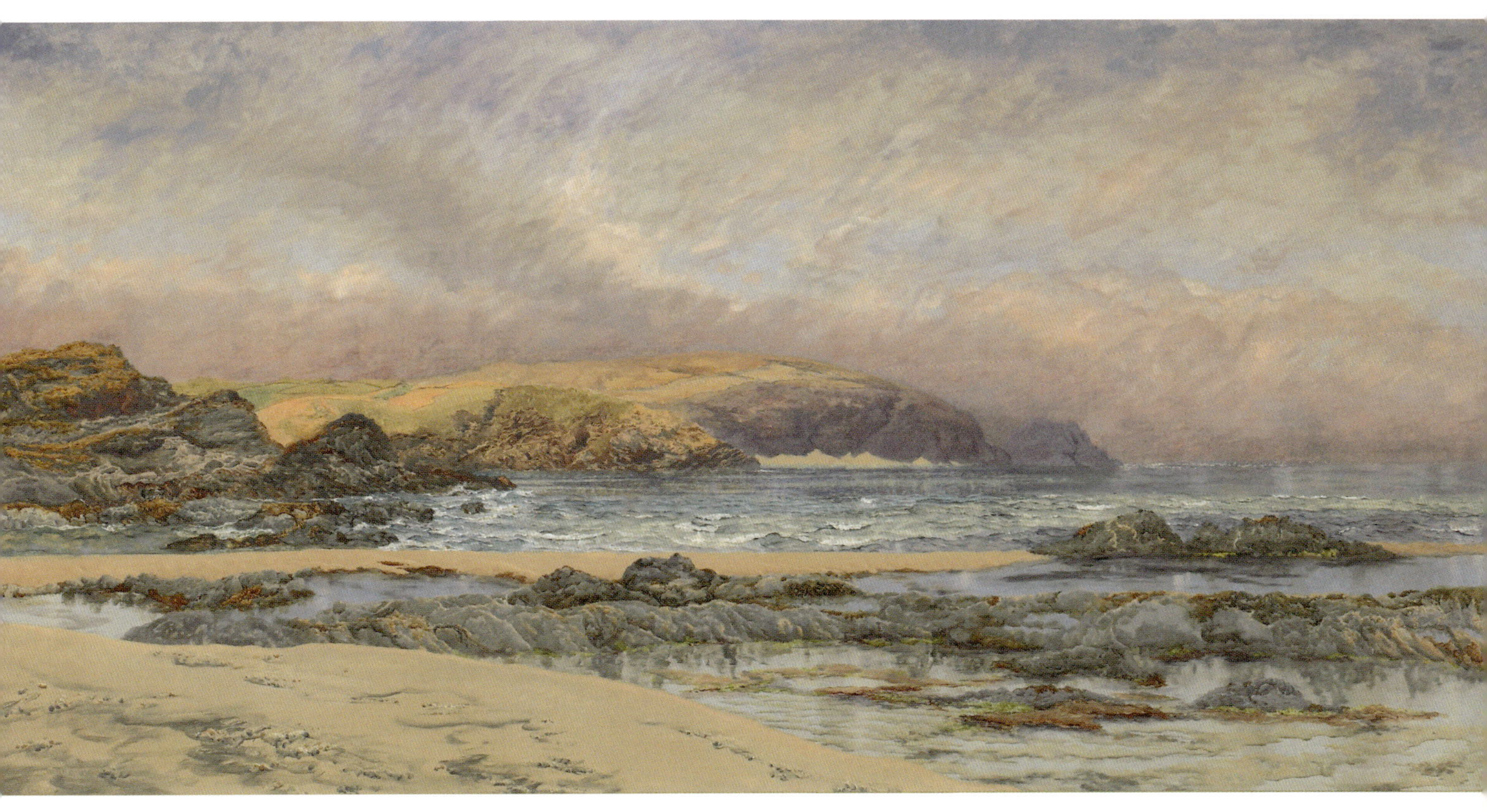

John Brett (1831–1902)

Trevose Head, 1897

Oil on canvas, 107.3 × 214.5 cm

Purchased in 1900; inv. no. WAG 2741

The Cornish coastline became a favourite subject for Brett in his later years. He holidayed there with his family in the summer months, making small oil sketches on the spot. In the winter months he would paint large-scale paintings from memory, using the sketches as *aide memoires* for colour. Beatrix Potter recorded in her diary that he was an enthusiastic photographer and used photographs to help him create the final composition. This was a considerable change from his earlier working methods when he followed the Pre-Raphaelite Brotherhood's dedication to painting their landscapes outside, directly onto the final canvas. His style also changed and, like Millais, he began to use broader brushstrokes. In this painting Brett depicts Trevose Head on the north coast of Cornwall. Having been painted from memory it is not a truly topographical landscape but captures the colours and atmosphere of the Cornish coast.

John Melhuish Strudwick
(1849–1937)

Love's Palace, 1893

Oil on canvas, size 64.7 × 114.9 cm

Bequeathed by Emma Holt in 1944; inv. no. WAG 304

Strudwick formed strong links to the second generation of Pre-Raphaelites by working as a studio assistant for John Roddam Stanhope Spencer (1829–1908) and Edward Burne-Jones. He also carved out a successful career in his own right, specialising in allegorical, literary and religious works. His paintings were particularly popular with Liverpool patrons including George Holt, whose collection at Sudley House is now part of National Museums Liverpool. Holt was a wealthy shipping magnate who lived at the house in the Mossley Hill suburb of Liverpool. He filled his home with works of art by largely contemporary artists. He tended to buy from dealers, rather than direct from the artist, but he commissioned Strudwick to paint three works for him, highlighting his strong admiration for the painter.

Love's Palace is an allegorical picture based on a poem by the architect and poet George Frederick Bodley (1827–1907). Enthroned in the centre of the composition sits Love. The three Fates are seated by the base of the steps. On either side of these figures are several young women. Some watch a bubble floating away - a symbol of both vanity and hope - and one cries in vain while the others listen to sweet music and read about love. Behind them are knights on horseback, those on the left symbolising the sorrow of love and on the right, its joy.

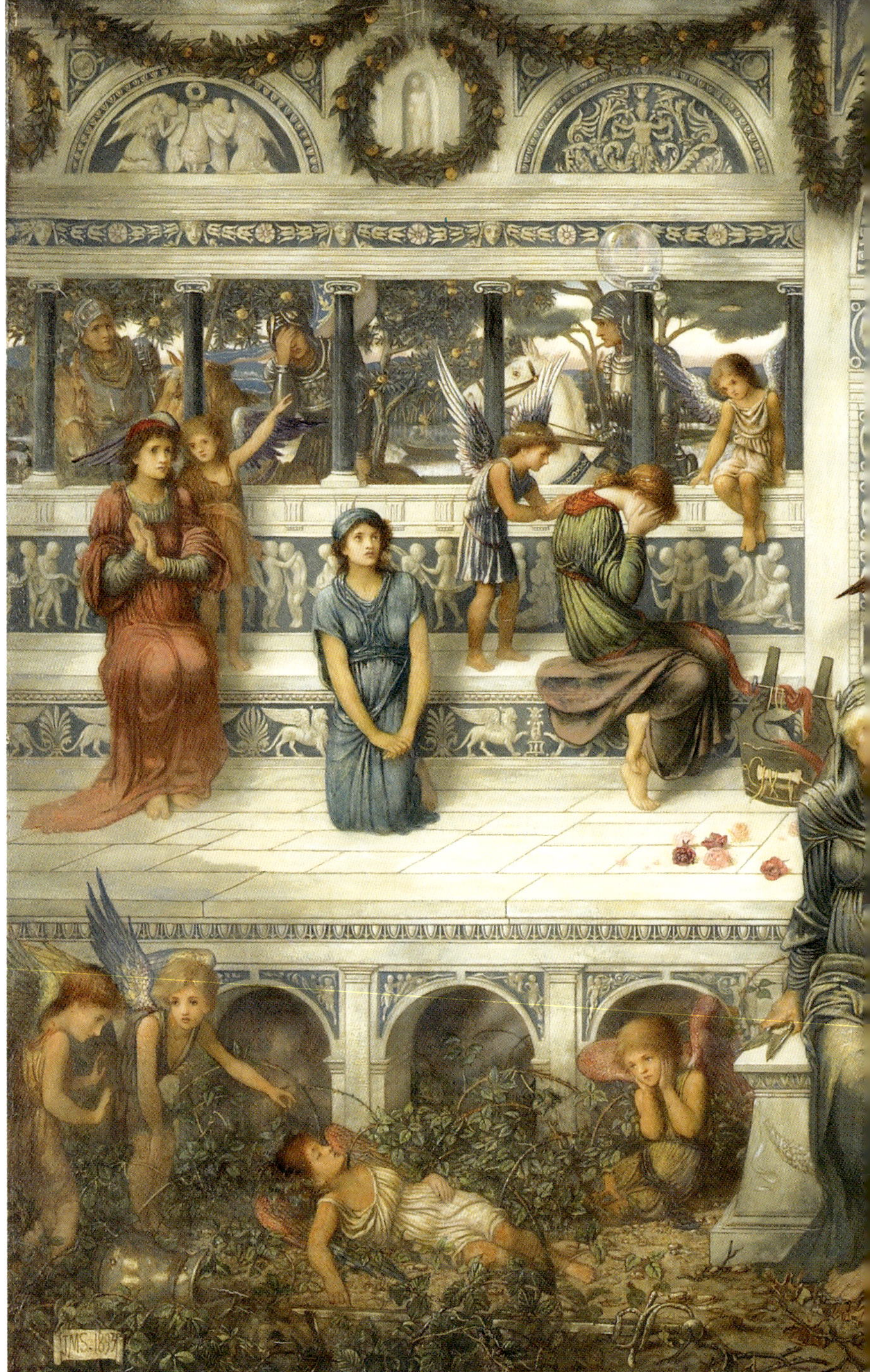

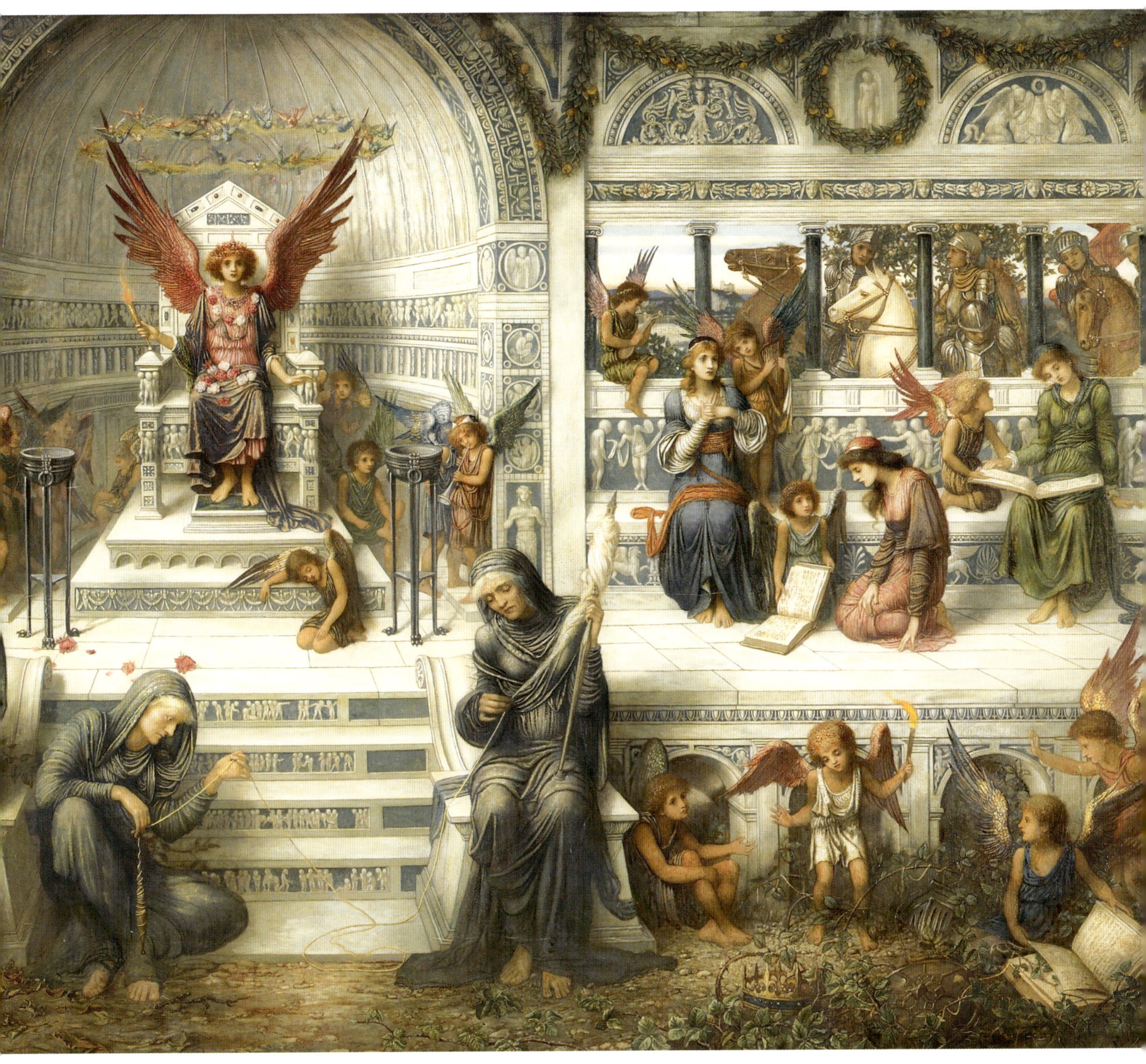

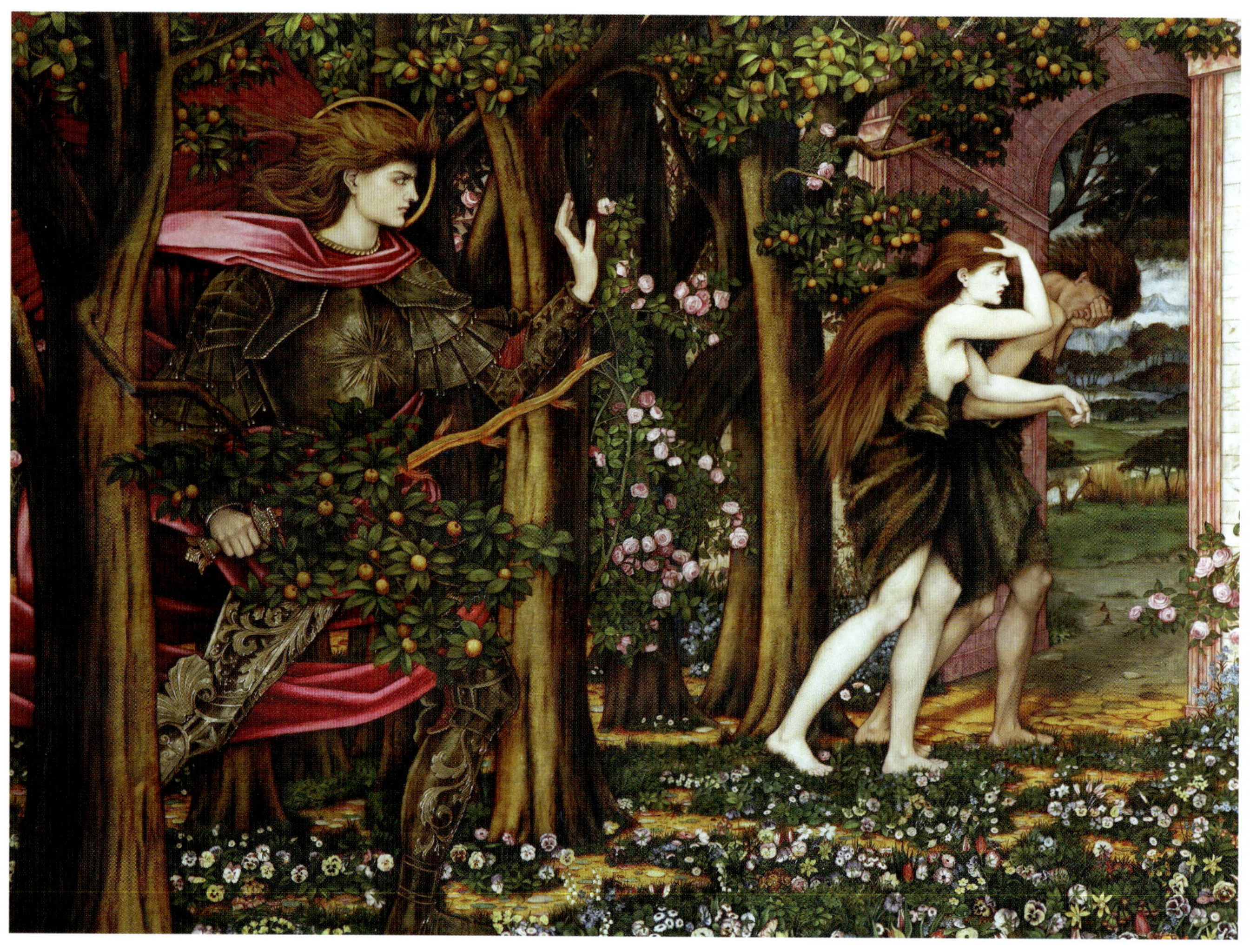

John Roddam Spencer Stanhope (1829–1908)

The Expulsion from Eden, about 1900

Tempera on canvas on panel, 136 × 176.8 cm

Presented by the Cohen family in 1925; inv. no. WAG 132

In 1857 Stanhope was one of the six young artists recruited by Rossetti to complete the Oxford Union murals. Like Burne-Jones, Stanhope visited Italy and was entranced by the work of 15th-century Italian artists such as Botticelli. Stanhope fused the archaic style of these masters with the modern colour harmonies and principles of the Aesthetic Movement. In 1880 he moved permanently to Florence but frequently sent works back to be exhibited in England, particularly at the annual Liverpool Autumn Exhibitions held at the Walker Art Gallery.

Stanhope was one of the leaders of the tempera revival. This traditional medium used egg yolk, rather than oil, to bind colour pigments. Its heyday was in the 15th century, before the invention of oil paint, and Stanhope's use of the medium gives this painting the archaic look he desired. Despite Stanhope's love of the past, the inspiration for the angel's 'flaming sword' appears to have been a modern gas poker.

Eleanor Fortescue-Brickdale
(1872–1945)

The Little Foot-Page, about 1905

Oil on canvas, 90.8 × 57 cm

Presented by an anonymous donor in 1909;
inv. no. WAG 1723

Fortescue-Brickdale was one of the last
followers of the Pre-Raphaelites and
adhered to their early style despite
beginning her career in the late 1890s.
The foliage in this painting shows her
unwavering dedication to their principle of
'Truth to Nature', in which everything,
including each blade of grass, is copied in
fine detail.

In a letter to the Walker Art Gallery the artist
said that the painting was based on the
ballad *Burd Helen* and features a girl who
cuts off her long hair and dresses up as a
page boy in order to follow her aristocratic
lover on his adventures. This ballad was
popular among Pre-Raphaelite painters as it
dealt with issues of social and gender
transgressions (see also William
Windus' *Burd Helen* [see p.83]).

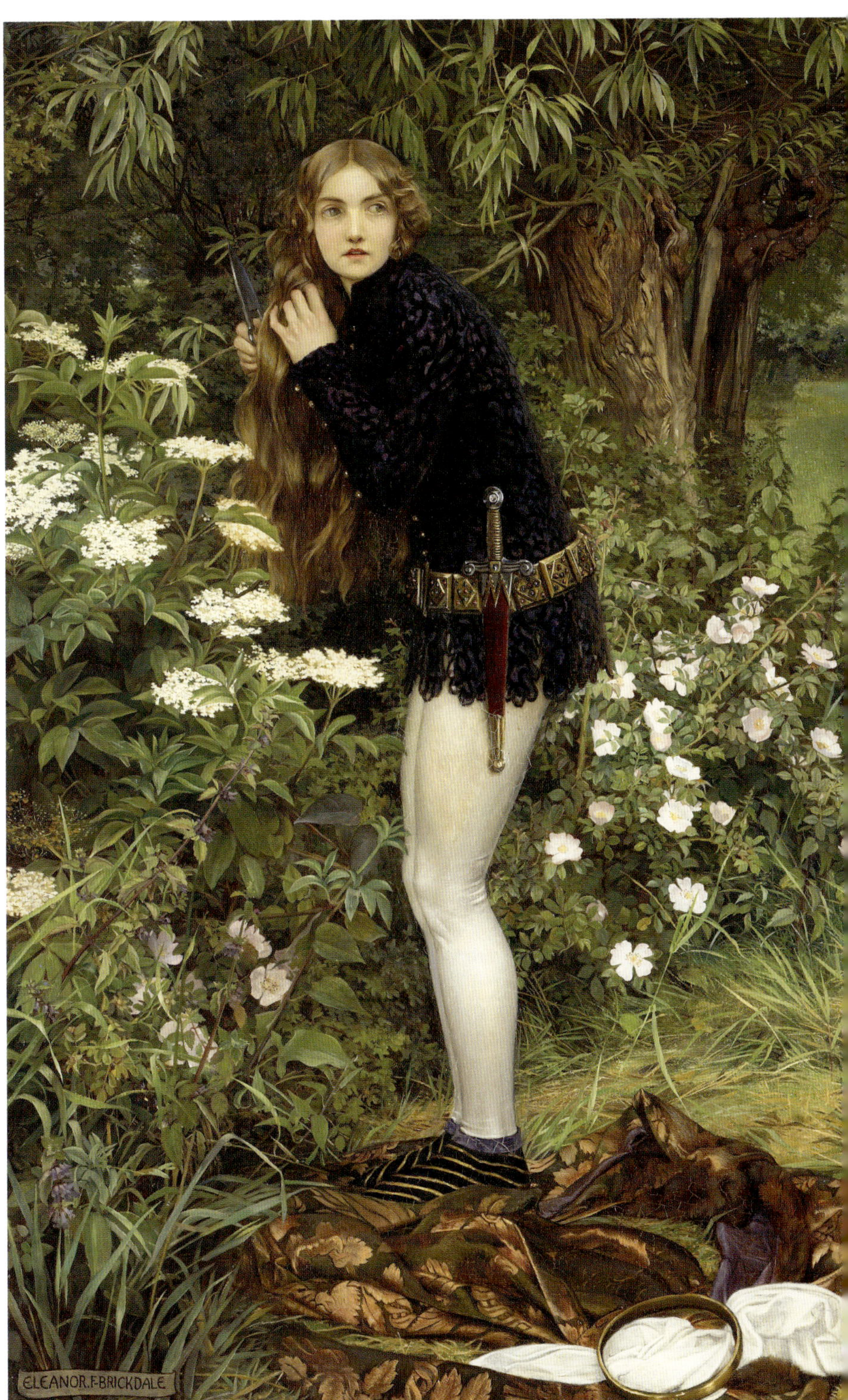

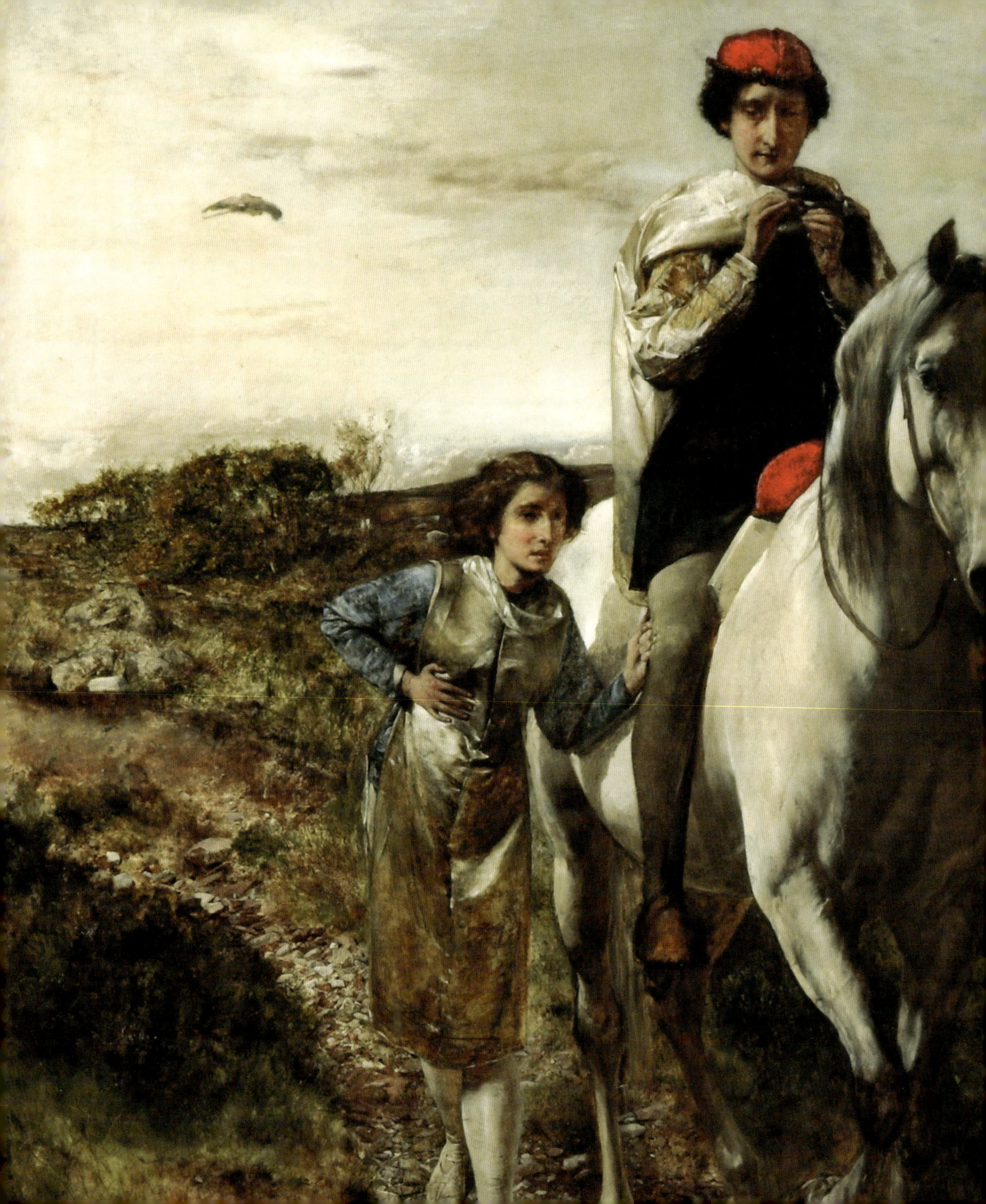

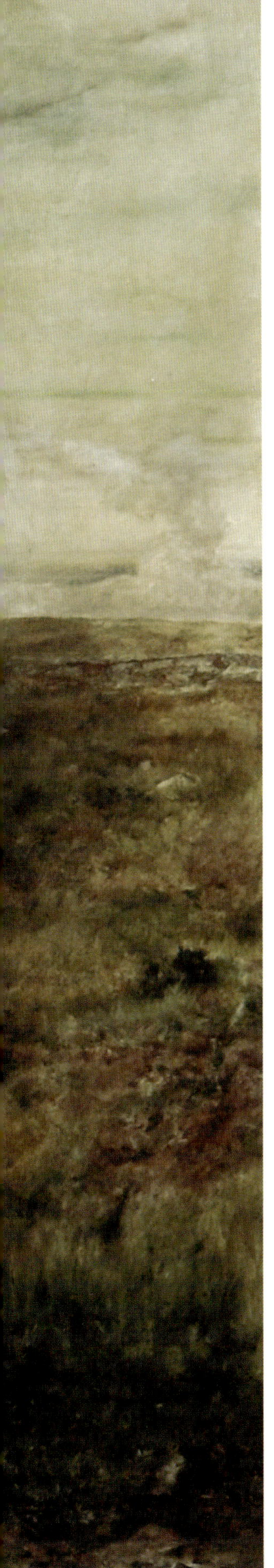

Liverpool Pre-Raphaelites

The Walker Art Gallery has the world's largest collection of works by the Liverpool Pre-Raphaelites, who rose to prominence in the 1850s. This group shared an enthusiasm for the bright colours, minute attention to detail and naturalism that were favoured by their London counterparts but they had their own distinct identity. They painted humble landscapes, views that were quietly beautiful rather than dramatic. They embraced the Brotherhood's passion for scenes from contemporary life but painted their figures in a more naïve, sometimes awkward, style.

Central to the spread of Pre-Raphaelite ideas within the city was the Liverpool Academy of Art. Here artists were able to debate and share their views about contemporary art. They were either elected as members of the Academy or exhibited their work in its annual exhibitions. Like the Royal Academy in London, the Liverpool Academy had its own art school. Many of the local artists who embraced Pre-Raphaelitism, such as William Lindsay Windus (1822–1907) and Joseph Edward Worrall (1829–1913), were taught there and their teachers, notably William Davis (1812–73), worked in the Pre-Raphaelite style in the 1850s.

Windus was a key member for the dissemination of Pre-Raphaelite principles at the Academy. His early admiration for the Pre-Raphaelite Brotherhood began in 1850 when he saw Millais' *Christ in the House of his Parents* (1849–50, Tate) at the Royal Academy. The trip to London to see the new art trends had been suggested by his patron, John Miller, a Liverpool merchant who was an important collector and supporter of both London and Liverpool Pre-Raphaelite painters. Inspired by the work of the Pre-Raphaelite Brotherhood, Windus returned to Liverpool and shared his enthusiasm with his fellow artists at the Academy. These artists had already begun to paint in a more naturalistic manner and were looking to embrace a new direction in contemporary art.

The people of Liverpool were able to see the work of the London Pre-Raphaelites first hand in the Liverpool Academy's annual exhibitions, which began in 1827. In the 1830s a £50 prize was introduced to encourage artists from the capital to send their work to be exhibited, raising both the profile of the Academy and the quality of the work shown. By the 1840s the Academy's annual shows were deemed the best provincial exhibitions in the country. They attracted the country's leading artists who saw them as a way to reach newly wealthy northern industrial and mercantile collectors. As young, ambitious painters, John Everett Millais, William Holman Hunt and Ford Madox Brown were the first Pre-Raphaelites to exhibit at the Liverpool Academy's annual shows. After Hunt won the £50 non-member prize in 1851 for his painting *Valentine rescuing Silvia from Proteus* (1850–51, Birmingham Museum and Art Gallery), other London Pre-Raphaelites began exhibiting at the Academy including Dante Gabriel Rossetti, John Brett, Henry Wallis, Edward Burne-Jones, Simeon Solomon and Arthur Hughes. This gave Liverpool artists and local collectors the chance to see the work of the Pre-Raphaelite circle on their own doorstep. In fact, by the time that Hunt won the £50 prize, many Liverpool artists, like William Davis, had already begun to appreciate the work of the Brotherhood and to see them as kindred spirits who were also interested in making art more naturalistic. Such was the admiration among a large group of members of the Liverpool Academy that a Pre-Raphaelite artist, or one associated with the group, won the £50 prize every year from 1851 until 1859.* This led to rifts among the various factions within the Liverpool Academy and criticism from the public and press who disliked the fact that one group of artists won almost every year. The controversy and ongoing differences of opinions between the conservative members and the more modern Pre-Raphaelites eventually led to the demise of the Academy in 1867.

The support the Liverpool Pre-Raphaelites showed for their London counterparts was rewarded by mutual enthusiasm, particularly from Ford Madox Brown, who exhibited at the Liverpool Academy almost every year from 1847 until 1865. He strongly admired the work of the Liverpool Pre-Raphaelites and got to know them on his visits to the city through their mutual patron, John Miller. Brown thought particularly highly of William Davis, whose humble but beautiful scenes of the English countryside matched his own approach to landscape painting. He championed the new Liverpool movement to his friends including Dante Gabriel Rossetti, who brought the work of both Davis and Windus to the attention of John Ruskin, the most eminent art critic of the 19th century. Ruskin's opinions could make or break an artist's career. Such was the admiration among the London artists for the Liverpool painters that when the Pre-Raphaelites held a group exhibition in London in 1857, paintings by Davis and Windus were included in the show. In 1858, James Campbell (1828–1893), William Davis and William Windus were all elected to join the Hogarth Club as non-resident members. This short-lived club was the brainchild of Brown and Rossetti who wanted an art club for Pre-Raphaelite artists and patrons, where members could meet socially but also exhibit their work. That three Liverpool painters were elected to join is another sign of how popular the Liverpool group had become in the Pre-Raphaelite circle.

It was not only the Academy and the artists who helped to create a Liverpool Pre-Raphaelite movement. The Liverpool art collectors who were buying Pre-Raphaelite works and encouraging Liverpool artists to embrace their principles also played a significant role. In particular, John Miller (1795/7–1876) of Everton, a Scottish-born tobacco merchant, was the central figure in the Liverpool circle of Pre-Raphaelites. He took pains to help them develop, notably encouraging Windus to explore new trends in contemporary art which led to the artist sharing his new passion for the Brotherhood with his Liverpool contemporaries. Despite his modest income Miller heavily supported these artists by commissioning, buying and selling their work. In the case of Davis he supported him single-handedly until his

---

*   William Holman Hunt, John Everett Millais and Ford Madox Brown each won the prize twice. Their friends Mark Anthony, Augustus Egg and William Dyce won in the other years (see Edward Morris and Emma Roberts *The Liverpool Academy and other exhibitions of contemporary art in Liverpool 1774-1867: a history and index of artists and works exhibited,* appendix 5 for the list of prizewinners).

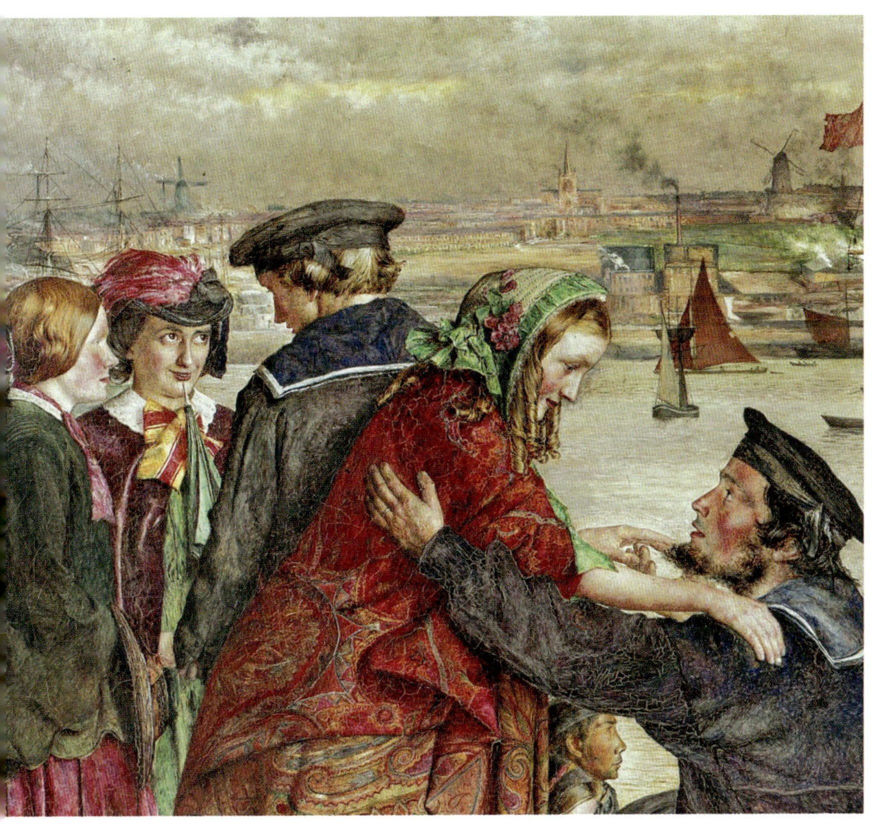

career took off. Furthermore, one of Miller's daughters, Augusta, married Peter Paul Marshall who, with a number of the Pre-Raphaelites, was one of the founding partners of Morris, Marshall, Faulkner & Co.* It was through Miller that the Birkenhead banker George Rae (1817–1902) discovered the Pre-Raphaelites. He went on to amass a considerable collection of their paintings including 19 works by Rossetti. Rae often lent works from his collection to the Liverpool Academy's exhibitions and like Miller he supported the local Pre-Raphaelites, particularly William Davis, from whom he bought 26 pictures. Miller also introduced Frederick Leyland (1832–92) to Rossetti. Leyland, who had started his career with the firm John Bibby and Sons, went on to make his fortune from his own shipping line. For a time he lived at Speke Hall, a Tudor mansion on the outskirts of Liverpool, and while there was visited by Ford Madox Brown and Rossetti. Leyland became a significant patron of Rossetti (and more notoriously of the leader of the Aesthetic Movement James McNeill Whistler).†

Despite the success of their Pre-Raphaelite works in the 1850s and 1860s, for most of the Liverpool artists this was a short-lived phase in their careers, and as mature artists they abandoned the Pre-Raphaelite emphasis on fine detail and bright colours. This is particularly true of William JJC Bond (1833–1926) whose later style owed more to JMW Turner than the Pre-Raphaelites. Like Joseph Edward Worrall he remained on Merseyside for the entirety of his career. The most successful of the group, William Windus, stopped painting professionally around 1862 and moved to London in the late 1870s. Others before him had already swapped Liverpool for London where they hoped to further their careers by moving to the centre of the British art market. In 1865 Alfred William Hunt (1830–96) moved to London and took over a house previously occupied by William Holman Hunt. In around 1866 John Lee (1839–82) also left Liverpool for the capital. James Campbell relocated to London but returned to his home city in the 1870s when his prospects failed to blossom. William Davis had also made the move by 1863 but died quite suddenly a decade later. Ford Madox Brown organised a memorial exhibition to raise an annuity to support his widow and their children. This compassionate act symbolises the depth of respect and friendship the London Pre-Raphaelites held for their northern contemporaries, who had, from the sparks kindled within the walls of the Liverpool Academy, created a significant impact upon the local and national art scene in the 19th century.

---

* In 1875 William Morris reorganised the firm, buying out Marshall, Rossetti and Madox Brown, and renaming it Morris and Co.

† The author would like to thank Sandra Penketh for the information on Miller's role in introducing both George Rae and Frederick Leyland to the Pre-Raphaelites and for the additional biographical information on Leyland.

William Joseph Julius Caesar Bond (1833–1926)

House at Oxton, 1854

Oil on board, 26.3 × 21.2 cm

Purchased in 1970; inv. no. WAG 7463

Bond was born at Knotty Ash near Liverpool. He was apprenticed to a picture restorer but was encouraged to become an artist by John Miller, Liverpool's most enthusiastic Pre-Raphaelite patron, who saw potential in his work. This is one of his earliest known pictures and was painted when he was just 21 years old. It shows the influence of the Pre-Raphaelites in its sharp detail and vivid colours painted on a white ground. Later in his career Bond focused on painting seascapes, adopting a style heavily inspired by Turner. Oxton village is a leafy neighbourhood on the Wirral, across the River Mersey from Liverpool.

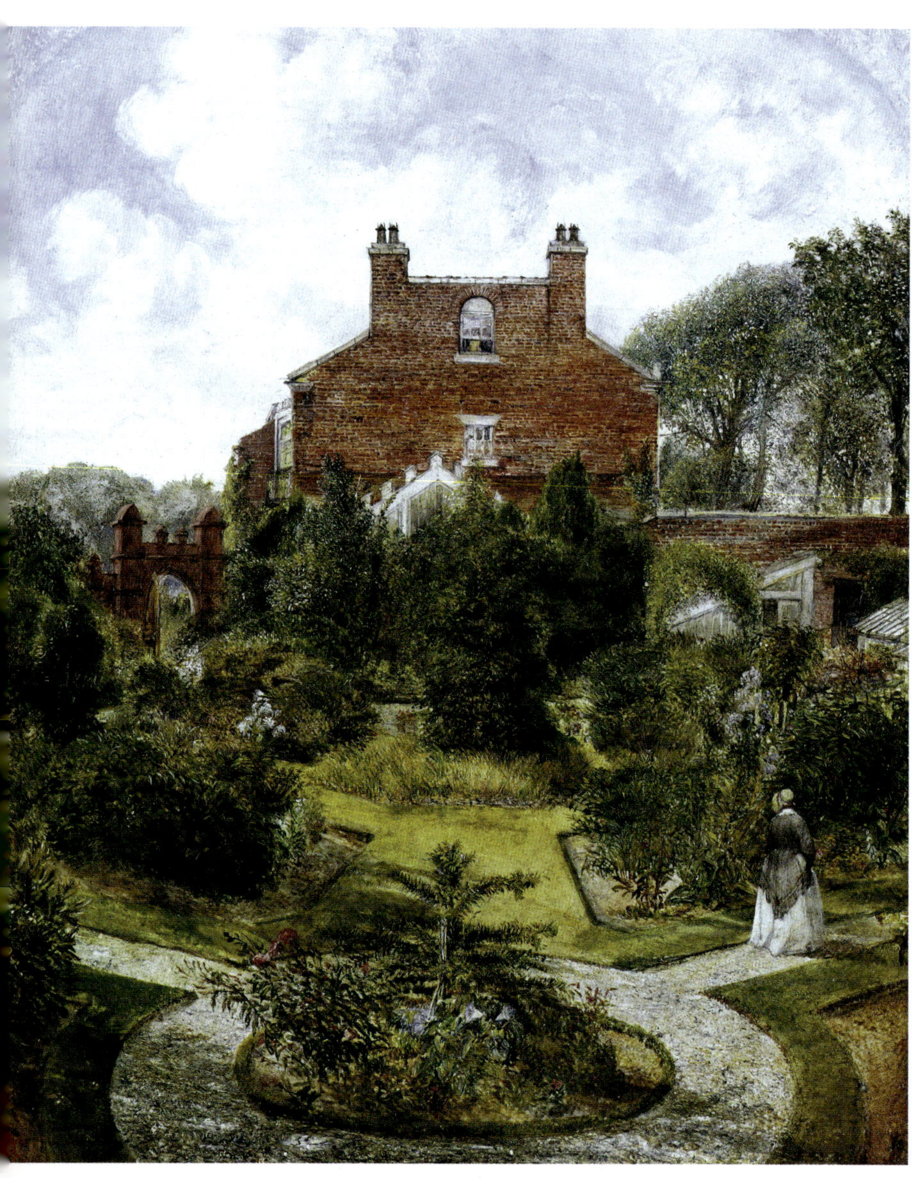

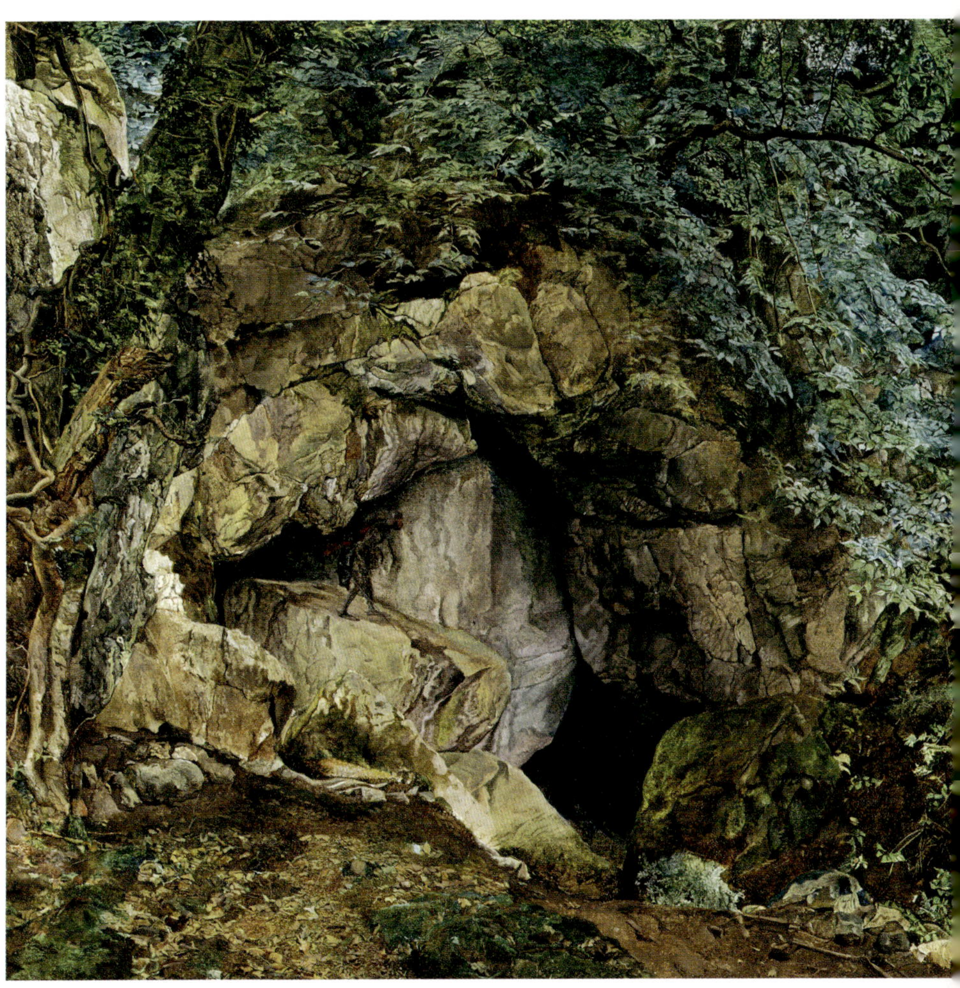

James Campbell (1828–93)

The Dragon's Den, about 1854

Oil on canvas, 40.1 × 40.1 cm
Purchased in 1980; inv. no. WAG 9742

James Campbell, son of a Liverpool insurance clerk, studied at the Liverpool Academy and in London at the Royal Academy. He painted this small picture from nature, choosing as his subject a cave known as Dunald Mill Hole close to the village of Nether Kellet, near Carnforth in Lancashire. His detailed painting of the cracks and crevices in the rocks shows the influence of the Pre-Raphaelites. To increase the appeal of the picture he added a knight peering into the dragon's den, perhaps hoping to take advantage of the Victorian enthusiasm for tales of medieval chivalry. The painting was bought by John Miller, the chief supporter of Pre-Raphaelitism in Liverpool and one of Campbell's best patrons.

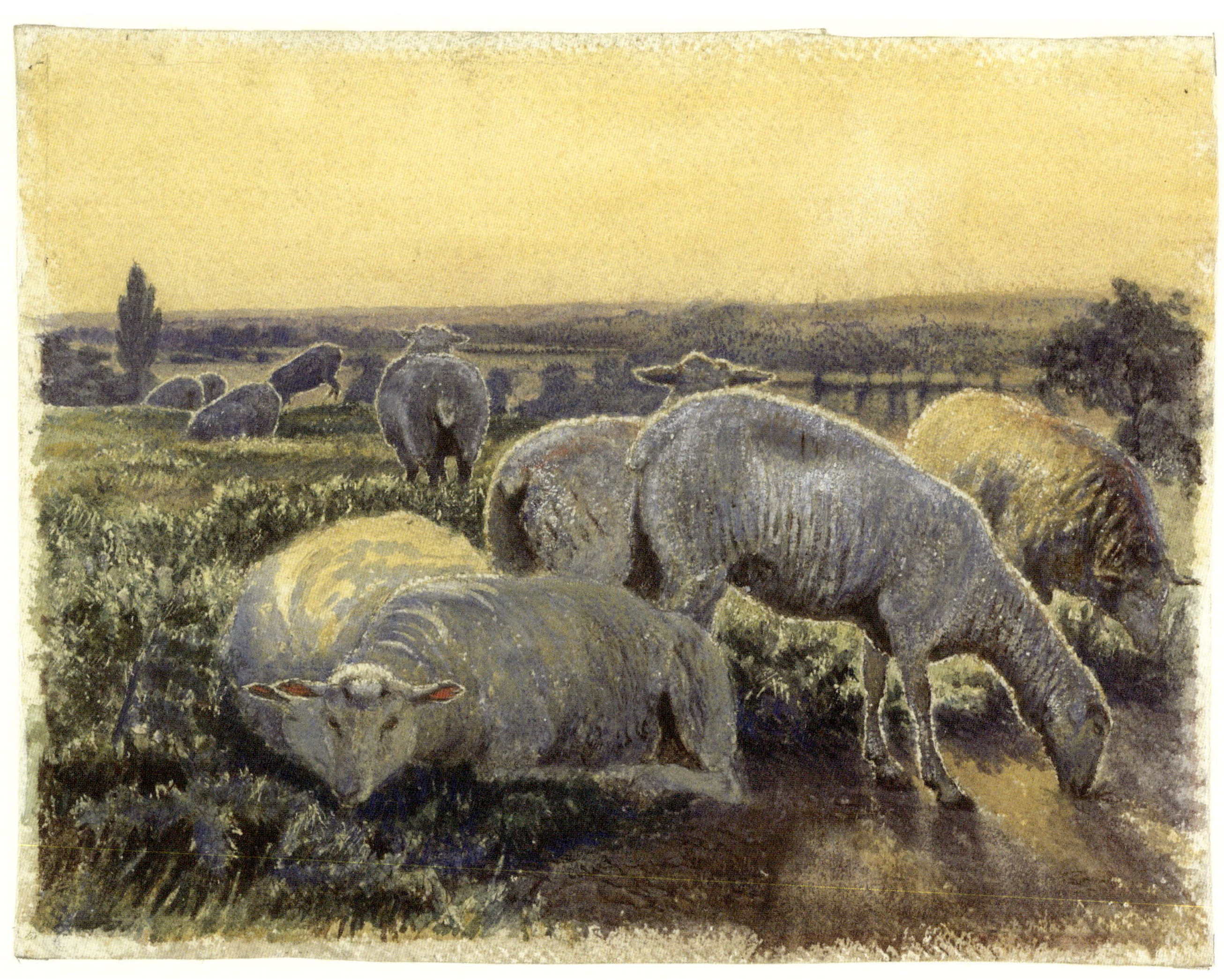

Daniel Alexander Williamson (1823–1903)

Early Morning Peckham, about 1855–60

Watercolour and gouache on paper, 22.9 × 30.3 cm

Bequeathed by James Smith of Blundellsands in 1923; inv. no. WAG 608

Williamson was born in Liverpool, but between 1849 and 1860 he lived in London, first in Peckham and then in Clapham. In the mid-19th century Peckham was a rural area and provided Williamson with suitable subject matter on his doorstep. The pastoral landscape in this watercolour, and the use of white gouache to capture the sparkle of the early morning sun on the backs of the sheep, indicate that Williamson admired the work of the early 19th-century British artist Samuel Palmer (1805–81). The leaping sheep in the background suggests that he might also have been inspired by Ford Madox Brown's painting *The Pretty Baa-Lambs* (Birmingham Museum and Art Gallery) which was exhibited at the Royal Academy in 1852, and included sheep frolicking on Clapham Common.

William Lindsay Windus
(1822–1907)

Burd Helen, 1856

Oil on canvas, 84.4 × 66.6 cm

Purchased in 1956; inv. no. WAG 158

When Windus exhibited this painting at the Royal Academy in London it became his most successful picture, bringing him the admiration of Dante Gabriel Rossetti and the highly influential art critic John Ruskin. Having seen *Burd Helen,* Rossetti was so excited that he forced Ruskin into a cab and rushed him to the Academy. Ruskin declared it 'a great Pre-Raphaelite painting'. He described it as 'thoughtful and intense to the highest degree' and 'of the grandest imaginative power'.

The painting is based on the Scottish border ballad of Burd Helen, a young woman who falls pregnant by her callous lover, Lord John. In order to stay with him she disguises herself as a page boy and runs alongside his horse, despite her condition. This subject allowed Windus to combine a tale of social transgression with his first naturalistic landscape background. Both of these elements were frequently found in works by the Pre-Raphaelite Brotherhood, whose work Windus greatly admired.

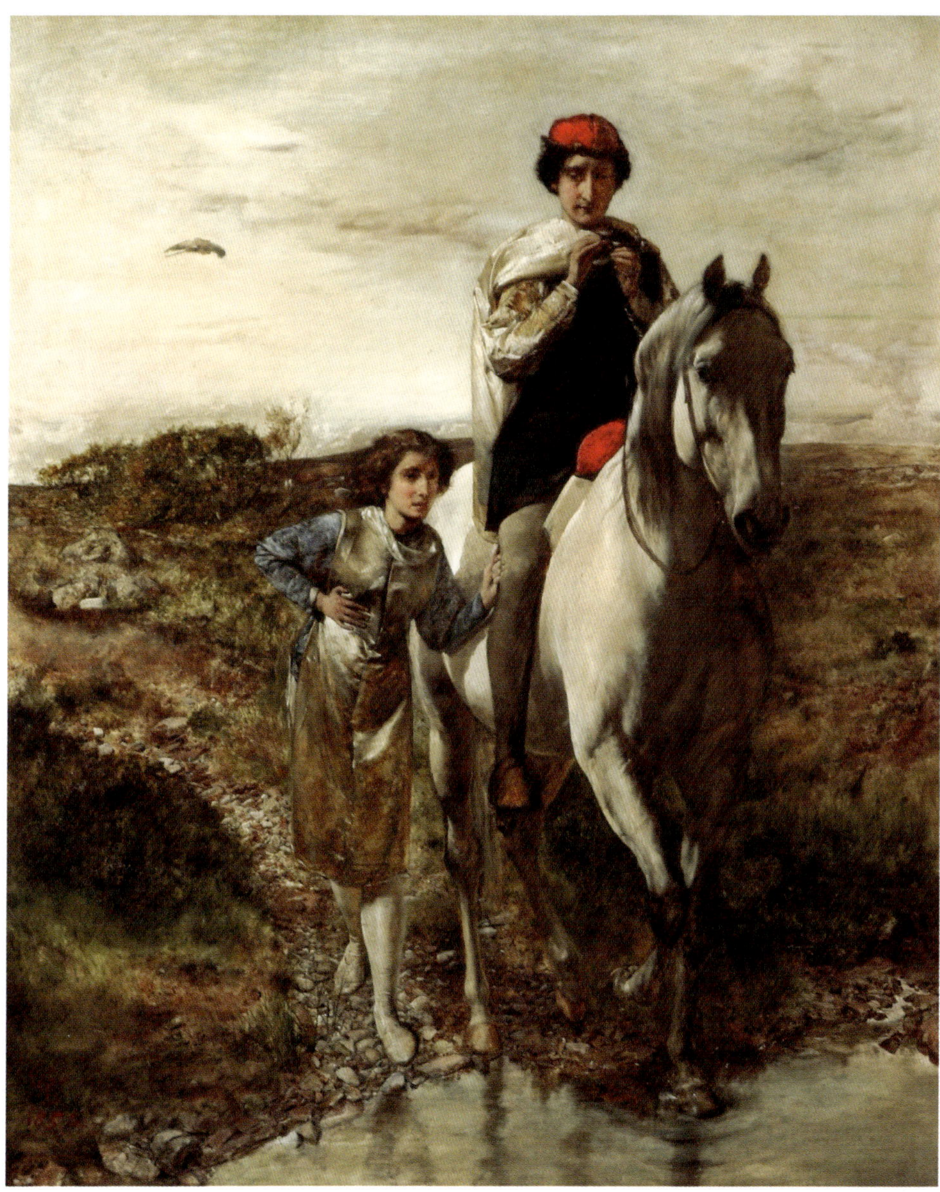

William Davis (1812–73)

Junction of the Liffey and Rye, near Leixlip, 1857

Oil on board, 20.3 × 30.5 cm

Purchased in 1964; inv. no. WAG 6248

Davis was born in Dublin but made his career in Liverpool. He attended classes at the Liverpool Academy from 1848 before becoming a full member in 1853, and taking over as Professor of Drawing in 1856. He made two visits to his native country in 1853 and 1857. This painting dates from the second visit and shows the church tower of Leixlip on the right and the boathouse in the grounds of Leixlip Castle on the left. As can be seen from this picture, Davis favoured a white ground and fluid oil paint to create light, bright colours on his canvases.

John Miller, the avid Liverpool supporter of Pre-Raphaelitism, bought this painting direct from Davis. In fact, despite Davis' popularity among the London Pre-Raphaelites, he found it hard to find patrons and was supported almost single-handedly by Miller for much of his career.

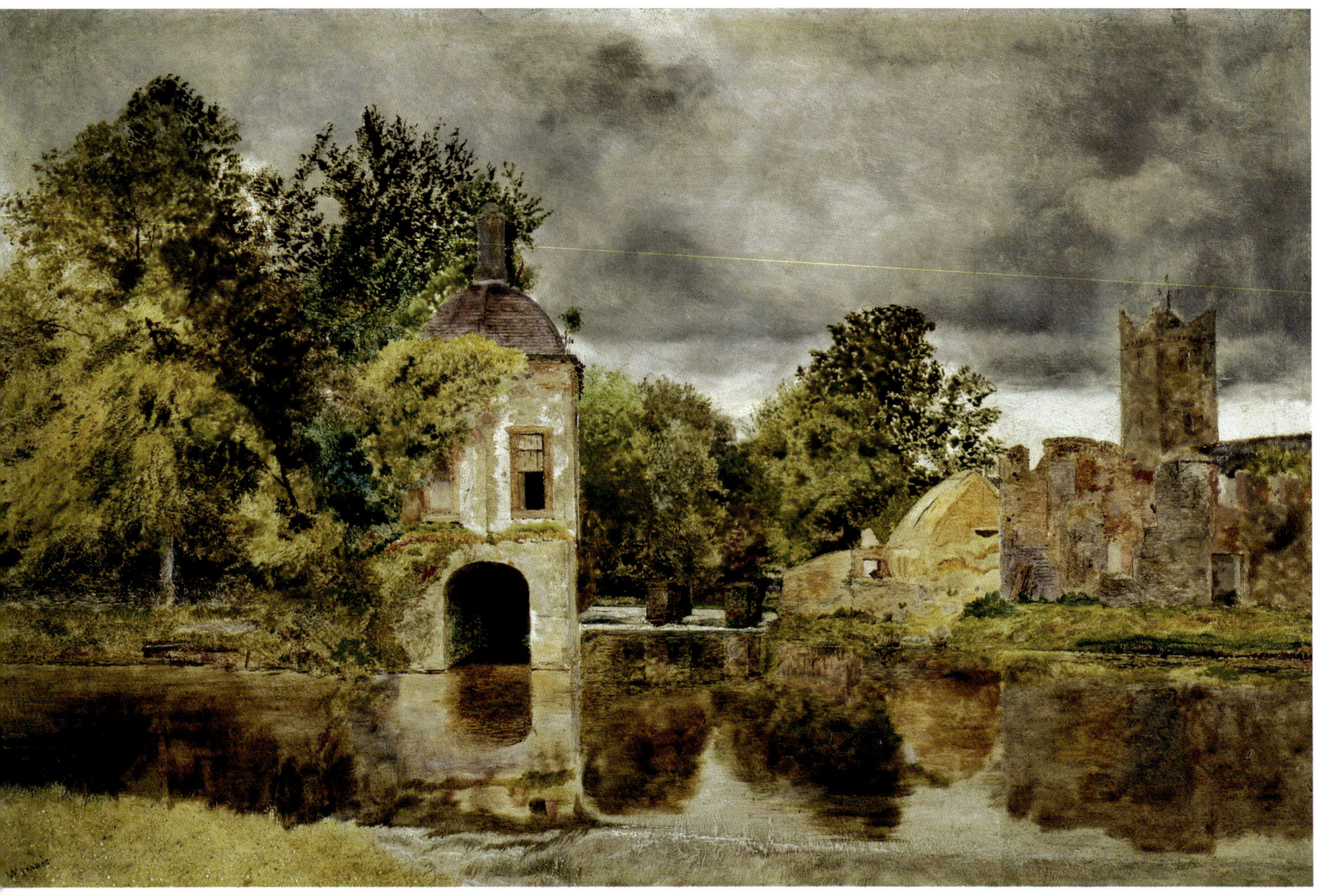

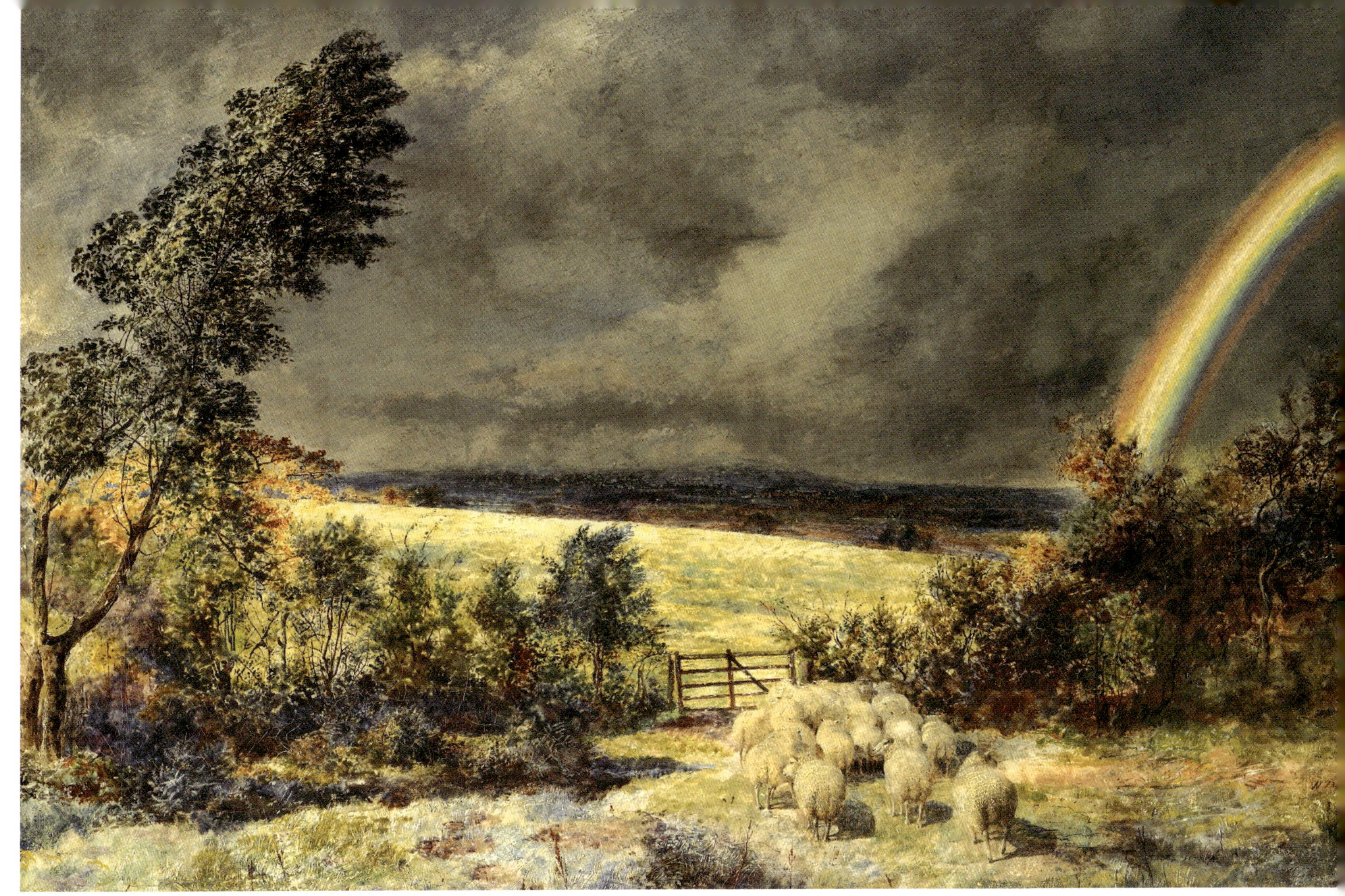

William Davis (1812–73)

The Rainbow, first exhibited in 1858

Oil on canvas, 45.5 × 65.5 cm

Presented by Mrs ACM Jones in 1974; inv. no. WAG 8724

In the mid-1850s, Davis began to focus on painting landscapes and he often found his subjects in the countryside around Liverpool. This picture shows a rainbow over fields near St Helens, east of Liverpool. His paintings earned the admiration of the London Pre-Raphaelites including Dante Gabriel Rossetti and Ford Madox Brown. On seeing a picture by Davis at the Royal Academy, Brown called it 'perfection' and wrote in his diary 'I do not remember ever seeing such an [E]nglish landscape, it is far too good to be understood'. What impressed Brown about Davis' landscapes was their ability to bring out the beauty of an everyday scene. As Brown had foretold, it was this quality which was misunderstood and led to criticism from Ruskin who preferred landscapes with drama or significance.

It seems that reviewers closer to home agreed with Ruskin. When this painting was exhibited at the Liverpool Academy in 1858 it was heavily criticised in the local papers. *The Courier* wrote that it 'can only excite a smile of pity' and *The Mercury* called it 'an offensive daub… which is difficult to realise as taken from… nature'. It appears that the artist took these reviews to heart and rolled up the right side of the canvas, concealing the rainbow which he felt was the focus of the criticism. In 1972 the rainbow was rediscovered, allowing this humble scene of the English countryside to regain its original beauty.

James Campbell (1828–93)

News from My Lad, 1858/9

Oil on canvas, 54.3 × 49.5 cm

Purchased in 1964; inv. no. WAG 6246

Campbell was a versatile artist, at ease painting landscapes or scenes of contemporary life. In this picture an elderly locksmith anxiously reads a letter from his soldier son. The painting is so detailed that much of the writing on the letter can be made out. It starts with 'Lucknow March 1858. My dear old Daddy, I dare say you will read this in the old shop and here I am under the burning sun of India.' The date and location are key to the narrative of the picture, as the son is one of the troops involved in putting down the Indian Mutiny. This rebellion began in May 1857 and lasted until June 1858.

Like many of the Liverpool artists, Campbell admired the work of the London Pre-Raphaelites and one painting in particular may have been the inspiration for *News from My Lad.* In 1856 Ford Madox Brown exhibited *Waiting: An English Fireside in the Winter of 1854–5* [see p.25] at the Liverpool Academy. The picture shows a woman in contemporary dress sewing by gaslight. On the table next to her are a letter and a miniature of her soldier husband, who is away fighting in the Crimean War. Like Brown's work, Campbell's picture capitalised on the public's interest in soldiers fighting abroad.

When the painting was exhibited at the Liverpool Academy in 1858, Campbell included an envelope on the floor in the scene, addressed to 'Enoch Smith, locksmith, Kirkdale, England'. Kirkdale is the area of Liverpool where Campbell lived with his father, but he painted out this local reference when he exhibited it at the Royal Academy.

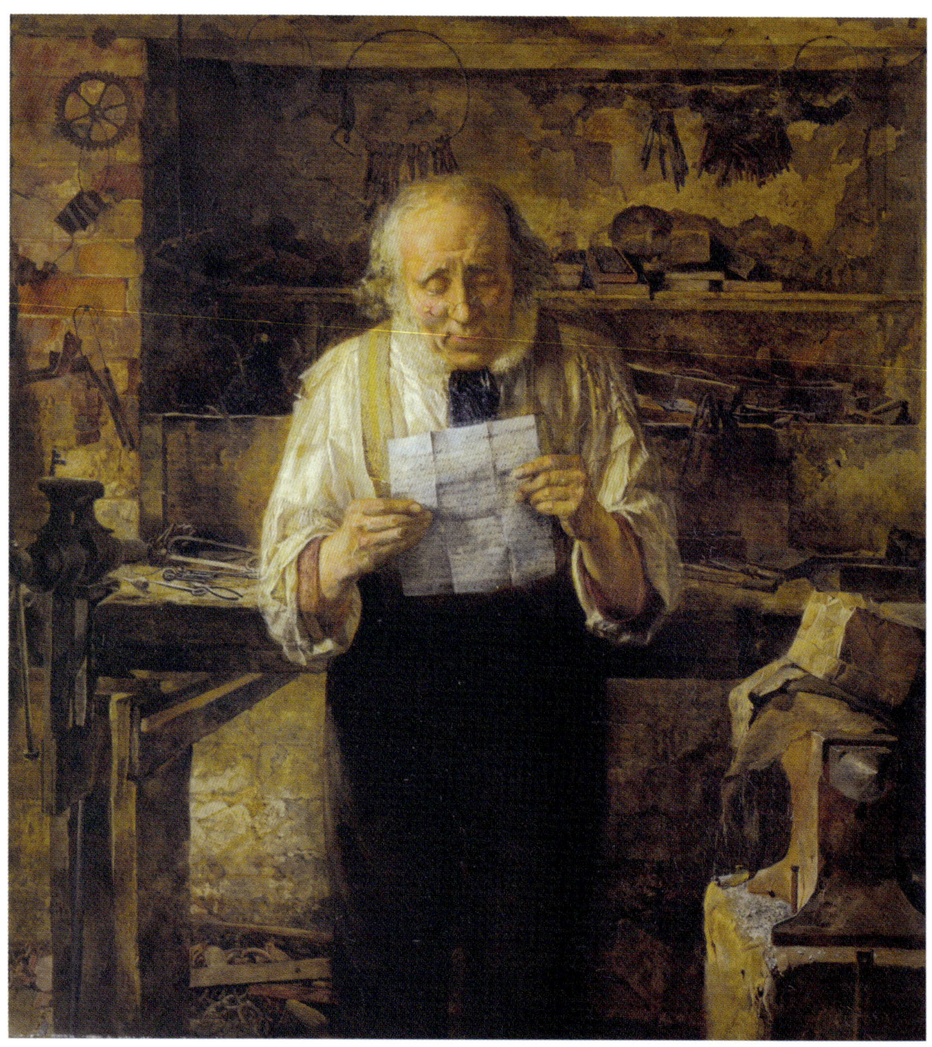

John Ingle Lee (1839–82)

Sweethearts and Wives, 1860

Oil on canvas, 84.5 × 71.3 cm

Purchased with the assistance of the Art Fund, the V&A Purchase Grant Fund and the Friends of Merseyside County Museums and Art Galleries in 1980; inv. no. WAG 9755

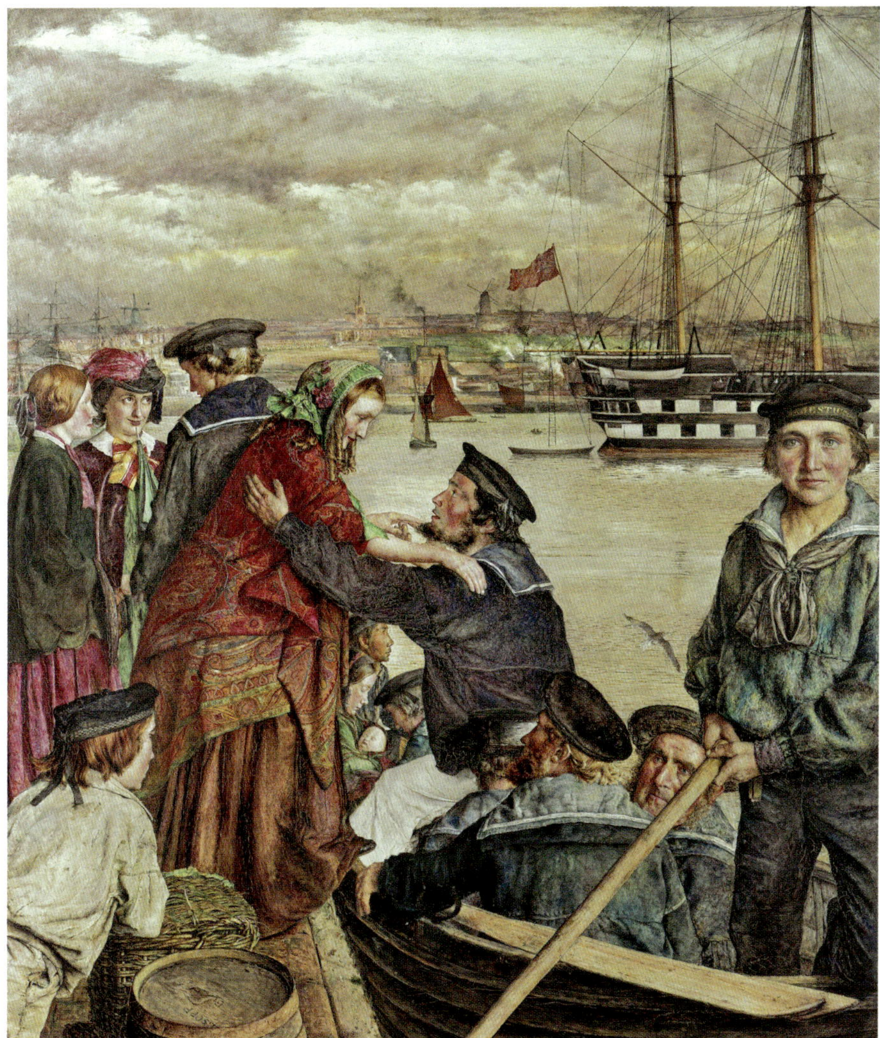

"Sweethearts and Wives" is the traditional Royal Navy toast used on Saturdays. The sailors in this painting are serving on HMS *Majestic*, an 80-gun, ex-Crimea wooden warship, anchored in the Mersey as part of the port defences. In 1863 she is recorded as having prevented two American Confederate battleships from leaving Laird's shipyard in Birkenhead.

Scenes showing soldiers or sailors parting from their loved ones were common in the Victorian period, but this is a rather more perplexing picture because it appears that some of women are going with the sailors. The bright colours of the women's clothes and the minute attention to detail highlight Lee's strong admiration for the Pre-Raphaelites.

Comparatively little is known about Lee and few paintings by him are known to exist. He was born in Liverpool into a family of some note - the family business became the well known department store, George Henry Lee & Co Ltd. After years of trading, Lee's father Henry became a photographer. One of his brothers, Joseph, was also a photographer, suggesting an artistic vein in the family. Lee moved to London in around 1866 and lived with his wife, Mary Ann, in the new middle-class enclave of Hampstead. During his career he exhibited at both the Liverpool Academy and the Royal Academy in London. Lee died near Glenorchy, Argyll, in 1882, leaving his widow a significant estate of almost £6,500.

Alfred William Hunt (1830–96)

Brignall Banks, about 1861

Oil on canvas, 28.5 × 46 cm

Purchased in 1910; inv. no. WAG 944

Hunt began his career as an academic and artist. He studied at Corpus Christi College, Oxford where he won the Newdigate Prize for composing poetry. When he was 23 he was elected a fellow, but combined his passion for academia with his love of painting. He inherited his artistic talents from his father, who was a drawing master and landscape painter. Hunt's early work shows the influence of his father's friend, the artist David Cox (1783–1859), but in the mid-1850s a new enthusiasm for the Pre-Raphaelites changed his style. This can be seen in the stippled brushstrokes in the foreground and background of this painting, and in the light, bright greens employed. Hunt's new style impressed the art critic John Ruskin and the two men formed a friendship that lasted for more than 20 years.

Brignall overlooks the River Greta near Barnard Castle in County Durham. The exact date of the picture is not known, but it is likely to have been painted around the time of his marriage in 1861 as his bride's home city was Durham. Having married, Hunt decided to give up his fellowship to focus on his career as an artist.

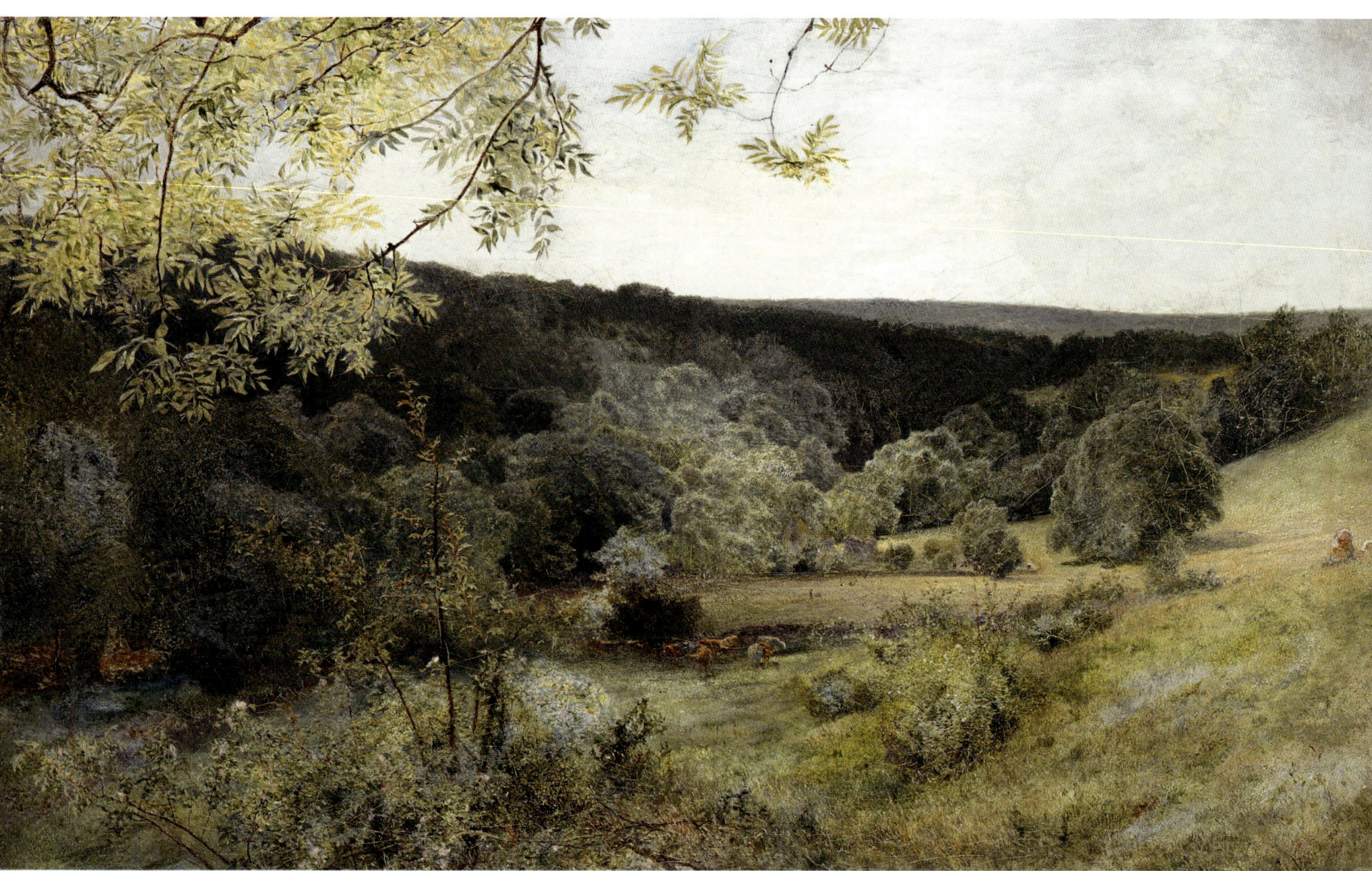

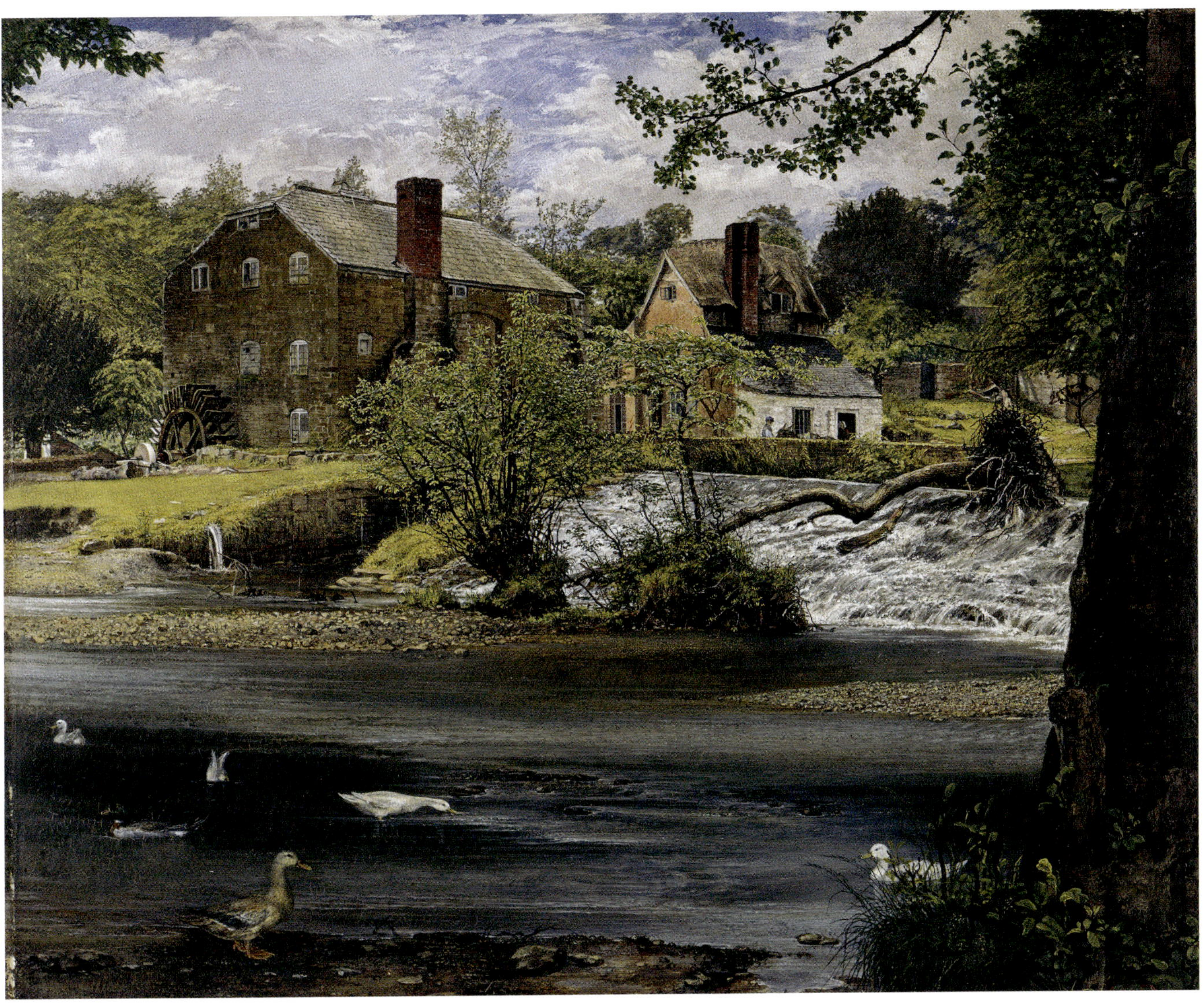

John Edward Newton (1834/5–1891)

Mill on the Alleyn, Denbighshire, about 1861

Oil on canvas, 30.5 × 36.8 cm

Purchased in 1964; inv. no. WAG 6250

The level of detail in Newton's early paintings is almost photographic. He specialised in still life pictures and landscapes, like this one, which enabled him to show off this talent. He was a particular friend of James Campbell and followed him to London in the late 1860s. In the capital his style broadened and he moved away from painting in minute detail. This picture shows a landscape in Denbighshire, Wales, but the exact spot has not been identified. Newton exhibited the painting at the Liverpool Academy in 1861. It was bought directly from the exhibition by the Birkenhead collector, George Rae, who had a large collection of paintings by both London and Liverpool Pre-Raphaelite artists.

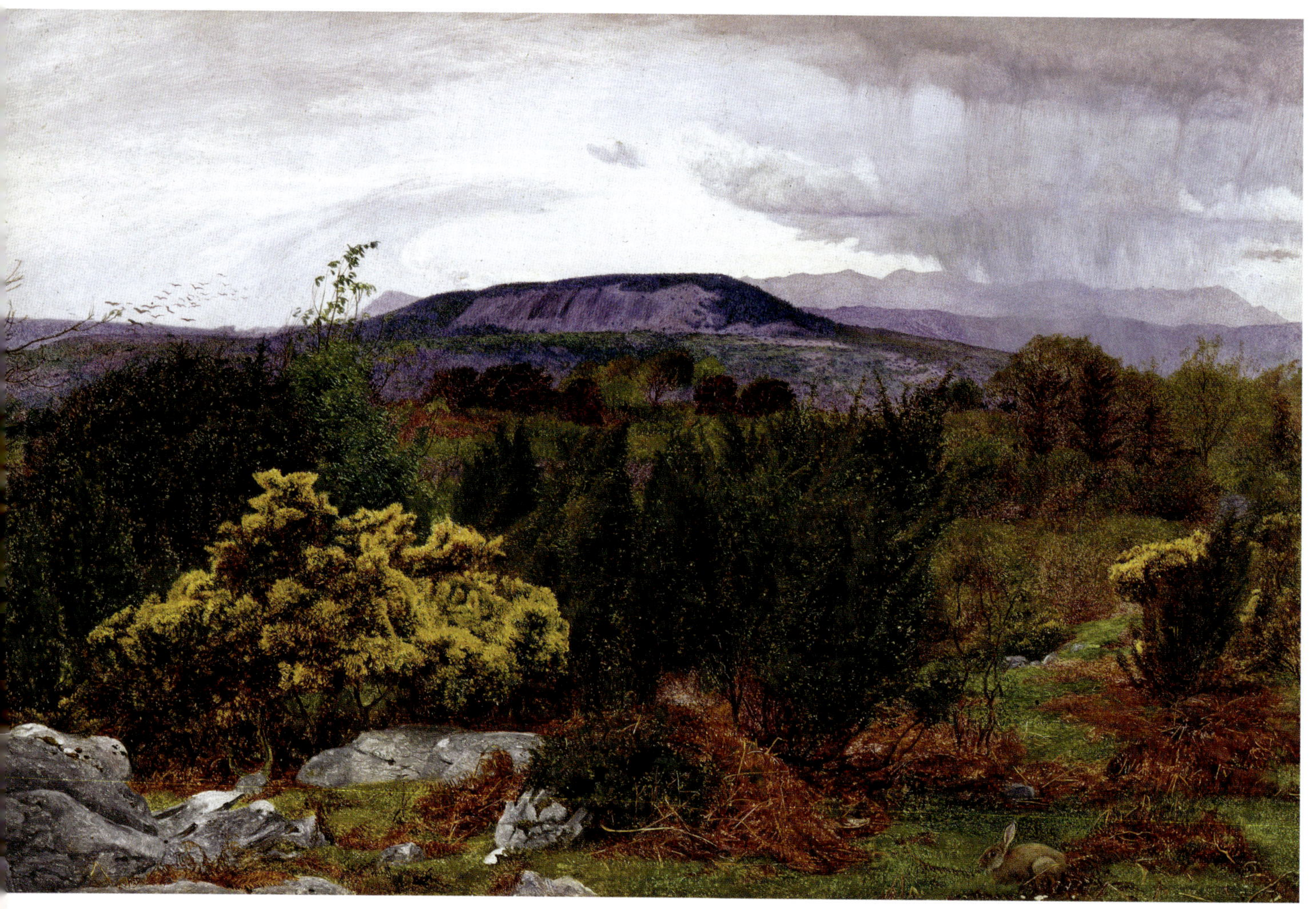

Daniel Alexander Williamson (1823–1903)

Spring, Arnside Knott from Warton Crag, 1863

Oil on canvas, 27 × 40.6 cm

Bequeathed by James Smith of Blundellsands in 1923; inv. no. WAG 784

Liverpool-born Williamson came from a family of landscape painters. In 1849 he moved to London and attended life-drawing classes with the idea of becoming a portrait painter. By the mid-1850s he had changed his mind and followed his father and grandfather by turning to landscape painting. He moved back up north and was living in Warton, near Carnforth, north Lancashire, when he painted this picture.

In the distance Williamson includes the famous landmark, the Old Man of Coniston, but draws the eye back to the foreground by including a minutely detailed rabbit, nestled in the lower right corner. The vivid colours and tiny brushstrokes he employs indicate that in the early 1860s his style was firmly influenced by the Pre-Raphaelites. This influence was short-lived, however, and by the 1870s his brushstrokes had become freer and his paintings more impressionistic.

The Baa Lamb: View on a Tributary of the River Duddon (also known as 'The Stray Lamb'), 1864

Oil on board, 21.2 × 30.5 cm

Bequeathed by James Smith of Blundellsands in 1923; inv. no. WAG 863

Windus was a great friend of the landscape artist Daniel Alexander Williamson [see pp. 82 and 90] who lived in north Lancashire, close to the Lake District. Windus visited him over several summers in the early 1860s and this picture is likely to have been produced on one of these trips. Painted with a Pre-Raphaelite eye for detail, it shows a section of the River Duddon in the south western Lake District. This river was a favourite of Wordsworth, and he wrote a series of sonnets dedicated to it between 1804 and 1820.

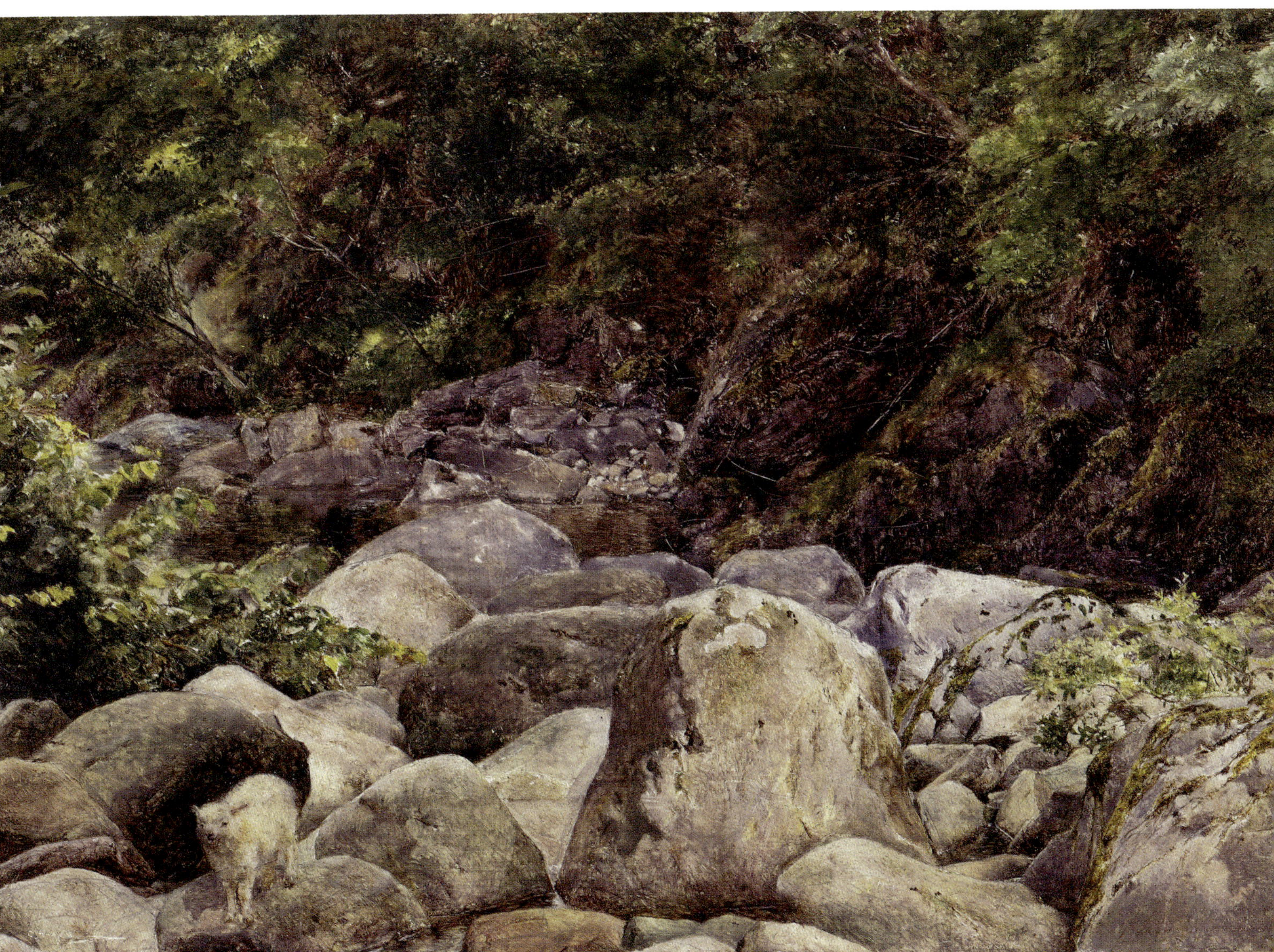

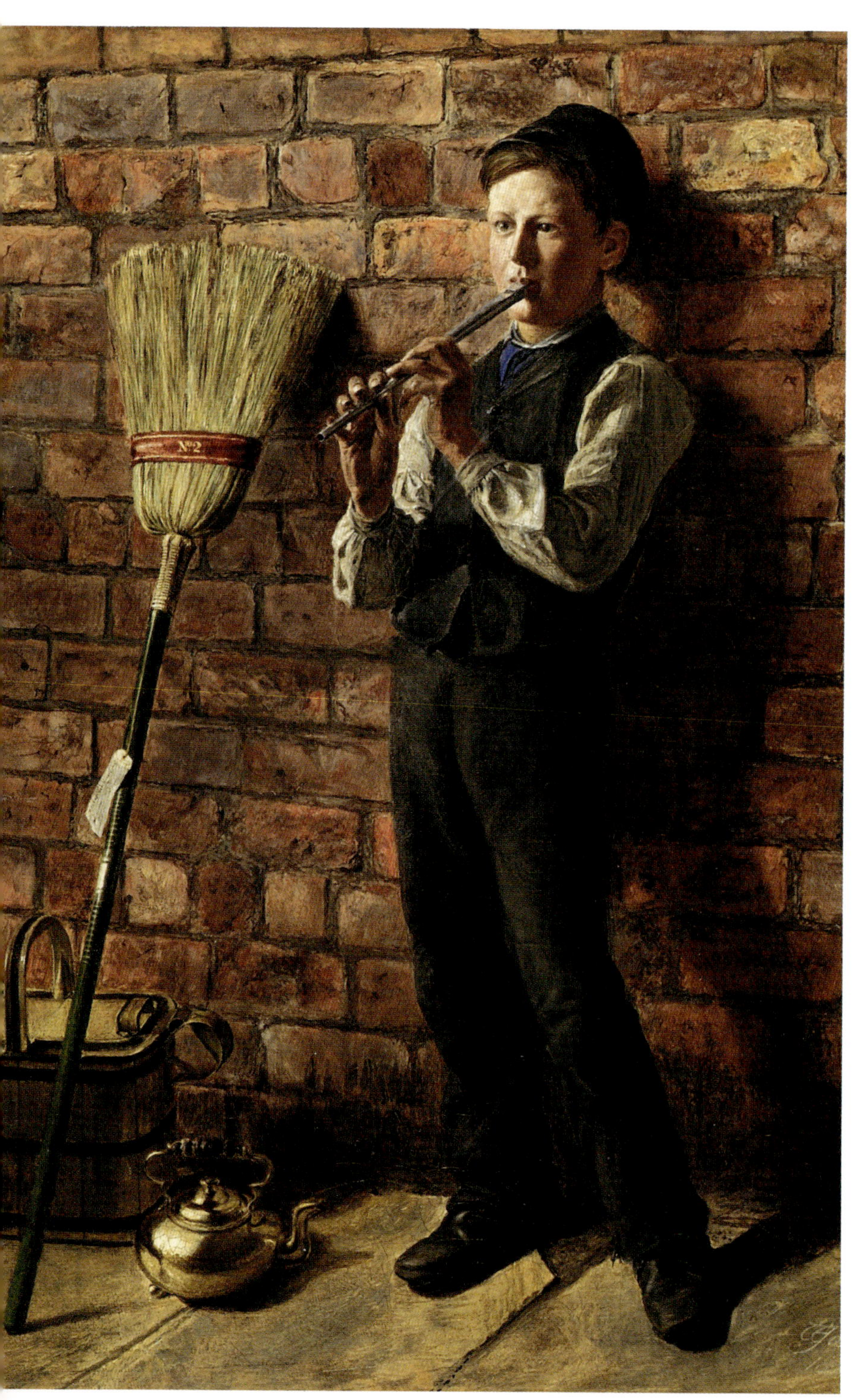

Joseph Edward Worrall
(1829–1913)

Music versus Work, 1864

Oil on canvas, 31.1 × 22.9 cm

Purchased in 2005; inv. no. WAG 2005.4

Worrall was born in Liverpool and lived there all his life. His received a thorough fine art training by attending classes at the Liverpool Mechanics' Institute and later at the Liverpool Academy. By 1861 he was working as a draughtsman and lithographer but his ambitions did not stop there. Only ten years later he had become a thriving landscape and figure artist with a studio employing three apprentices.

In this painting a servant boy has cast aside his sweeping brush to play his tin whistle. When the picture was exhibited at the Royal Academy in London it brought a smile to the face of one critic who wrote, 'We are always so glad when it is possible to steal a laugh within the solemn propriety of the walls of the Academy'.

William Lindsay Windus (1822–1907)

The Young Duke, about 1865

Oil on board, 38.2 × 24.5 cm

Bequeathed by James Smith of Blundellsands in 1923; inv. no. WAG 480

This is said to be Windus' last major picture as he gave up painting professionally suddenly following the death of his wife. He continued to paint as a pastime, but according to William Michael Rossetti he felt, despite his early fame, that the need to look after his young daughter would prevent him from pursuing a successful career as an artist. His decision may also have been influenced by the harsh criticism he received from Ruskin in 1858, when he exhibited his painting *Too Late* at the Royal Academy. He was so hurt by Ruskin's review of it that he never exhibited there again and struggled to rebuild his confidence, destroying many of his sketches in the late 1870s. This light, bright work is sketchier than his other Pre-Raphaelite pictures but sticks to the theme of knights and chivalry, a typically Pre-Raphaelite subject.

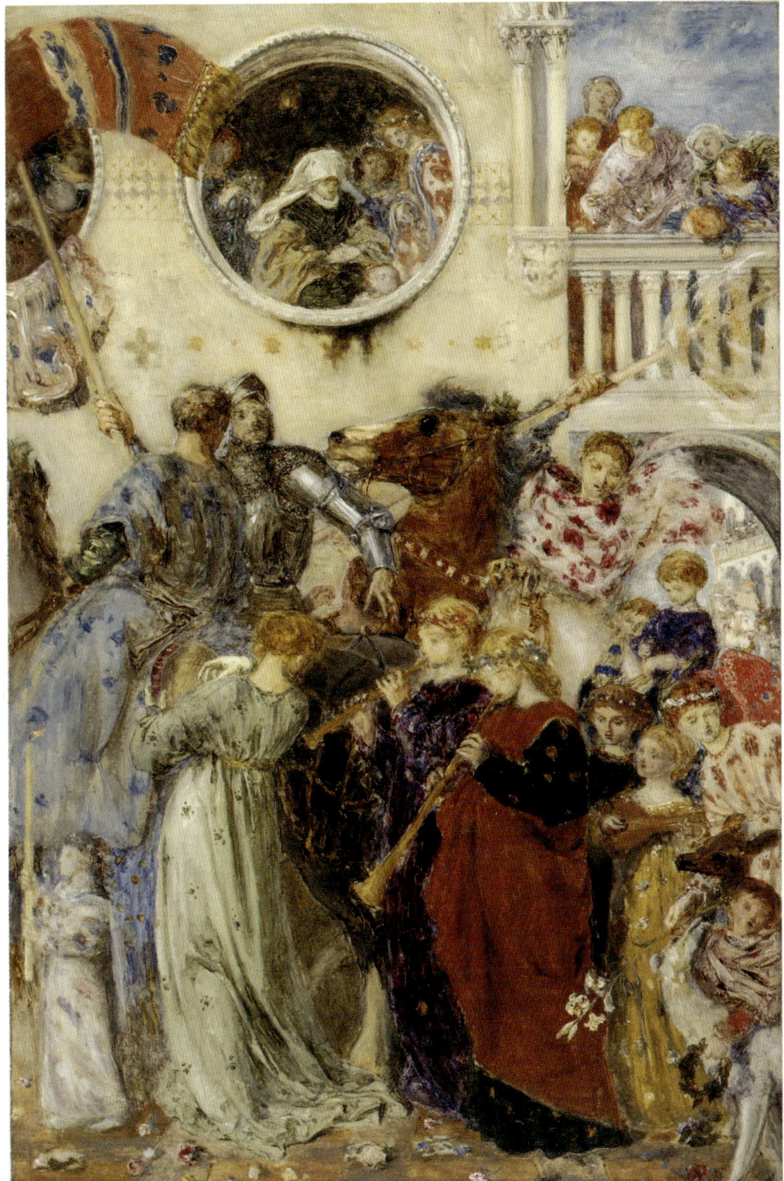

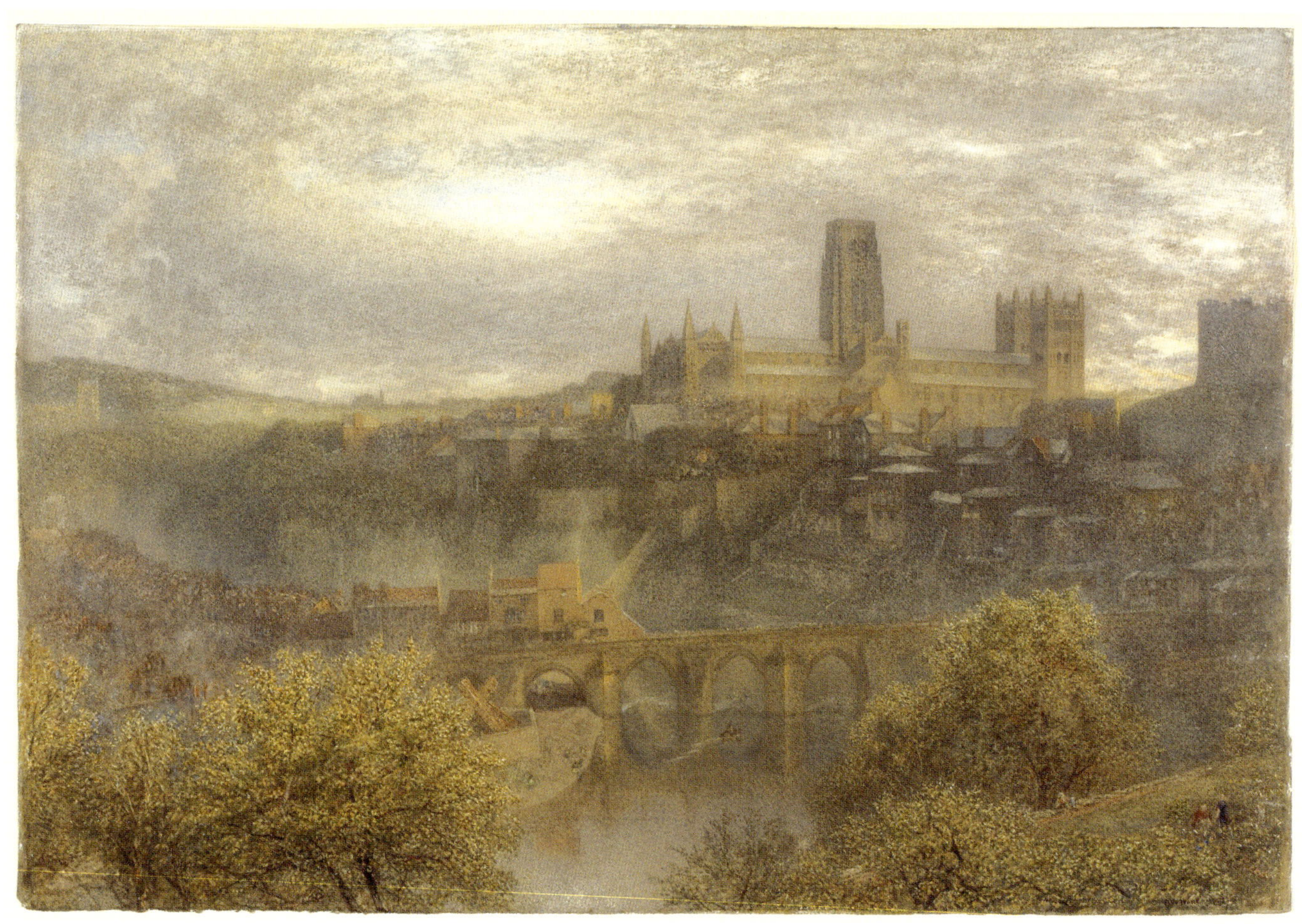

Alfred William Hunt (1830–96)

Durham, first exhibited 1881

Watercolour on paper, 37.7 × 54.2 cm

Bequeathed by the Reverend EC Dewick in 1919; inv. no. WAG 386

In the early 1860s Hunt focused on painting in watercolour. He was
skilled at producing detailed, highly finished atmospheric scenes
such as this topographical view of Durham. In this landscape he has
caught the effect of the sun glimmering through a break in the clouds
on a misty morning. Following his marriage in 1861, Hunt moved to
Durham for four years. He found ready subjects for his watercolour
paintings in the city and the surrounding countryside. His success in
the medium was rewarded by being elected an associate of the Old
Watercolour Society in 1862, and a full member in 1864.

Further reading

Pre-Raphaelite Drawing, exhib. cat., Colin Cruise, Thames and Hudson, 2011

Pre-Raphaelite Painting Techniques, Joyce H Townsend, Jacqueline Ridge and Stephen Hackney, Tate Publishing, 2004

Pre-Raphaelites: Victorian Avant-Garde, exhib. cat., Tim Barringer, Jason Rosenfeld and Alison Smith, Tate Publishing, 2012

Pre-Raphaelite Vision: Truth to Nature, exhib. cat., Allen Staley and Christopher Newall, Tate Publishing, 2004

Pre-Raphaelite Women Artists, Jan Marsh and Pamela Gerrish Nunn, Thames and Hudson, 1998

Reading the Pre-Raphaelites, Tim Barringer, Yale University Press, 2003

The Art of the Pre-Raphaelites, Elizabeth Prettejohn, Tate Publishing, 2000

The Diary of Ford Madox Brown, ed. Virginia Surtees, Yale University Press for the Paul Mellon Centre for Studies in British Art, 1981

Victorian Painting, Julian Treuherz, Thames and Hudson, 1993

www.preraphaelites.org.uk - Birmingham Museums and Art Gallery's award winning Pre-Raphaelite website